WHEN POLITICS BECOMES PERSONAL

Can we be good partisans without demonizing our political opponents? Using insights from political science and social psychology, this book argues for the distinction between positive and negative partisanship – with significant implications: Strong support for a political party does not have to be accompanied by the vilification of the opposing party and its members. Utilizing data from five different countries, Alexa Bankert demonstrates that positive and negative partisanship are independent concepts with distinct consequences for political behavior, including citizens' political participation and their commitment to democratic norms and values. The book concludes with the hopeful message that partisanship is an essential pillar of representative and liberal democracy.

Alexa Bankert is Assistant Professor in the Department of Political Science at the University of Georgia. Her work has appeared in peer-reviewed journals such as the *Journal of Politics*, *Political Psychology*, and *Political Behavior*. She is the recipient of several awards, including the *Distinguished Junior Scholars Award*, given by the Political Psychology Section of the American Political Science Association.

T0371531

Contemporary Social Issues

General Editor: Brian D. Christens, *Vanderbilt University*

Contemporary Social Issues is the official book series of the Society for the Psychological Study of Social Issues (SPSSI). Since its founding in 1936, SPSSI has addressed the social issues of the times. Central to these efforts has been the Lewinian tradition of action-oriented research, in which psychological theories and methods guide research and action addressed to important societal problems. Grounded in their authors' programmes of research, works in this series focus on social issues facing individuals, groups, communities, and/or society at large, with each volume written to speak to scholars, students, practitioners, and policymakers.

Other Books in the Series

Developing Critical Consciousness in Youth: Contexts and Settings
Luke Rapa and Erin Godfrey, editors

Critical Consciousness: Expanding Theory and Measurement
Erin Godfrey and Luke Rapa, editors

When Politics Becomes Personal

The Effect of Partisan Identity on Anti-Democratic Behavior

Alexa Bankert

University of Georgia

CAMBRIDGE
UNIVERSITY PRESS

CAMBRIDGE
UNIVERSITY PRESS

Shaftesbury Road, Cambridge CB2 8EA, United Kingdom

One Liberty Plaza, 20th Floor, New York, NY 10006, USA

477 Williamstown Road, Port Melbourne, VIC 3207, Australia

314–321, 3rd Floor, Plot 3, Splendor Forum, Jasola District Centre, New Delhi – 110025, India

103 Penang Road, #05–06/07, Visioncrest Commercial, Singapore 238467

Cambridge University Press is part of Cambridge University Press & Assessment, a department of the University of Cambridge.

We share the University's mission to contribute to society through the pursuit of education, learning and research at the highest international levels of excellence.

www.cambridge.org
Information on this title: www.cambridge.org/9781316511343

DOI: 10.1017/9781009052290

First published 2023

A catalogue record for this publication is available from the British Library.

Library of Congress Cataloging-in-Publication Data
NAMES: Bankert, Alexa, 1987– author.
TITLE: When politics becomes personal : the effect of partisan identity on anti-democratic behavior / Alexa Bankert.
DESCRIPTION: Cambridge, United Kingdom ; New York, NY : Cambridge University Press, 2023. | Series: Contemporary social issues series | Includes bibliographical references and index.
IDENTIFIERS: LCCN 2023013309 (print) | LCCN 2023013310 (ebook) | ISBN 9781316511343 (hardback) | ISBN 9781009055512 (paperback) | ISBN 9781009052290 (epub)
SUBJECTS: LCSH: Party affiliation. | Political participation. | Political sociology. | Democracy–Social aspects.
CLASSIFICATION: LCC JF2071 .B36 2023 (print) | LCC JF2071 (ebook) | DDC 323/.042–dc23/eng/20230501
LC record available at https://lccn.loc.gov/2023013309
LC ebook record available at https://lccn.loc.gov/2023013310

ISBN 978-1-316-51134-3 Hardback
ISBN 978-1-009-05551-2 Paperback

To Brandon, who reminds me every day that happiness is life's greatest accomplishment.

CONTENTS

FIGURES

TABLES

ACKNOWLEDGMENTS

While I am listed as the sole author of this book, many people have contributed to it, in various ways – all of them incredibly meaningful. For that, I am truly grateful. First, I would like to thank my dissertation advisor, Leonie Huddy, whose thoughtful, creative, and meticulous work on social identities as well as her invaluable guidance throughout graduate school had a profound impact on my own work but also on my own identity as a scholar. Not surprisingly, Leonie's work is featured prominently in this book.

I owe a similarly significant debt to my colleagues at the University of Georgia, especially Stephen Nicholson who supported my research unconditionally and provided the necessary funds for collecting high-quality data samples in five different countries. Without his generous financial help, this book would have required many more sleepless nights and many more years for completion. For other vital forms of support – words of encouragement, professional advice, and candy – I would also like to thank Jamie Carson, Christy Boyd, Geoff Sheagley, David Cottrell, Michael Lynch, Tony Madonna, Wendi Finch, my former department chair Scott Ainsworth my current department chair Susan Haire, my college's associate dean John Maltese and my college's dean Matt Auer.

I would also like to express my gratitude to my editor at SPSSI, Brian D. Christens, who – to my delightful surprise – had been reading my work on group identities and partisanship. Brian also offered vital feedback on my initial proposal for the book which helped me see more clearly what I would like to accomplish with the book. His enthusiasm for my work kept me motivated throughout the pandemic and beyond. I am also utterly grateful for the wonderful people at Cambridge University Press, namely Janka Romero and Rowan Groat, who guided me throughout the publication process, continuously offered their help, and never got mad at any of my multiple requests to extend the submission deadline. I am grateful for their patience and kindness.

I would be remiss if I did not mention the crucial contributions from my research assistants, Andrew L. Stone and Tabitha Lamberth. Their detail-oriented and prompt work made my life much easier.

For delicious culinary assistance, I express my deep gratitude to Café Racer who, in my humble and constantly hungry opinion, make the best burger in Athens, Georgia. I also need to mention The Lark and Normaltown Brewing Company for providing the most delectable distractions after a long day, or week.

Finally, I am indebted to my family and friends. I thank my family in Germany, Anke and Rolf Hoffmann, for allowing me to have two equally meaningful homes – one in Germany and one in the United States. It is thanks to my mother, Kati Bankert, that the idea of pursuing research as a profession never seemed like a lofty and outrageously outsized goal for a girl from a family that frequently struggled to pay the bills. Neither my transcontinental move to America nor my career in academia would have been possible without my family.

I would certainly not have survived graduate school, life on the tenure track, or just the process of writing this book without the unwavering support of my friends: David Stack, Joerg Mayer, Janet Martin, Molly Williams, Hanna Kleider, Eliza Banu, Jenni Mathis, Nick Maulding and Erin Towery, Kate Fortmueller, David Lerner, Annie Gilbert, David Cottrell, Chad and Rachel Clay, David Fung, Daniel Moody, Will Harvey (and his famous Mac 'n' Cheese!), Andy Flowers, Patrick Ayers, Angelina Mattus, and Erich Fietkau.

I owe the most to my favorite person, Brandon Pool, and his wonderful parents Melody and Eddie Pool with whom I built a home and a family in Georgia. Without Brandon's unfailing support and encouragement, I would never have learned to be kind to myself, especially when I fail to live up to my own expectations. I am a better and a happier person for having him in my life.

To all of you: Thank you *so* very much.

Introduction to the Book

> It's only natural for unbridled partisanship to lead to chaos. This is the great danger George Washington saw in political parties.
>
> John Avlon in the book *Washington's Farewell* (2017)

It is undoubtedly ironic that one of the Founding Fathers of the United States – the birthplace of hyper-partisanship and polarization – had a premonition of the dangers of "unbridled partisanship" in the early days of the American republic. Fast-forward 245 years, as Washington's warning comes to fruition in the form of partisan acrimony that culminated in the January 6th insurrection at the US Capitol, the symbolic core of American democracy. A YouGov poll conducted the day after the insurgency revealed that 45% of Republicans approved of the storming of the Capitol while 52% of Republicans blamed Joe Biden for the actions of those who attacked the Capitol.[1] This was not an isolated incident. Only a few weeks later, members of Congress called for the removal of Representative Marjorie Taylor Greene, a Republican from Georgia, following revelations about past social media posts in which she called for violence against Democratic politicians.[2] In August 2021, the US Department of Homeland Security issued a bulletin warning of a continued threat from domestic violent extremists whose actions are fueled by false narratives about fraud in the 2020 US presidential election.[3] Critics might argue that political violence is not a completely novel phenomenon in US history. After all, violent fringes on both sides of the ideological aisle have been in existence since the late 1960s, committing violence in

---

[1] This poll can be accessed here: https://today.yougov.com/topics/politics/articles-reports/2021/01/06/US-capitol-trump-poll (last accessed, November 9, 2021).

[2] Representative Greene also filed Articles of Impeachment against President Biden the day after his inauguration on January 20, 2021, to "be the voice of Republican voters who have been ignored."

[3] Department of Homeland Security, Summary of Terrorism Threat to the U.S. Homeland, www.dhs.gov/ntas/advisory/national-terrorism-advisory-system-bulletin-august-13-2021 (last accessed, November 10, 2022).

support of social causes, such as the far-left Weather Underground Organization as well as the anti-abortion group Operation Rescue. However, the political violence in the twenty-first century is no longer exclusively driven by a few ideologically extreme fringe groups. Instead, the January 6th insurrection was driven by a "broader mass movement with violence at its core" (Chicago Project on Security and Threats 2021, p. 4) that, in contrast to past extremists' groups, includes older, employed Americans *without* an affiliation to a militia such as the Proud Boys or the Aryan Nation but *with* a strong party affiliation.[4] Indeed, a recent nationally representative survey reveals that among Americans who identify as Democrat or Republican, one in three now believe that violence could be justified to advance their parties' political goals.[5] These patterns constitute a textbook example of "unbridled partisanship" and its damaging effect on Americans' commitment to democratic norms and values including the peaceful transition of power, the recognition and protection of fair and legitimate elections regardless of their outcome, as well as civil and respectful discourse between leaders and members of opposing parties.

Yet the United States is not the only country that has been struggling with the dangerous consequences of uncritical party loyalties and violent rhetoric: Many of Europe's mainstream political parties are facing off with populist challengers who frequently espouse anti-democratic and illiberal values. Italy, for example, is equally familiar with claims of election fraud by a losing party: In 2006, Forza Italia, led by Berlusconi, did not accept its defeat and called the election outcome illegitimate, which marked the beginning of hostile and confrontational relations between the parties in the legislature (Donovan 2008). This emerging conflict was further exacerbated when Berlusconi returned to office in 2008, creating a political climate that normalized the demonization of and aggression toward opposing parties (Bosco and Verney 2020). Indeed, the partisan vitriol became so intense that, at the time, President of the Republic Giorgio Napolitano described Italy as "torn by hyper-partisanship, a daily guerrilla, a reciprocal delegitimization."[6] The Italian version of hyper-partisanship resembles its American counterpart in the sense that it, too, is driven by polarizing party elites who benefit from the partisan rancor, such as Berlusconi and, in contemporary Italy, Northern

---

[4] Chicago Project on Security and Threats, Understanding American Domestic Terrorism, https://d3qioqp55mx5f5.cloudfront.net/cpost/i/docs/americas_insurrectionists_online_2021_04_06.pdf?m

[5] Politico, Americans increasingly believe violence is justified if the other side wins, www.politico.com/news/magazine/2020/10/01/political-violence-424157 (last accessed, November 10, 2022.

[6] Grasso, Benedetta, Giorgio Napolitano, a cosmopolitan Italian, www.iitaly.org/magazine/focus/op-eds/article/giorgio-napolitano-cosmopolitan-italian?mode=colorbox (last accessed, July 20, 2022).

League leader Matteo Salvini whose "innovative use of the social media, dialectic ability and aggressive language polarised and divided the electorate as only Berlusconi had done in the past" (Bosco and Verney 2020, p. 275). Concurrently, anti-racist groups in Italy report increasing violence against migrants, including 12 shootings, 2 murders, and 33 physical assaults recorded in just the two months after the leader of the far-right Northern League, Matteo Salvini, took office in 2018.[7] More such incidences are predicted in the aftermath of the electoral victory of Italy's far-right Brothers of Italy in the 2022 general election – a party that originated in the neofascist Italian Social Movement and that is known for its aggressive rhetoric against migrants, the LGBTQ community, and reproductive rights.[8]

Even in Sweden – otherwise known for its progressive policies – a nationalist, anti-immigrant party, the Sweden Democrats, is steadily gaining support. The party was long seen as marginal; but in 2022, it is Sweden's third-largest party, holding 60 seats in the 349-seat parliament (Ahlander and Johnson (2021). As their electoral appeal is growing, so are levels of animosity toward the Sweden Democrats (Reiljan and Ryan 2021) with 43% of Swedish citizens reporting that they would never vote for the Sweden Democrats – followed, in second place of Sweden's most unpopular parties, by the left-wing Feminist Initiative, which only 10% of Swedes would never vote for (Bankert 2020). Note the large gap between these two parties: almost half of the Swedish electorate appears to be unified in their aversion to the Sweden Democrats. These numbers align with the prediction that successful populist parties can collapse and divide political competition into a struggle between "liberal democracy" as represented by establishment parties in the political center and "populism" as represented by the strongest populist party (Mudde and Kaltwasser 2018). This struggle has also been accompanied by higher levels of partisan acrimony whereby many Swedes share more negative, rather than positive, feelings toward their political parties (Bankert 2020). Concurrently, researchers have also been documenting "an increasing frequency of threats and hatred voiced against politicians and officials" (Oscarsson et al. 2021, p. 5) as was exemplified by the stabbing of a public health official at the hands of a Neo-Nazi supporter at Sweden's annual democracy festival in July 2022 (Pelling 2022).

The rise of negativity toward one or several political parties is also characteristic of the Netherlands, where Dutch voters report more negative feelings for people from different political parties than for people from

[7] *The Guardian*, Warning of dangerous acceleration in attacks on immigrants in Italy, www .theguardian.com/global/2018/aug/03/warning-of-dangerous-acceleration-in-attacks-on-immigrants-in-italy (last accessed, November 9, 2021).

[8] Open Democracy, The anti-women agenda of the woman set to be the next Italian prime minister, www.opendemocracy.net/en/5050/giorgia-meloni-far-right-brothers-of-italy-election-prime-minister-racism-gender/ (last accessed, November 10, 2022).

nonpolitical groups such as those from different religious, educational, or ethnic backgrounds, a startling trend given the Netherlands' tradition of a consociational and consensus-oriented democracy. This negativity directed at political out-groups illustrates the emergence of hostility along party lines, especially between those who support and oppose the populist radical right parties (Harteveld 2021) – similar to Italy and Sweden. While many Dutch citizens fiercely oppose the populist right, its supporters feel a similarly deep disdain for adherents to establishment parties, which leads to a "'double boost' of antipathy to the system by [the populist right] being both the object and subject of unique antipathy" (Harteveld 2021, p. 10). Yet even more generally, some Dutch partisans report more negative feelings and a sense of greater social distance toward opposing parties while also ascribing more negative traits toward their supporters (Heeremans 2018) – a partisan division that has intensified during the COVID-19 pandemic (Krastev and Leonard 2021).

Last, the United Kingdom too has seen a rise in political threats and violence against politicians (Parker, Pickard, and Wright 2021). Most recently, conservative Member of Parliament (MP) Sir David Amess was assassinated in Essex in October 2021. He is the second serving MP to be killed in the past five years, following the murder of Labour MP Jo Cox in 2016. Again, these are not isolated cases. Between 2016 and 2020, the Metropolitan Police recorded 678 crimes against MPs, including 582 reports of malicious communications, 46 cases of harassment, and 9 relating to terrorism (Parker, Pickard, and Wright 2021). Some political pundits consider the hostile rhetoric between party leaders responsible for these violent trends. Indeed, there are many examples of violence in political elites' rhetoric such as referring to their colleagues across the aisle as "a bunch of scum" and "absolute vile" and even suggesting that a bomb should be planted in their office (*The Guardian* 2021). This bellicose political discourse has downstream effects on the mass public since partisans mirror the behavior and attitudes of their party elites (Huddy and Yair 2021). Not coincidentally, British partisans discriminate against members of the opposing party more so than they favor their own (Westwood et al. 2018). In other words, the disdain for the opposing party and its members exceeds the support for one's own party. The negativity that permeates the political discourse is also connected to lower levels of satisfaction with democracy. While 47% of Britons in 2017 reported feeling dissatisfied with the way democracy was working in their country, this number increased to 69% in 2019,[9] which constitutes a substantial jump within a short time period.

---

[9] These numbers are taken from a Pew Research poll which can be accessed here: www .pewresearch.org/fact-tank/2019/10/28/brexit-divides-the-uk-but-partisanship-and-ideology-are-still-key-factors/ (last accessed, November 9, 2021)

The United States, the United Kingdom, Italy, Sweden, and the Netherlands – these countries differ dramatically in their political culture, the socio-demographic makeup of their voters, as well as the institutional features of their political systems such as the number of parties, their ideological distinctiveness, and their degree of collaboration within or outside a governing coalition. Yet despite these stark differences, these countries seem to face a similar challenge relating to the increasingly acrimonious way citizens perceive and engage with their political opponents. These antipathies have a negative impact on more than *just* relationships between political parties; they are also connected to a weakened commitment to democratic norms and values that leads partisans to be more accepting of violence toward opposition party leaders and their supporters as well as more willing to infringe upon their democratic rights and freedoms. To illustrate this point, let us have a cursory look at some of the data that I will introduce and analyze in subsequent chapters: In one of my recent surveys of partisans in the United States, almost half of respondents considered their political opponents a serious threat to the country; among those, 25% believe that some parties and candidates should be barred because of their beliefs and ideologies, and 15% agree that violence might sometimes be necessary to fight against parties and candidates that are bad for the country. These indicators of partisan rancor are not just an American phenomenon. Even in Sweden, 31% of partisans consider their opponent a threat to the country, 41% of those would prefer banning certain parties, and 19% agree that violence against these parties might be necessary. The number of partisans who are willing to at least consider violence is also substantial in the United Kingdom (32%), the Netherlands (35%), and Italy (28%).[10] Clearly, partisanship is not just a powerful and complex concept in the United States and its infamous two-party system, but also in many European multi-party systems, which warrants a close and comprehensive examination of its origins, expressions, and impact on political behavior – both from a theoretical as well as empirical perspective. This is, at its core, the purpose of this book.

Despite the ubiquity and necessity of political parties in mass democracies, there is a lively scholarly debate regarding the nature and consequences of partisanship: In its classical definition, partisanship reflects a voter's well-defined political preferences as well as a reasoned and informed understanding of the parties' positions and their leadership's performance. I refer to partisanship grounded in this type of responsive and informed deliberation as *instrumental*. The instrumental model of partisanship closely builds on the idea that people can approximate the ideal of a rational decision maker. This

---

[10] All these numbers are taken from recent surveys of partisans in each country. The data was collected by the author. More information about the data collection process can be found in subsequent chapters; sample features can be found in the Appendix.

Rational Choice paradigm has shaped political science and its adjacent fields for a long time. From this perspective, strong policy preferences and ideological convictions *precede* and shape our party affiliation. For example, an American voter might strongly oppose abortion and therefore decide to support the Republican Party. Thus, the causal arrow points from policy preference to partisanship. And indeed, there is some evidence supporting this instrumental model, showing that partisanship is grounded in partisans' assessment of their leaders and party platforms (e.g., Dalton and Weldon 2007; Garzia 2013). At the same time, however, researchers have found mixed results for voters' ability to recognize and adjust to ideological changes parties' political platforms. While Adams and colleagues (2011) find that the public remains unaware of changes in a party's policy positions, Fernandez-Vazquez (2014) reports a slight change in voters' perceptions that, nevertheless, falls far short of the magnitude of actual change. These findings constitute a challenge to the instrumental model of partisanship: If shifts in parties' platforms are not registered by voters, then how can they influence voters' party affiliation?

In response to the limited evidence in support of instrumental partisanship, an alternative *expressive* approach to partisanship has developed and gained credence in the United States. This model considers partisanship a social identity rather than a reflection of political preferences. This internalized identity minimizes partisans' responsiveness to and acknowledgment of negative information about their political party, including poor performance, weak leadership, and changing party platforms. Indeed, when partisanship operates as a partisan identity, it *motivates* partisans to defend their party even in the face of such negative information – which results in a relatively stable political identity (Green et al. 2002) in spite of leadership and policy changes over time. This expressive approach to partisanship is grounded in Social Identity Theory (Green et al 2002; Huddy 2001; Huddy et al.; 2015 Tajfel and Turner 2004) – a socio-psychological theory that will serve as the main theoretical lens through which I will examine partisanship in this book.

While the predictions derived from the expressive partisanship model appear rather at odds with normative expectations of democratic decision-making, it is important to understand and acknowledge what the nature partisanship is rather than what it should be. After all, partisanship is a powerful influence on people's political behavior, including but not limited to their voting decisions. Thus, comprehending the nature and origins of our party attachments is a crucial step in understanding how people engage with their political system, even if that means abandoning high ideals of democratic citizenship (see, for example, Achen and Bartels 2017). As the famous political scientist Schattschneider astutely put it: "We become cynical about democracy because the public does not act the way the simplistic definition of democracy says that it should act, or we try to whip the public into doing things it does not want to do, is unable to do, and has too much sense to do.

The crisis here is not a crisis in democracy but a crisis in theory" (Schattschneider 1960:127). The expressive model of partisanship offers a possible answer to that crisis in theory; it does not just encompass a rich theoretical framework to derive predictions about *actual* political behavior, it also provides a blueprint for identifying the causes of partisanship's negative impacts, such as the dehumanization of political opponents (e.g., Cassese 2021; Martherus et al. 2019), as well as possible interventions that can counteract them. Only after realistically assessing how partisanship operates can we find solutions for its blind spots.

Cynics might argue that political parties themselves are the problem. Indeed, demands for more direct democracy are common (*US News & World Report* 2016). While efforts to re-think and reinvent democracy are important and valuable, it is not my intention to convince the reader of the necessity and utility of political parties in democratic societies. This book builds on the assumption that modern mass democracies *require* political parties. While representative democracy has its flaws, there is no shortage of examples of direct democracy gone wrong: From opposition to fluoride in drinking water in the 1950s and 1960s to conspiracy theories about vaccinations against measles and COVID-19; citizens will inevitably fall for other motivational and cognitive biases – with or without political parties.

Given these considerations, this book serves a crucial purpose: It provides a comprehensive overview and extension of contemporary research on partisanship, including not just a review of existing scholarship but also extensive analyses of recently collected data on partisanship and its consequences in the United States, the United Kingdom, Sweden, Italy, and the Netherlands. However, in contrast to prior work, I examine two different types of partisanship: positive partisanship – that is, strong identification with and attachment to a political party – and negative partisanship – that is, strong internalized hostility toward a political party and its supporters. With this distinction, I arrive at a more nuanced assessment of partisanship: Across multiple countries and their political systems, I find that positive partisanship encourages a range of desirable political behaviors such as turnout and even other forms of effortful or costly political participation such as donating to or volunteering for a political campaign. At the same time, most of the problematic attitudes and behaviors that we associate with democratic erosion such as the vilification and demonization of political opponents are more strongly, if not exclusively, related to negative partisanship. Crucially, I demonstrate that these types of partisanship can exist and operate independently of each other, which is important for how we evaluate partisanship and its (anti-) democratic influences.

More generally, I would like the book to function as a field guide for scholars who work in disciplines that are inevitably affected by partisanship's growing reach, including political science, psychology, anthropology, sociology, and economics. At the same time, I aim to make this book accessible to citizens outside of academia who try to make sense of the partisan rancor and political violence that might have befallen their own country and community. From this perspective, this book might also be relevant for local civic organizers and activists who wish to understand the origins of entrenched partisan divisions in their own communities. While the book relies heavily on scholarly work and statistical analyses, I provide a summary of the results as well as a conclusion at the end of each empirical chapter to make them more accessible to readers from all backgrounds.

The book is organized into two theoretical sections and five empirical parts. The first theoretical section (Chapters 1–2) provides the reader with an understanding of the two main models of partisanship; it compares the socio-psychological conceptualization of partisanship (i.e., expressive partisanship) to its rational choice–based counterpart (i.e., instrumental partisanship). I highlight their different theoretical assumptions about the way people develop political preferences, the empirical evidence in their support (or lack thereof), as well as the normative implications of both approaches for our assessment of democratic decision-making. In the second theoretical section (Chapters 3–4), I introduce the reader to positive and negative partisanship, including a review of prior work on these types of partisanship, their grounding in Social Identity Theory, and a justification for why we should care about their distinctive origins and nature.

After laying the theoretical groundwork, I shift gears and embark on the first empirical section of the book (Chapters 5–6), focusing on the measure-ment of positive and negative partisanship in survey research. If partisan-ship – positive and negative – is an identity, then this should be reflected in the way we capture it. The measurement approach I utilize in this book is informed by Social Identity Theory and has been validated by prior scholar-ship, including my own (see Bankert, Huddy, and Rosema 2017 as well as Bankert 2020). The second empirical section (Chapter 7) examines the psychological origins of positive partisanship (PPID) and negative partisan-ship (NPID) whereby I focus on prominent personality traits such as Social Dominance Orientation, Authoritarianism, the Need for Closure, and the Big 5 Personality Traits. Aligned with my expectation, PPID and NPID are related to different sets of personality traits, providing evidence for their independent nature.

The third empirical section (Chapter 8) examines the impact of strong positive and negative partisanship on a range of democratic behaviors, including turnout, vote choice, and other forms of political engagement. For this analysis, I utilize original, individual-level survey data from the United States as well as four European multi-party systems, namely Sweden, the Netherlands, Italy, and the United Kingdom. I focus on these countries since I am somewhat familiar with their political systems due to my prior work but also because this case selection allows me to compare the magnitude and impact of positive and negative partisanship across five drastically different political systems and cultures. The comparative nature of these analyses can also assess the generalizability of the results beyond the US two-party system, which has attracted a large share of attention in prior scholarship. Across all five countries, the evidence shows that negative and positive partisanship differentially impact political behavior. Chapter 8 also includes a brief excursion into a somewhat neglected part of the electorate, namely political independents. I demonstrate that even independent voters can develop negative partisanship – even though they, by definition, lack a positive party attachment. This finding reasserts the notion that negative partisanship can exist independently of any positive party attachments. At the same time, it also sheds light on how even the disdain for a political party can promote political engagement.

In the fourth empirical chapter (Chapter 9), I examine the relationship between partisanship – both positive and negative – and anti-democratic attitudes such as the use of violence against members of the opposing party and the willingness to ban political parties and limit their free speech. The evidence suggests that negative partisanship is the main driver of these disconcerting attitudes and behaviors. While positive partisanship is not completely unrelated to these symptoms of democratic erosion, negative partisanship is much more strongly and more consistently associated with them across all five countries.

The final empirical part of the book (Chapter 10) examines possible ways to foster positive partisanship without intensifying its negative counterpart. For this purpose, I draw from prior experimental research in political psychology that aims to identify interventions to reduce partisan hostility. Utilizing their theoretical insights and experimental designs, I implement three original survey experiments that test the effect of superordinate identities and crosscutting identities, as well as the impact of party elites' rhetoric on positive and negative partisanship. Taken together, these experimental results emphasize the power and responsibility of party elites in promoting good partisanship among their supporters. In Chapter 11, I conclude the book with a few reflections on the future of research on partisanship in the United States and beyond as well as a normative assessment of the past and present challenges to democracy posed by negative partisanship.

Overall, I hope to leave the reader with a more informed, more positive, and more nuanced perspective on partisanship; one that enables all readers to critically assess their own party loyalties and one that enables academic readers to identify promising avenues for future research. A healthy and robust democratic system depends, in no small part, on the character of our party affiliations. There is a world in which partisans can strongly identify with their party without vilifying their opponents. The stakes are too high to dismiss such an alternative.

2

From Rational Choice to Partisan Identity

A Paradigm Change

2.1 WHAT IS IN THIS CHAPTER?

In this chapter, I introduce two models of partisanship – both of which differ dramatically in their assumptions about the origins of citizens' political behavior. First is the *instrumental* model of partisanship, which is based on Rational Choice Theory (RCT). Instrumental partisanship assumes that citizens bring their political preferences into the political arena and then decide to support a political party that satisfies these preferences. From this perspective, partisanship is determined by the proximity between a party's platform and a voter's political preferences. While this model has dominated political science for a long time, there is an abundance of scholarship showing that partisans do not always follow traditional notions of rational decision-making. In response to these inconsistencies, I introduce and review prior scholarship on the *expressive* model of partisanship, which, based on Social Identity Theory (SIT), conceptualizes partisanship as an identity that can operate relatively independently of political convictions and ideologies. After reviewing prior scholarship's evidence in support of the expressive model, I discuss its implications for democratic behavior as well as its current place in the academic discourse on partisanship.

2.2 WHY DOES THIS MATTER?

It is important to understand the origins of partisanship. Do partisans merely disagree on political issues or are they motivated to defend their party – regardless of actual policies or party performance? In other words, are partisans concerned about policies or about winning? The answers to these questions have vast implications for how we assess the nature of partisan conflict and its solutions. If the conflict between partisans is based on policies, then policy compromise is one possible solution. However, if it is based on status, then even shared policy preferences might do little to lessen partisan hostility, since it is not about policies but about seeing your team win at all costs.

∗∗∗

Partisanship plays a central role in political science. It is a key predictor of a host of important political outcomes, including the vote (Brader and Tucker 2009; Green et al. 2002), political issue preferences and core values (Gerber et al. 2010; Goren 2005), as well as political engagement (Huddy et al. 2015; Nicholson 2012). While the impact of partisanship on political behavior is well documented, there is still a lively debate regarding the origins of partisanship. Intuitively, partisanship should reflect people's political preferences and ideological convictions. Following this logic, citizens choose to support a political party based on their informed understanding of the party's platform and its alignment with their own political priorities. This notion, however, conflicts with the fact that citizens are generally uninformed about politics and tend to know little about concrete policy proposals (Lupia 2016). How do we square this lack of knowledge with the fierce partisan battles that characterize the political landscape in the United States and beyond? Put even more simply: What do we argue about if not about political issues? How can we explain "unbridled partisanship" – even in the face of unaware voters, changing ideologies, weak leadership, and poor governance? Rethinking partisanship as an identity, rather than just the sum of political preferences, can help solve some of these mysteries. To fully understand the theoretical innovation behind the expressive model, it is helpful to first review how political science has traditionally conceptualized partisanship. For this purpose, the following section discusses the instrumental model that, based on RCT, highlights the role of political issues and ideological convictions in shaping partisanship.

2.3 VOTER ECONOMICUS? RATIONAL CHOICE AND THE INSTRUMENTAL MODEL

The instrumental model is based on RCT, which has shaped the methodological and theoretical approaches of political scientists, psychologists, and economists for decades. RCT describes how people should behave if they complied with the ideal of the *homo economicus* – a self-interested agent whose actions are guided by the logic of optimization and utility-maximization. According to this logic, people's decisions are dictated by their anticipation of the value associated with possible future outcomes. Put differently, we are motivated to maximize the expected value of our actions. While this prediction may sound reasonable (and desirable), it builds on many underlying assumptions about how people arrive at these rational decisions: First, people need to gather sufficient information about their plausible courses of action since rational decision-making requires people to be well informed. Second, people need to assess the value of each plausible outcome and weigh that value by its expected probability of occurring. In other words, it is not enough to identify the outcome with the highest value to us. We also need to consider the probability of this outcome actually occurring. If the probability is low, then this will negatively affect the expected value of this outcome. For example, an American voter might consider voting for a third party such as the Green Party in a presidential election. Since the United States has a two-party system, the chance of the Green Party winning the election is quite slim, thereby reducing the expected value of voting for a third party. Eventually, the *homo economicus* compares the functions of plausible outcomes and chooses the one with the greatest expected value. These steps make up the ideal decision-making process; it specifies how people *should* act under optimal circumstances. From this perspective, RCT is a normative theory with strong built-in assumptions about how people make decisions.

It does not require a social science degree to raise objections to these assumptions. The bar for rationality is high, and in everyday life, the circumstances of our decision-making are anything but conducive to a *rational* choice. We are chronically short on time – certainly too short to gather sufficient information about plausible outcomes; and even if we have an abundance of time, access to critical information might not always be granted or easy to comprehend. Think about the complexities of tax policies or even just buying a car! To further complicate the matter, people are not always motivated to improve the quality of their decisions, particularly if they do not consider the decision at hand important. To illustrate this point: People might aim to be well informed when choosing a car that represents the best possible purchasing decision, but for how many people does that logic hold true when it comes to evaluating a party's tax policy proposal? Indeed, prior research has demonstrated that voters generally perform poorly when asked to place political parties on an ideological spectrum (Levitin and Miller 1979) or even to merely define the parties' ideological orientations (Converse 1964). These pieces of evidence call into question the notion of the well-informed voter as well as voters' ability to seek out a party that matches their political preferences or ideological convictions.

Despite these objections, RCT has greatly influenced the study of mass political behavior and propelled the development of instrumental partisanship. According to this model, various contemporary factors such as economic evaluations, presidential approval (MacKuen et al. 1989), policy preferences, party performance (Fiorina 1981), and candidate evaluations (Garzia 2013) shape party loyalties. Put simply, citizens select a party that aligns with their own policy preferences and has a track record of good governance and strong economic performance. This, in turn, also means that partisans abandon their party if it no longer satisfies these *instrumental* considerations.

With the implementation of the first *American National Election Study* panel survey in 1948, the instrumental model became directly testable with individual-level data of both party preferences and political attitudes over time. This data allowed political scientists to examine how party identification and political attitudes relate to each other, how that relationship changes over time, and if a change in one factor precedes a change in the other. If the instrumental model holds, we should observe that a change in political attitudes precedes a change in party preference since the former shapes the latter. However, the panel data revealed patterns conflicting with these predictions:

Despite some decline in the average level of partisan loyalty (and despite the inter-vention of the Watergate scandal and the resignation and subsequent pardoning of Richard Nixon between 1972 and 1976), the stability of individual partisanship was just as great in the 1970s as in the 1950s. Meanwhile, the continuity of individual issue preferences (for issues included in both sets of surveys) was no greater in the 1970s than in the 1950s – and thus well below the corresponding level for party identification. (Bartels 2008, p. 15)

Bartels (2008) identifies the crux of the issue: The instrumental model is unable to explain the extraordinary stability of partisanship in the face of volatile political attitudes. Citizens seem to change their political preferences without changing their partisanship. At the same time, partisanship remains relatively unaffected by shifting party platforms: Adams et al. (2011) show that when a party alters their policy platform, these changes either go unnoticed or have a small and delayed effect on partisanship.

In addition to partisanship's resistance to changing political attitudes and party platforms, another complication challenges the instrumental model: Voters do not assess instrumental concerns – party performance, leadership quality, and economic evaluations – in an objective fashion. A large share of research demonstrates the impact of partisan biases in the evaluation of many instrumental factors. For example, Lebo and Cassino (2007) show that "partisan groups generally do reward and punish presidents for economic performances, but only those presidents of the opposite party." This suggests that partisans are less likely to hold their party accountable, let alone change their party loyalties. Similarly, Bisgaard (2015) demonstrates partisan bias in the attribution of responsibility for the national economic downturn in the United Kingdom: While party supporters were generally capable of admitting that the British economy had deteriorated between 2004 and 2010, government party supporters were much less likely to blame their party for it while oppositional party supporters considered the government to be the primary culprit. This asymmetry in blame attribution is an unequivocal sign of partisan-motivated reasoning – another observation that seems to conflict with the instrumental model.

Overall, partisanship is much more enduring and resistant to changes in the political environment than the instrumental model would predict. There are cases in the history of American politics that can illustrate the stickiness of

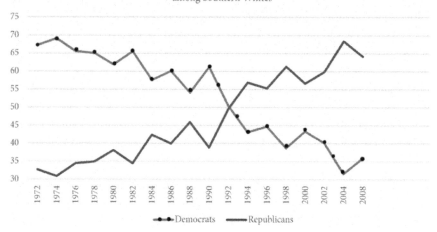

FIGURE 2.1 Party identification levels among White Southerners, 1972–2008
Note: Data taken from the ANES cumulative file. Graph includes Whites in the South only, who identify as both a strong or weak Democrat/Republican and who oppose government involvement in supporting minority groups.

partisan loyalties, even as the parties dramatically change their policy stances. Figure 2.1, for example, displays partisanship levels (as percentage of Democrats and Republicans) among White Southerners who oppose government involvement in supporting minority groups (i.e., civil rights legislation). The graph nicely illustrates partisans' resistance to change: Even though the Republican Party enjoyed several political successes in the South during the 1960s, it was not until 1992 that the partisan majority in the South flipped in favor of the Republican Party. Hence, it took almost three decades after the passage of the Civil Rights Act in 1964 before White Southerners who opposed civil rights legislation abandoned their former loyalties to the Democratic Party.

While the graph admittedly only shows aggregate levels of party identification, it nevertheless suggests that people only reluctantly reconsider their party affiliations – despite the drastic change in the parties' stance on civil rights. These findings might be driven by people's lack of attention to their party's policy platform (as Adams et al. [2011] demonstrate), but it could also be driven by their desire to protect and align themselves with their party. For example, Johnston et al. (2004) show that conflicts between party identification and liberal-conservative ideology tend to be resolved in favor of the party because partisans are motivated to be "good team players." Rather than abandoning their party because of a policy disagreement or poor performance in government, partisans try to defend their party, even to themselves.

Critics might advocate for a more generous application of the instrumental model. Rather than specific policy preferences, voters can utilize more general political principles and core values such as limited government, free enterprise, and individualism to judge which political party best represents their interests. While this argument certainly has face validity (and, again, can be considered desirable from a normative standpoint), Goren (2005) finds that party identification is more temporally stable and enduring than political core principles such as equal opportunity, limited government, or traditional family values. It is hard to explain these patterns if we keep assuming that core values determine partisanship. Instead, Goren's results suggest that even political core values – the basic building blocks of political attitudes – might be shaped by partisanship.

All these findings have one thing in common: they reverse the causal arrow suggested by RCT and the instrumental model. Partisanship is relatively resistant to changes in voters' core political values and preferences as well as to changes in their party's platforms. It thus becomes clear that changes in partisanship are the exception, not the norm, and are most likely to occur under unusual circumstances. As Campbell et al. (1960) – the authors of the pioneering book *The American Voter* – put it, "Only an event of extraordinary intensity can arouse any significant part of the electorate to the point that its established political loyalties are shaken" (p. 151). In other words, instrumental considerations might be neither the only reason people acquire their party affiliations nor the only reason they remain loyal to them.

2.4 PARTISANSHIP AS AN IDENTITY: THE EXPRESSIVE MODEL

As the gap between the instrumental model's expectations and the empirical evidence widened, an alternative conceptualization of partisanship gained credence, known as the expressive model. Campbell et al. (1960) depart from the paradigm of rational decision-making and its assumption about the nature of partisanship. Instead of viewing partisanship as the product of careful reflections on policies and party performance, the authors define partisanship as a psychological attachment to a political party, arguing that – rather than malleable – party loyalties tend to transcend "elements of historical circumstances" (p. 8) such as fluctuations in party performance, changes in policies, and even in the state of the economy. Partisans are motivated to defend and protect their party – even in bad times – because their partisanship is part of who they are; protecting the party is thus analogous to protecting a part of their self-image. From this vantage point, partisanship turns into an identity similar to other social group memberships that are important to people such as religion, race, or even loyal support of a football team. Motivated by this partisan identity, partisans strive to select information that presents their party in a positive light and deny or distort information that presents their party in a negative light. Consequently, partisans' efforts to protect the party – and by extension the self – create a form of echo chamber that filters out or distorts adverse information about their party, its leadership, and its supporters. Accordingly, Campbell et al. (1960) consider partisanship an "unmoved mover" that drives partisans' perceptions and evaluations of their political environment, thereby highlighting how difficult it is for partisans to be truly objective in assessing their party's merits.

What explains the enduring power of these identities? Partisan identities develop at an early stage in people's political socialization – oftentimes before their political convictions and preferences have fully formed. This creates a feedback loop whereby young partisans adopt the political positions of their party, which further strengthens their party attachments. Over time, this reciprocal process diminishes the impact of information that might challenge their party loyalties, including changes in the party's platform or bad party leadership. From this perspective, the expressive model does not assume partisans to be well informed about politics or even to have well-defined prior preferences. Instead, partisanship can operate somewhat independently and motivate partisans to align their political beliefs with their party's stances. This identity-driven process can explain the oftentimes uncritical and unconditional loyalty we see among strong partisans.

Given the reinforcing nature of partisanship over time, it is important to examine more closely the process by which people acquire partisanship in the first place. In their seminal work *Partisan Hearts and Minds*, Green, Palmquist, and Schickler (2002) argue that partisanship links an individual's self-image to the social groups that are emblematic of each political party such as race, ethnicity, religion, gender, or even groups based on lifestyle choices such as vegetarianism, parenthood, or gun ownership. Thus, the process by which people come to identify with a political party starts with the question: "What kinds of social groups come to mind as I think about Democrats, Republicans, and Independents? Which assemblage of groups (if any) best describes me?" (p. 8) rather than "Which party best represents my political positions?" From this perspective, partisanship is the result of a self-categorization or matching process during which people compare themselves to the types and groups of people that are associated with each party and then sort themselves into the party where this matching process yields the best fit.

This process can also help explain under what circumstances partisanship can change. If the social group composition of a political party influences partisans' attachment to that party, then we would expect that a major socio-demographic change in the party's leadership and its base can impact existing partisan loyalties. Green et al. refer to these changes as alterations in the party's public persona: "By stressing how difficult it is to alter the partisan balance, we do not mean to suggest that parties are altogether incapable of producing change. From time to time, a party alters the social group composition of its leadership and, by extension, its public persona" (2002, p. 13). Green and colleagues also use the gradual party realignment process in the

American South as an example to illustrate the face validity of their argument: the inclusion of Black Americans into the Democratic Party's base gradually altered the social group composition of the party's public persona. Over an extended period, this change led White Southerners, who sought to preserve the existing racial hierarchy, to abandon the Democratic Party. Other factors such as the increased presence of White Southern leadership in the Republican Party further accelerated the *Republicanization* of the South. These realignments of party loyalties were driven by voters' changing perceptions of which regional and racial groups "go with" each party. Since these perceptions are sticky and hard to change, it is not surprising that the exit of White Southerners from the Democratic Party occurred so incrementally over the course of decades.

2.5 SOCIAL IDENTITY THEORY AND THE EXPRESSIVE MODEL OF PARTISANSHIP

The expressive model and the idea of a partisan *identity* did not develop in a vacuum; they are derived from Social Identity Theory (SIT) – a prominent theory in social psychology that examines the role of identity in intergroup relations. With the integration of social and cognitive psychology into political science in the past few decades, SIT and its offshoots have become a prolific theoretical framework for the study of partisan identities (e.g., Huddy et al. 2015; Mason et al. 2015) and other social and political identities such as gender, race, religion and ethnicity (see Huddy 2001 for a review). Since SIT is the main theoretical framework of this book, I review the theory's key tenets in the remainder of this chapter.

Social Identity Theory (Tajfel and Turner 1979) originated as a model of intergroup behavior, examining the psychological processes that promote the development of group identifications. According to SIT, people are motivated to achieve a positive "social identity," which is defined as "that part of an individual's self-concept which derives from his knowledge of his membership in a social group (or groups) together with the value and emotional significance attached to that membership" (Tajfel 1981, p. 255). Put differently, people's sense of self is defined by their membership in social groups such as their nationality, occupation, religion, race, or even their hobbies and lifestyle choices. For example, when people are asked to describe themselves, they might say "I am an American" and "I am a Muslim" if their nationality and religion are an important part of who they are. Alternatively, one might value "being a UGA football fan" as an integral part of one's self-concept. Thus, membership in these social groups is important to us and we aim to defend and protect them because they are a part of who we are. Turner et al. (1987) further describe this motivation as a need for people "to differentiate their own groups positively from others to achieve a positive social identity"

(p. 42). We are motivated to see the groups we belong to in a positive light – especially in comparison to other social groups – since it reflects well on us as a member of that group too.[1]

The ease with which people attach to their groups and internalize their membership has been empirically demonstrated by the so-called minimal group paradigm – a methodology in social psychology that investigates the conditions for conflict and discrimination between groups (Tajfel 1970). Experiments that have utilized this method consistently show just how *minimal* the conditions for in-group favoritism and out-group prejudice can be. In fact, even experimentally imposed and thus arbitrary distinctions between groups of respondents, such as the color of participants' shirts or preferences for certain paintings, can motivate participants to systematically favor their "own" group at the expense of other groups – despite the trivial and random nature of these group distinctions (see Tajfel, Billig, Bundy, and Flament, 1971). This in-group favoritism is driven by the motivation to achieve a positive social identity in relation to other groups, even if the group was artificially created for the purpose of the experiment.

These predictions are even more applicable to real-world identities that have been practiced over time, such as partisan identities: Partisans are motivated to defend their party, precisely because the party's status is intertwined with their self-understanding. This helps explain not just partisans' motivation to discredit information that portrays their own party (i.e., in-party) negatively but also the hostility partisans show toward the opposing party (i.e., out-party) in zero-sum situations – the latter poses a threat to the positive image and status of the in-party. From this vantage point, Social Identity Theory can explain many of the partisan behaviors that are hard to reconcile with the expectations of rational decision-making, including biased and selective information processing (Bolsen et al. 2014; Druckman et al. 2013; Lebo and Cassino 2007) as well as disdain toward the opposing party – even when they endorse similar policies as the in-party (Mason 2015; Westwood et al. 2015). Indeed, as Mason (2015) shows, partisans who strongly identify with their party care about more than *just* policies; they want their party to win. Electoral victory is not just a means to an end (i.e., implementing desired policies), it is also an end to itself (i.e., positive status). The desire for victory also helps us understand why partisans are much less

[1] While the authors of *Partisan Hearts and Minds* refer to partisanship as a social identity, they explicitly distance themselves from Social Identity Theory (SIT). In fact, Green et al. (2002) state that their theoretical approach differs from SIT: "The [theory] emphasizes an individual's drive to achieve positive self-esteem. People attach themselves to socially valued groups, and those who are trapped in low-status groups either dissociate themselves or formulate a different way of looking at groups. This depiction is very different from ours ... [we] remain agnostic about the underlying psychological motives that impel people to form social identities such as party attachments" (p. 11).

likely – if at all – to punish their party for poor policies. While many political pundits might assume that these powerful partisan identities are an American phenomenon, recent scholarship has demonstrated the validity of expressive partisanship in European multi-party systems (Bankert et al. 2017), as well as in newly formed (Carlson 2015) and politically changing democracies (Baker et al. 2015), highlighting the universal applicability of Social Identity Theory and the expressive model of partisanship.

2.6 EXPRESSIVE VERSUS INSTRUMENTAL MODEL

Considering all the evidence, it is clear that the origins of expressive partisanship stand in sharp contrast to its instrumental counterpart. However, that contrast should not create the wrong impression that expressive and instrumental partisanship are two irreconcilable theories. For example, Green and colleagues do not categorically rule out the importance of issue positions in shaping partisanship: "To be sure, party issue positions have something to do with the attractiveness of partisan labels to young adults, much as religious doctrines have something to do with the attractiveness of religious denominations. But causality also flows in the other direction: When people feel a sense of belonging to a given social group, they absorb the doctrinal positions that the group advocates. However party and religious identification come about, once they take root in early adulthood, they often persist. Partisan identities are enduring features of citizens' self-conception" (2002, p. 4). Here the authors make the crucial point that the expressive and instrumental models are not mutually exclusive. Both models can shape the development of partisanship, a notion that is further supported by Huddy et al. (2015): "Distinct expressive and instrumental approaches to partisanship have coexisted in political science research since at least the early 1980s …. Both models can claim empirical support, and there is growing evidence that instrumental and expressive accounts of partisanship may explain vote choice and public opinion at different times, under differing conditions, and among distinct segments of the electorate" (pp. 1–2).

Indeed, the applicability of expressive and instrumental partisanship might depend significantly on characteristics of voters, including their age, education, political knowledge, but also personality traits (more on this in Chapter 7). Equally important might be the political culture and the institutional features of an electoral system. For example, partisanship in multi-party systems might be more influenced by instrumental considerations like ideology[2] since it is a more salient dimension that voters use to categorize political parties and coalition blocs (see, for example, Huddy, Davies, and

---

[2] Note though that even a seemingly instrumental factor like ideology can function as an identity (see Malka and Lelkes 2010; Mason 2018; and Oshri et al. 2021).

Bankert 2018 for a review of partisan identity in Europe, as well as Bankert, Del Ponte, and Huddy 2017 for a case study of partisan identity in Italy). From this perspective, rather than asking which model is "correct," a theoretically more interesting question would be which model is more applicable *under what conditions.* An answer to that question requires studying partisan identity across different political systems. Such a comparative setup can detect the cultural and contextual factors that might accentuate expressive and instrumental facets of partisanship such as the number and ideology of political parties in the electoral space, the voting system, the campaign finance system, the regulation and distribution of public and private media ownership as well as the length and quality of the election campaign cycle. Chapters 8 and 9 aim to propel that kind of research by providing a comparative assessment of partisanship in the United States as well as four different multi-party systems in Europe – Sweden, the Netherlands, the United Kingdom, and Italy. These countries differ vastly in their political culture as well as in the architecture of their political institutions, providing a comprehensive test of the validity of the expressive model.

2.7 SUMMARY

Partisanship originates in a mix of both expressive and instrumental factors. While the instrumental model considers partisanship the product of careful evaluation of a party's platform and their leadership's performance, the expressive model conceptualizes partisanship as a social identity that is part of partisans' self-image and thus motivates them to protect and defend the in-party – even in the face of changing policies and poor performance. From this perspective, partisan identities are self-reinforcing: Strong partisans aim to be good team players that support and align themselves with their party. Over time, this practiced loyalty becomes a habit that further strengthens their party attachments and creates a perceptual lens through which partisans assess their political environment This reciprocal relationship can be disrupted by major changes in the party's social composition or stances on highly salient policies such as the inclusion of southern Whites in the Republican Party's leadership or the Democratic Party's decision to promote civil rights legislation in the 1960s.

3

Partisan Identity and Political Behavior

A Review of Prior Scholarship

3.1 WHAT IS IN THIS CHAPTER?

In this chapter, I offer a thorough review of the scholarship that investigates the impact of partisan identity (i.e., expressive partisanship) on political behavior, including political attitudes, turnout, voting, and other forms of political participation. While most of that work focuses on Democrats and Republicans in the US two-party system, there is a growing number of scholars who apply the expressive model to their studies of partisanship in European multi-party systems and beyond. I will emphasize these studies and their value in advancing the generalizability and applicability of the expressive model beyond partisans in the United States.

3.2 WHY DOES IT MATTER?

The current chapter serves two purposes. First, it provides an assessment of partisan identities' influence on citizens' political behavior, thereby illustrating how partisanship anchors people in their political system and fosters political engagement – a pillar of democratic citizenship. At the same time, it also documents partisanship's negative side effects, which constitutes a first step in trying to rectify them. Overall, this chapter poses a conundrum to the reader: How can we benefit from partisanship's positive influence on people's political engagement without its seemingly negative influence on the relationship between partisans?

***

In their seminal work *The American Voter*, Campbell and his colleagues early on observed that a political "party has a profound influence across the full range of political objects to which the individual voters respond" (1960, p. 128). Since then, there has been a flourishing literature in political science, documenting the profound effects of partisanship on partisans' political attitudes and evaluations as well as their political engagement. In many cases, this plethora of research aligns with the expressive model's predictions – as well as Campbell and colleagues' early observation – that partisanship influences how partisans select and process political information. This finding has crucial implications for the instrumental model. Rather than representing the sum of citizens' policy preferences, their ideological convictions, and assessment of the government's performance, partisanship also shapes these instrumental concerns by motivating partisans to support and align themselves with their party. In political psychology, this phenomenon is oftentimes referred to as "partisan-motivated reasoning." Another feature of strong partisan identities is their ability to generate powerful emotions among partisans, such as anger and enthusiasm, especially when their in-party and its status are threatened – a scenario that occurs frequently during ever-expanding election cycles. This threat motivates partisans to become politically active on behalf of their party in an attempt to promote and secure its success. These are powerful predictions that can help explain partisans' fierce disagreements in assessing the performance of their political parties as well as the heightened tensions between partisans as elections approach. In the following, I will take a closer look at partisan identities and their impact on partisans' political attitudes and engagement.

3.3 PARTISANSHIP'S EFFECT ON POLITICAL ATTITUDES AND VALUES

For expressive partisans, political parties are more than just a proxy for their preferred policies; they are also a reference point to develop these preferences. Even without partisan-motivated reasoning, it is not surprising that partisans take cues from their party to decide which policies to support or oppose. Policy proposals are complex, nuanced, and might require some level of political knowledge, time, and motivation to comprehend. Thus, partisans turn to short cuts to form their political preferences. As Goren et al. (2009) explain: "Most people do not analyze systematically the messages they encounter. Instead, they usually turn to simple heuristics such as whether or not they like or trust the source, when evaluating a message" (Goren et al. 2009, p. 806). These simple heuristics, or cognitive shortcuts, often involve signals from party elites that guide and shape citizens' political attitudes. From this perspective, partisanship serves a crucial function for voters by facilitating their political decisions, assessments, and judgments (Campbell et al. 1960; Goren et al. 2009). Prior scholarship has provided several examples of these effects. For example, partisanship shapes partisans' perceptions of the economy's performance (Bartels 2002; but see Bullock, Gerber, Hill, and Huber 2015), their evaluations of policy debates (Druckman et al. 2013; Slothuus and de Vreese 2010), and even their core political values such as traditionalism and limited government (Goren, Federico, and Kittilson

2009). In the messy political world, partisan shortcuts provide an invaluable benefit, especially to voters with less political knowledge.

In one of the most illustrative studies to test this argument, Cohen (2003) designs an experiment that demonstrates that partisans' "attitudes toward a social policy depended almost exclusively upon the stated position of one's political party. This effect overwhelmed the impact of both the policy's objective content and participants' ideological beliefs" (p. 808). Cohen's study shows that both liberal and conservative participants adjust their stance on welfare programs if they are led to believe that their party endorsed them. This adjustment leads to obvious ideological mismatches: Liberal respondents in the experiment reported support for more stringent welfare policies if the Democratic Party supposedly proposed them while conservative respondents reported support for more generous welfare programs if the Republican Party supposedly advocated for them. This experimental evidence convincingly demonstrates that partisans alter their own policy preferences to align with their party – even if that policy conflicts with their self-declared ideological convictions. Notably, when asked to justify their opinions, partisans denied that they had been influenced by their political party's stance on welfare programs. Instead, they claimed their *own* political convictions guided their support for the policy proposal. Clearly, partisans either rationalize or are being oblivious to their party's influence. It is this unawareness – conscious or not – that can turn a healthy party attachment into uncritical tribalism. To further complicate things, respondents in Cohen's experiment also believed that the members of the out-party were much more likely to be influenced by their political party – which, in line with Social Identity Theory, illustrates the effects of in-party favoritism as well as partisans' need to positively distinguish their party from the out-party and its supporters.

While the evidence of partisanship's effects in Cohen's study is persuasive, such experimental work is often criticized on the grounds of lacking external validity. This concern can affect the results discussed here in two distinct ways: Experimentally manipulated party cues might not be perceived as credible by the respondent, or one-shot exposure to party cues is simply not sufficient to affect respondents' political attitudes. If these concerns were valid, however, we would expect null results for most studies that examine the effect of party cues. Alternatively, it is possible that the experimental setting creates an unrealistic scenario by allowing respondents to experience undisturbed exposure to party cues, free from daily life distractions. Indeed, during an ordinary day, people might not read any political news at all, or if they do, they might do so with only partial attention or interest. From this perspective, real-world partisans might mostly be deaf to their party leaders' cues. If this concern holds, then prior results on the effects of partisanship might be overstated.

In a rare quasi-experimental panel study, Slothuus and Bisgaard (2020) address the issue of external validity by examining Danish voters over the course of five waves between 2010 and 2011 – a period that was marked by a recession in the Danish economy. During that time, several major political parties announced far-reaching policy reforms related to unemployment insurance and retirement programs. Slothuus and Bisagaard (2020) tracked respondents' attitudes on these polices before and after the proposed cutbacks in these programs. The real-world political results were astounding and worth quoting directly:

> We find that citizens' policy opinions immediately moved by around 15 percentage points in response to their party's new issue position compared to similar citizens whose party did not change its position. Moreover, the marked opinion change was not just driven by citizens already (partly) supportive of welfare cutbacks. To the contrary, parties were successful in reversing opinions among their supporters, moving them from opposing cutting down welfare to supporting it. (p. 897)

These findings, generated in a multi-party system, neatly align with Cohen's early study on the effect of partisanship on welfare attitudes among Democrats and Republicans – despite the lack of a captive audience that experimental studies are often criticized for. Even more impressively, the authors find that these effects lasted for several months, and in the case of unemployment reform, even more than a year. As Slothuus and Bisagaard note, this is a far longer duration than the one detected in most experimental studies in which effects evaporate after a few weeks (Gerber et al. 2011; Hill et al. 2013). From this perspective, it is even possible that many prior experimental studies underestimate the effect of party cues on partisans' political attitudes.

Critics might argue that these studies merely demonstrate partisan cheerleading – "cheap talk" to express support for the in-party at no personal cost. However, partisanship even drives people's perspectives on issues that they clearly have a personal stake in. Conducting a survey experiment in Denmark, Slothuus and Bisgaard (2021) demonstrate that even in the context of collective bargaining conflicts over salary and labor rights, party cues significantly shape public employees' attitudes toward these personally relevant and costly policies. Yet the authors also show that these effects are not limitless: In-party support did not motivate these public employees to completely forgo their self-interest; instead, "party cues worked by tempering the most extreme policy demands among public employees, leading them to take a more moderate position on the issue" (p. 1095). This is an interesting finding that demonstrates the power of partisanship in shaping attitudes even on policies that directly affect partisans' pocketbooks.

Yet one could challenge the interpretation of these results. Perhaps these alignment processes are not driven by partisans' motivation to be loyal to their team, as predicted by the expressive model of partisanship. Instead, voters might rely on these party cues simply because doing so has worked well for them in the past. From this vantage point, adopting the in-party's position is a result of a repeatedly successful match between the party's policy positions and voters' own preferences. Conceptually, this is different from the motivational process that the expressive model suggests by which partisans adopt and support the in-party position because it strengthens a sense of belonging to that group. However, recent work by Carlson (2015) demonstrates expressive partisanship's impact even in new (semi-)democracies such as Uganda, where party cues have not yet developed the level of stability and reliability common in established electoral systems like the United States and Europe. In particular, the author shows that partisans of the incumbent president's party systematically overestimate the benefits they obtained from the government, while opposition supporters tend to underestimate them. This is indicative of partisan-motivated reasoning, supporting the notion that partisanship is a readily adoptable identity even in new electoral systems where partisan cues have not been "vetted" yet.

Partisanship also influences voters' political core values – predispositions that we normally tend to think of as more stable than political attitudes: Goren (2005) uses panel data from the *American National Election Study* to demonstrate that party identification is more temporally stable than political core values such as support for equal opportunity, limited government, family values, and moral tolerance. If causes are more stable than effects, then these results suggest that support for these political values is shaped by party cues, especially by the rhetoric of party elites. Goren's results "suggest that political elites activate latent partisan biases in the minds of citizens, which in turn subtly affect their core political values. Party identification does not determine value positions, but it appears to shape them" (2005, p. 894).

In another study, Goren and colleagues (2009) provide causal evidence for this argument. Using a survey experiment, the authors show that partisan cues shape the level of support for political core values such as equal opportunity, moral traditionalism and tolerance, and beliefs in self-reliance, concluding that "while it is true that people can work out what they believe is best for society irrespective of their group loyalties, it seems fair to say that group attachments usually weigh rather heavily on such beliefs" (p. 819). In a similar vein, McCann (1997) shows that beliefs about equality and traditional morality are influenced by candidate evaluations, but the author finds no comparable influence of these core values on candidate evaluations. Since candidate evaluations are also subject to partisan biases, the impact of candidate evaluations on core beliefs provides indirect evidence for partisanship's influence on beliefs about equality and morality rather than vice versa.

By extension, partisan-motivated reasoning also leads to ideologically more consistent attitudes and beliefs among partisans – a concept that political scientists refer to as attitude constraint (Converse 1964). Strong partisans are ideologically much more consistent across political issues than their nonpartisan counterparts (Baldassarri and Gelman 2008; Lau and

Redlawsk 2001; Lupia 1994; Zaller 2004). Note once again the unusual direction of the relationship between ideological consistency and partisanship: Ideological consistency among partisans is heightened because they align their political attitudes to match their party's policies. Thus, as political parties – especially in the United States – have become ideologically more homogenous, so have their supporters, especially if they are strong partisans and display some level of political awareness (Layman and Carsey 2002). For example, the 2016 *American National Election Study* reveals that about 64% of strong Democrats (and only 38% of weak Democrats) claimed a liberal ideology. Compare this number to the 26% of strong Democrats who called themselves liberals back in 1990 when the Democratic Party was ideologically much more heterogeneous. Thus, partisans learn ideological association from their party elites. The flipside of this argument has implications for citizens without a party affiliation (i.e., independents) who might display lower levels of ideological preferences because they do not have an in-party that they could use as an ideological benchmark. Indeed, almost 34% of pure independents in the 2016 *American National Election Study* identified as moderates and 39% were unable to place themselves on an ideological spectrum, compared to only 19% of partisans who called themselves ideologically moderate and 19% who were unable to place themselves on the ideological spectrum. These numbers shrink even further when examining strong Democrats and Republicans only (13% and 18%, respectively).

 Overall, there is plenty of evidence supporting a key prediction of the expressive model of partisanship: Motivated by strong party attachments, partisans align their political attitudes and even core beliefs with their party's stances.

 Nevertheless, there are also a number of recent studies that find evidence for the impact of instrumental factors such as actual policy preferences and expert evaluations. Rather than trying to refute the expressive model of partisanship, these studies examine the expressive model's limitations as well as the conditions under which instrumental factors outweigh partisan cues (e.g., Boudreau and MacKenzie 2014; Malhotra and Kuo 2008; Nicholson 2011, 2012; Tomz and Houweling 2009). For example, Mummolo, Peterson, and Westwood (2021) demonstrate that partisanship is especially dominant in the context of less salient political issues such as tariffs, school curricula, health insurance coverage of birth control, and interior department spending – issues that generate much less interest and partisan fervor than highly salient issues such as the discrimination of the LGBTQ community, Obamacare, assault rifle bans, and abortions. The authors find that if their own party's candidate disagrees with them on four or more of these highly salient and divisive issues, the average partisan is more likely to support a candidate from the opposing party. While these results constitute evidence for the limits of partisan loyalties, they also clearly show just how much it takes for partisans to abandon them. As Mummolo et al. (2021) note: "Even after a co-partisan candidate takes dissonant positions on three high-salience issues, the average voter is still more likely than not to select this candidate" (p.959). Partisans are thus more likely than not to support their party's candidates, even if they advocate for policies that contradict their party's established platform. Notably, the authors remain agnostic about the underlying mechanism that drives partisans to defect eventually from their party: Is the defection motivated by voters' self-interest, as the instrumental model would predict? Or is it motivated by their desire to protect the party from "faux" candidates who might obfuscate the party's brand? Either way, the study strongly suggests that partisan loyalties have *some* limits when highly salient issues are at the forefront. This finding underlines the notion that some political issues, such as abortion, are more resistant to partisanship than others, reiterating the point that expressive and instrumental partisanship can operate differently across different issues and contexts.

This is also echoed by Peterson (2019) who argues that, when examining partisanship's impact on political attitudes, we need to distinguish between assimilation and tolerance: While the former aligns with the expressive assertion that partisans adopt their party's policies, the latter proposes that partisans "merely tolerate policy divergence to a greater extent in the presence of partisan cues (i.e., they support a particular elite-endorsed policy proposal even as their own preferred policy outcome remains unchanged)" (p. 336). The author shows that many partisans will *tolerate* an in-party–endorsed policy that conflicts with their own preferences – but they will not change their own underlying policy preference. Like Mummolo and colleagues (2021), Peterson's study focuses on the manipulation of highly salient issues such as abortion, budget deficit reduction, and the minimum wage – political issues that are linked to a political party's identity and that partisans have strong feelings about. Thus, tolerance might be more common in these cases than assimilation. On the flipside, this means that political issues with low salience – and thus less familiarity among voters – might be more susceptible to assimilation. Thus, the type of political issue at hand determines whether partisans will internalize their party's policies or merely tolerate them. In support of this notion, Arceneaux and Vander Wielen (2017) find that partisans – in the absence of crystallized attitudes – merely adopt their party's stances if the issue at stake is not very salient in the political discourse. However, "parties appear to lose this leverage over voter positions in the domain of high salience issues" (p. 110).

Cumulatively, this prior scholarship builds an integrative perspective that considers expressive and instrumental partisanship as two distinct but compatible conceptualizations. Despite this book's focus on expressive partisanship, it is important to note that both types of partisanship can shape political attitudes in a complementary, rather than competitive, fashion.

3.4 PARTISANSHIP'S EFFECT ON VOTING

In the instrumental model, the vote is considered the result of various considerations that voters take into account before making a decision, such as the party's handling of the economy, the quality of the party's leadership and its platform, and their own policy preferences. In contrast, the expressive model of partisanship considers voting an expression of partisans' motivation to secure and advance their party's electoral success and status. Indeed, strong partisans are not only more likely to turn out to vote (Wattenberg and Brians 2002), but they are also significantly more likely to vote for the party they identify with (Bartels 2000; Green, Palmquist, and Schickler 2002; Huddy et al. 2015; Lewis-Beck et al. 2008) even as political parties change their leadership and substantive policy platform (Lewis-Beck et al. 2008).

As obvious as it seems, the notion that partisanship predicts voting behavior was contested in the early 1970s as the share of "independent" voters and the prevalence of split ticket voting increased. Political scientists interpreted these patterns as symptoms of partisan decline (Broder 1971; DeVries and Tarrance 1972). Despite these early volatilities, "the impact of partisanship on voting behavior has increased markedly in recent years, both at the presidential level (where the overall impact of partisanship in 1996 was almost 80 percent greater than in 1972) and at the congressional level (where the overall impact of partisanship in 1996 was almost 60 percent greater than in 1978)" (Bartels 2000, p. 35). Since then, partisanship has been a stable key predictor of the vote in the United States (Brader and Tucker 2009; Green et al. 2002) and continues to grow in influence, especially among the increasing share of strong partisans in the United States (Mason 2013). The 2020 US election results illustrate this point quite well: Among self-identified Democrats, 95% voted for Biden – despite the lukewarm response he provoked among many supporters of the Democratic Party.[1] Similarly, 94% of Republicans voted for their party's candidate, namely Donald Trump – despite the controversial nature of his presidency and candidacy leading up to the elections.[2]

This close relationship between partisanship and vote choice is amplified in the US two-party system where only two parties define the entire ideological space: one party for the liberal side and one party for the conservative side of the spectrum. Thus, a vote for the opposing party would not just violate party loyalties but also voters' ideological self-understanding (e.g., being a Democrat and being a liberal). Due to this partisan-ideological

---

[1] The Christian Science Monitor, The left is lukewarm on Biden. Will they turn out for him anyway?, www.csmonitor.com/USA/Politics/2020/0429/The-left-is-lukewarm-on-Biden.-Will-they-turn-out-for-him-anyway (last accessed, December 13, 2021).

[2] These numbers are taken from a report by the Pew Research Center, www.pewresearch.org/politics/2021/06/30/behind-bidens-2020-victory/ (last accessed, December 13, 2021).

alignment, it might not be too surprising that partisanship powerfully predicts vote choice in the United States. But does this connection also emerge in multi-party systems?

Indeed, there are reasons to believe that party affiliations are only weakly related to vote choice in these systems since they offer voters the chance to switch between political parties within the same ideological bloc. Thus, voters in multi-party systems can vote for a different party without contradicting their ideological affiliation. This liberty to trade within families of ideologically similar parties might weaken partisans' identification with one particular party, thereby diminishing its impact on the vote. Moreover, multi-party systems often generate coalitional governments along ideological lines that can further blur loyalty to one single party (Gonzalez et al. 2008; Hagevi 2015; Meffert et al. 2009). Given these concerns, we might reasonably expect partisanship to be a much weaker predictor of vote choice in multi-party systems. Yet recent scholarship has provided evidence to the contrary: Bankert, Huddy, and Rosema (2017) show that levels of in-party voting – that is, voting for the party voters identify with – is quite high across several European countries, with 88% in Sweden, 76% in the United Kingdom, and 61% in the Netherlands. Even in these multi-party systems, partisan identity has a strong impact on vote choice: My colleagues and I show that the probability of voting for the in-party – ranging from 0, the lowest probability, to 1, the highest probability – differs dramatically across the strength of partisan identity, from a low of roughly 0.45 in the Netherlands and 0.5 in the United Kingdom at the weakest levels of partisan identity to a high of 0.9 among the strongest partisans. We further demonstrate far weaker effects for voters' strong ideological positions – a more instrumental facet of partisanship. These results suggest that expressive partisanship is not limited to the US two-party system, as partisan identity is a strong and powerful predictor of vote choice even among European voters. Our findings also align with other scholarship demonstrating a tight link between partisanship and the vote in the British parliamentary elections (Berglund et al. 2005), the Italian national elections (Huddy et al. 2018), the German federal elections (Arzheimer 2017), in several developing democracies across Latin America (Lupu 2015), and in African democracies where scholars traditionally thought of ethnicity – based on shared language, dialect, and region – as the most crucial social and political identity rather than partisanship (Mattes and Kroenke 2020).

Yet, despite their strong connection across so many different countries and continents, it is important to note that partisanship and vote choice are not interchangeable; they might neatly overlap in many cases, but they nevertheless are not the same and do not always go hand in hand. Consider the following scenario: Partisans might identify with a particular party and yet vote for the candidate of another or abstain from voting altogether. This choice might be grounded in instrumental concerns such as poor party performance. However, it can also be motivated by strategic voting calculations in an attempt to secure the party's success in the long run. Green and colleagues (2002) illustrate this point nicely with the example of Democrats' withdrawal of support for President Carter's second term: "Partisans do not want their own leaders to become a liability to the team. [In the case of Carter and Clinton], liberals were angered by their president's move to the right, but Carter was regarded by Democrats as a weak leader and an electoral liability, whereas Clinton was tolerated as an unusually gifted campaigner" (p. 220). From this perspective, partisans can vote against their party's candidate, not despite their party attachment but because of it: Partisans are loyal to their party and committed to its success – even if that means temporarily deserting a weak party leader.

The distinction between the vote and partisanship is also relevant when examining independent voters who – by definition – have no prior party attachment. Their vote for a particular party might be driven by two very different motivations: One the one hand, it can indicate a temporary support *for* a political party. On the other hand, it can also be an expression of a negative vote, that is, a vote *against* a particular party. This is especially likely in the two-party system, in which voting for one party directly reduces the chances of electoral victory for the other. Treating partisanship and the vote as interchangeable masks these distinct motivations among independents and partisans alike.

Last, partisanship also increases turnout. A plethora of studies on electoral behavior consistently shows that independent voters care much less about election outcomes and thus – not surprisingly – also turn out at significantly lower rates than their partisan counterparts. These different turnout rates align with the expressive model's expectation that partisans are driven by the desire to see their team succeed. There is no equivalent motivation among independent voters since they do not have a team to root for. As Green, Palmquist, and Schickler (2002) put it so eloquently: "Like people who lack an allegiance to a football team but who nevertheless find themselves at a Super Bowl party, nonpartisans look on with a certain sense of indifference. They do not regard a victory of one side as victory for themselves" (p. 219). From this perspective, partisanship serves an important normative function in democratic societies: It anchors people in their political system and promotes their engagement with it. If voting is the foundation of democratic citizenship, then partisanship significantly contributes to its attainment.

3.5 PARTISANSHIP'S EFFECT ON POLITICAL ENGAGEMENT

Political engagement goes beyond turnout and vote choice. Classic studies of political behavior (e.g., Verba et al. 1995) examine a broad array of ways that are at citizens' disposal to participate in the political world. Notably, and in contrast to voting, these activities can greatly vary in the amount of time and effort they require from citizens, ranging from discussing politics with people on social media to volunteering time or even money to a political campaign.

The decision to become politically active can be grounded in instrumental as well as expressive components of partisanship. The instrumental model would suggest that citizens actively support their party to see their preferred policies implemented. From this vantage point, we would expect that citizens with strong political preferences are most likely to become politically active on behalf of the party that best represents these preferences. In contrast, in the expressive model, partisans become active on behalf of their party to see their "team" win. Note the subtle difference between the expressive and instrumental partisans' motivation. For instrumental partisans, their party's electoral victory is a means to an end, namely the implementation of valued policies. For expressive partisans, electoral victory is an end in itself, independent of policy preferences; seeing their party succeed makes them feel good about themselves because they are part of the winning team. From this perspective, the strongest party supporters, whose self-esteem is most closely intertwined with the party's success, work most actively on behalf of their party (Ethier and Deaux 1994; Fowler and Kam 2007). Accordingly, Huddy and colleagues (2015) aptly compare strong partisans to passionate sports fans: "The social identity model of partisan politics is not very different from that advanced to explain the ardor and actions of sports fans. Weakly identified fans may attend games when the team is doing well and skip those where defeat is likely, but strong fans persevere and participate, even when the team is sure to lose, in order to boost their team's chances of victory" (p. 3). Indeed, Social Identity Theory emphasizes the role of threat to the group's status in shaping collective action among strong group identifiers (Tajfel and Turner 1979; Van Zomeren, Postmes, and Spears 2008). Partisans' engagement is thus especially high during times of electoral competition, when the status of their party – their team – is most at risk.

This desire to win as well as the fear of losing can generate strong emotions among partisans. These emotions are essential in driving political action (Huddy, Feldman, and Cassese 2007; Lerner and Tiedens 2006). While emotions have traditionally been seen as an obstacle to democratic citizenship by clouding people's judgment, a substantial amount of research has demonstrated the positive effects of anger and enthusiasm on political interest and even more effortful forms of political action such as protest and attending campaign rallies (Groenendyk and Banks 2013; Marcus, Neuman, and MacKuen 2000; Valentino et al. 2011; van Zomeren, Spears, and Leach 2008). Not surprisingly, emotions run high shortly before as well as in the aftermath of a competitive election (see Green, Palmquist, and Schickler

2002), especially among strong partisans who feel anger and enthusiasm more intensely in the face of their party's ever-changing odds of electoral victory (Rydell et al. 2008; van Zomeren, Spears, and Leach 2008).

In the instrumental model, emotions can play a vital part in driving political action too. Yet, once again, the origin of these emotions differs from the expressive model: Instrumental partisans feel angry if their favored policies or ideological convictions are being challenged and they feel enthusiastic if their preferred policies are likely to be implemented. From this perspective, emotions are not a prerogative of the expressive model; instead, they are a vital driver of political action among both instrumental and expressive partisans. The notable difference lies only in the origin of these action-driving emotions, whether it is a strong partisan identity and the resulting concern for the party's status or strong policy preferences and closely held ideological convictions. In their pioneering work, Huddy, Mason, and Aaroe (2015) provide a comprehensive test of the role of expressive and instrumental factors in shaping partisans' campaign involvement in the United States. Utilizing four different samples of respondents with varying levels of prior political engagement, the authors show that partisan identity is a significantly stronger predictor of campaign involvement – such as working for or donating money to a political party or candidate – than strong ideological convictions or political issue preferences. Utilizing an experimental message that portrayed the in-party either as the likely loser or winner in an upcoming election, Huddy and colleagues show that strong partisans reacted to the threat of losing with significantly greater anger than weak partisans and with greater enthusiasm to the reassurance of their party's upcoming electoral victory. There is thus a close connection between the strength of partisans' identity and their emotional reactions to the prospect of their party winning or losing an election. However, the authors show that instrumental components generate emotions too, albeit in a much more muted and less coherent fashion: In response to an experimental message that reported a likely failure of highly salient policies related to health care and same-sex marriage, respondents with strong positions on these issues did not report greater anger than respondents without them, but they were slightly more likely to react positively to an experimental message that provided reassurance of those policies' future success. Overall, these results suggest that emotions are a key ingredient to political action and are more powerfully predicted by expressive components of partisanship than by instrumental ones.

Given these considerations, it should not come as a surprise that partisans – both strong and weak ones – do not just vote at significantly higher rates but also participate more actively in politics and follow it more closely than political independents (Brady, Verba, and Schlozman 1995; Campbell et al. 1960). This leads to stark differences in political engagement between independents and partisans: Only 5% of independents reported having attended a political rally in 2016 in contrast to 10% of strong partisans (*American National Election Study* 2016). Independents do not have a team to root for, so they do not receive the psychological gratification that comes with seeing their party succeed. This lack of political engagement poses a dilemma since political alienation[3] is self-reinforcing. People who do not feel like they belong to any political party are less likely to become politically involved, which, in turn, makes them feel even more estranged from their political system over time. From this perspective, partisanship serves a vital function in a democratic system; it makes citizens care about and participate in the world of politics.

3.6 SUMMARY

This chapter reviewed a slice of the abundant scholarship on the impact of partisanship. The review underscores the notion that vote choice, turnout, and political participation can be driven by a mix of expressive and instrumental factors. In addition to their empirical evidence, it is also important to consider the different normative implications of these two models. Instrumental partisans participate in the political system because they care about policies; they support a political party because that party runs on a platform that aligns with their own political preferences. In an ideal world, instrumental partisans might be the norm. However, as this chapter has demonstrated, to many partisans, their party is more than just a vessel for the implementation of preferred policies; instead, they identify with their party as a social group whose success is intimately tied to their self-image. While this psychological attachment strongly motivates partisans to become politically active, it also means that, for some partisans, elections are less about actual policies and more about their team's victory.

---

[3] Note that being a self-identified independent does not have to equal political alienation. While it is true that independents are much less engaged with politics than their partisan counterparts, they can still follow current affairs and care about politics. Indeed, preliminary work by the author suggests that "independent" can be a political identity on its own that, if strongly internalized, can boost political engagement among those who are politically unaffiliated.

4

Negative Partisanship

4.1 WHAT IS IN THIS CHAPTER?

In this chapter, I introduce the reader to the concept of negative partisanship and its distinction from positive partisanship. Generally, negative partisanship captures the notion that disdain for the opposing party is not necessarily accompanied by strong in-party attachments (i.e., positive partisanship). Despite the wealth of research on positive partisanship, negative partisanship has only recently regained scholarly attention on its own. With the help of Social Identity Theory, I describe the psychological process that underlies the formation and effects of negative partisanship. I then highlight the conceptual distinction between negative and positive partisanship with the example of multi-party systems and independent voters in the United States. I explain why this distinction matters and how it changes our overall assessment of partisanship and its role in a healthy democratic society.

4.2 WHY DOES IT MATTER?

Partisanship has become the culprit behind almost everything that pains democratic societies around the world, ranging from blind loyalty to the in-party to heightened levels of resentment toward the out-party. Yet research in social psychology has long made the case that strong in-group attachments do not have to be accompanied by out-group animosity. This notion is critical since it suggests that partisans are able to feel deeply connected to their party without feeling deep disdain for the opposition party. From a normative standpoint, this is good news for the role of political parties in representative democracies and provides a strong impetus for future research to explore the factors that allow partisans to root for their team without vilifying their opponent.

***

When we hear the word "polarization," there is a narrative that unfolds quite easily in our minds: Republicans and Democrats strongly and unconditionally support their own party while strongly and unequivocally disdaining the opposing party. The notion of polarization, thus, seems to suggest an equal growth of two poles: more intense in-party love accompanied by more intense out-party hatred, while the gap between them is widening. Yet the past few presidential elections in the United States have been marked by an asymmetry between the two, whereby partisans' strong opposition to the out-party is a more powerful motivator than their embrace of the in-party. Indeed, In a poll conducted by the Pew Research Center in the months leading up to the 2016 elections, Americans overwhelmingly reported feeling angry with the other party, while a much smaller share cited feeling enthusiastic about their own party.[1] This asymmetry is not just an election artifact: In February 2018, another nationally representative poll revealed that 71% of Republicans and 63% of Democrats cite the harm from the opposing party's policies – rather than the in-party's policies – as a major reason to affiliate with their own party.[2] These polls indicate that the opposition to a political party can sometimes influence citizens' political behavior independently of (or even without) their support for a political party, a phenomenon that has been labeled "negative partisanship" in the political science literature.

The concept of negative partisanship tries to capture the idea that strong disdain and resentment for a political party can develop without equally strong attachments to an in-party (i.e., positive partisanship). This separation has important implications for our assessment of partisanship: If in-party support is not automatically connected to out-party hostility, then partisans can strongly identify with their party without developing deep disdain for the opposing party. However, on the flipside of this argument, it also means that citizens can develop hostility for a political party without strongly supporting another, turning them into *negative* partisans. Despite the wealth of research on affective polarization (e.g., Iyengar and Westwood 2015; Iyengar et al. 2012; Lelkes and Westwood 2017; Mason 2015; Miller and Conover 2015; Rogowski and Sutherland 2016), negative partisanship has not received much scholarly attention on its own. As Caruana and colleagues (2015, p. 771) put it: "The volume of scholarship that investigates negative partisanship is dwarfed by the body of literature that considers positive partisanship." While recent work on polarization has shown a strong correlation between partisan strength and disdain for the out-party (Mason 2015; Miller and

---

[1] This poll can be accessed here: www.people-press.org/2016/06/22/6-how-do-the-political-parties-make-you-feel/ (last accessed, December 20, 2018).

[2] This poll can be accessed here: www.pewresearch.org/fact-tank/2018/03/29/why-do-people-belong-to-a-party-negative-views-of-the-opposing-party-are-a-major-factor/ (last accessed, December 20, 2018).

Conover 2015), some earlier research in political science (Maggiotto and Pierson 1977; Weisberg 1980) and social psychology (Allport 1954; Brewer 1999) suggests that strong in-party attachments do not have to involve hostility toward the out-party. This argument has strong normative implications because it suggests that strong partisans are not condemned to demonizing the other party – a promising perspective that warrants a closer look at the research on negative partisanship in prior and contemporary scholarship.

4.3 PRIOR SCHOLARSHIP ON NEGATIVE PARTISANSHIP

Most prior research on negative partisanship does not necessarily call it that; instead, scholars of affective polarization have been relying on feeling thermometer scores to measure *negative affect* toward political parties. This body of work demonstrates a strong relationship between the strength of positive party attachments and negative affect toward the out-party in the US two-party system (Abramowitz and Webster 2016; Bafumi and Shapiro 2009; Mason 2015; Miller and Conover 2015; Rogowski and Sutherland 2016). Yet a strong correlation does not necessarily mean that strong party attachments are *naturally* accompanied by negative affect toward the out-party.

One of the few contributions to address this concern comes from Abramowitz and Webster (2015) who demonstrate that positive and negative partisanship do not move in parallel. Instead, even weakly identified partisans in the United States now hold very negative views of the out-party, suggesting that strong partisan ties are not a requirement for the development of negativity toward the other party. This notion is also echoed by Iyengar and colleagues (2012): Using the *American National Election Study*, the authors show that partisans' feeling thermometer ratings of the out-party have become increasingly negative over time. At the same time, partisans' affect toward their in-party has remained relatively stable. Taken together, these findings neatly align with each other and support the notion that negative affect toward the out-party does not move in tandem with positive affect toward the in-party, thereby hinting at the distinction between the two.

While the focus on negative affect toward the out-party emerged recently within the context of affective polarization in the United States, Campbell and colleagues (1960, p. 121) already suggested the possibility of negative *partisanship* in their pioneering work *The American Voter*, stating that "the political party serves as the group toward which the individual may develop an identification, positive or *negative*, of some degree of intensity" (emphasis added). It is striking that the concept of negative partisanship originated at the same time that political scientists started to embrace the idea of partisanship as an identity. Yet positive partisanship has remained at the core of political science research, with only a few exceptions: Maggiotto and Pierson's work (1977) questions the relationship between the strength of positive in-party identification and negative out-party evaluations, stating that "there is no reason to expect the traditional measure of partisan identification to be perfectly related to attitudes toward the opposition party" (p. 747). The authors test this idea empirically and show that evaluations of Democrats and the Republicans are indeed relatively independent of one another. Thus, a positive evaluation of the Democratic Party does not necessarily imply a negative evaluation of the Republican Party and vice versa.

Outside the context of the US two-party system, Rose and Mishler (1998) make the case for negative partisanship in post-Communist countries. The authors develop a fourfold typology of open, negative, closed, and apathetic partisans: Open partisans exhibit positive partisanship toward their in-party without negative partisanship toward an opposing party. Negative partisans, on the other hand, exhibit negative partisanship toward a political party without positive partisanship. Last, closed partisans possess both a negative and positive party identification while apathetic partisans possess no identification at all. Rose and Mishler argue that these four combinations also have different consequences for partisans' political behavior, thereby emphasizing the important distinction between positive and negative partisanship. Indeed, the authors find that the latter is much more common than the former in four post- communist European countries: More than half of respondents held negative partisanship views toward at least one party, but positive partisanship views toward none (i.e., negative partisans). Interestingly, in these multi-party systems, negative partisanship was particularly strong toward political parties with extreme ideologies and more exclusive electorates such as the ones based on ethnicity and race.

In other European democracies such as Italy, Germany, and Sweden, negative partisanship has emerged with the rise of right-wing populism. Populism is often associated with a polarization of the political system (Ignazi 1992; Mudde and Kaltwasser 2018), not just along political but also cultural lines, thereby creating an even stronger contrast between the in-party and the out-party. Mudde and Kaltwasser note that "in many West European countries, the party with the highest negative partisanship is the populist party, which is generally considered to hold a radical ideology" (2018, p. 20). As more and more European citizens develop negative partisanship toward a populist party, political competition collapses along a single dimension, with the populists on one end and more established center parties on the other. In this scenario, negative partisanship works essentially the same as in a two-party system: A vote for the populists is a vote against the established party system, while a vote against the populist is a vote in favor of liberal democratic values. There are many examples of this one-dimensional collapse of the political space in Latin America, such as the political battles between Peronism vs. Anti-Peronism in Argentina, Fujimorismo vs. Anti-Fujimorismo in Peru, and Chavismo vs. Anti-Chavismo in Venezuela (Mudde and Kaltwasser 2018).

This prior scholarship on negative partisanship leads to three different conclusions: First, negative partisanship can exist independently of positive partisanship. Second, negative partisanship can influence political behavior, even in the absence of positive partisanship. Third, negative partisanship is not just a feature of the US two-party system but can also develop in multi-party systems, especially toward parties with radical ideological profiles and narrowly defined electoral bases.

Despite the accumulated evidence in support of negative partisanship's independent nature, the concept itself, let alone its measurement, has not nearly received as much attention as its positive counterpart. Part of this imbalance, I think, is the difficulty in conceptualizing negative partisanship. Is it just negative affect, or can it indeed be a social identity, similar to expressive positive partisanship? It is hard to imagine what an identity looks like when it centers on the opposition of a social or political group rather than its embrace. To address this challenge, I once again turn to Social Identity Theory.

4.4 THE CASE FOR NEGATIVE PARTISAN *IDENTITY*

Social Identity Theory (Tajfel and Turner 1979), I argue, can also be used to derive an understanding of negative partisanship. Identities cannot only develop in response to common characteristics among in-group members but also in opposition to groups. Thus, the identity is negative in the sense that it centers on the rejection of a group and its members; it prescribes what we are *not* rather than what we *are*. Zhong et al. (2008) refer to this type of identity as *negational*.[3] In the political realm, psychologists have demonstrated that Americans form negative identities in response to third parties (Bosson et al. 2006) as well as political organizations like the *National Rifle Association* (Elsbach and Bhattacharya 2001), turning the opposition to a group – the "not being one of them" – into a meaningful social identity.

Naturally, questions arise regarding the origins and development of these negative identities. Some researchers assume the psychological primacy of the in-group in forming negative identities (Allport 1954; Gaertner et al. 2006), meaning that a positive identification with a group promotes and anchors the development of a negative identity. However, Zhong et al. (2008) disagree with that notion and argue instead that for negative identities, "out-groups are 'psychologically primary,' in the sense that dissimilarity or distance from one's out-group comes before similarity to or attachment with in-groups" (p. 797). Relevant examples include *Occupy Wall Street*, the *NeverTrumpers*, the anti-nuclear movement, and anti-feminism campaigns since all these groups formed in response to what they oppose, rather than what they

---

[3] In the following, I use the terms "negational identities" and "negative identities" interchangeably as well as "negative partisanship" and "negative partisan identity".

support. Indeed, even the slow and gradual transition of White Southerners with racial grievances from the Democratic to the Republican Party can be interpreted as an example of negative partisanship. It took these White Southern Democrats such a long time to finally abandon their party not just because of their strong attachment to the Democratic Party but also because they strongly rejected Republicans. After all, Republicans were considered the "aggressors" against the South in the Civil War. From this perspective, the Southern party realignment in the 1960s might be an early example of negative partisanship in US politics.[4]

At the same time, there is no set of common in-group characteristics among the members of these negational social and political movements; their members may not have much in common except for the rejection of a political group that binds them together. From this perspective, negative identities can effectively unify a diverse coalition of groups and people.

Negative and positive identities also differ in their psychological origins: Referring to Balance Theory (Heider 1958) and Optimal Distinctiveness Theory (Brewer 1991), Zhong et al. (2008) argue that positive identities satisfy both basic human desires: the need for inclusion as well as the need for distinctiveness by emphasizing similarity within the in-group (i.e., belonging to other in-group members) as well as differences across groups (i.e., being distinct from out-group members). Negative identities, on the other hand, satisfy the need for distinctiveness to a much larger extent than the need for inclusion; they emphasize the dissimilarity from an out-group but they do little to provide a sense of belonging to the other in-group members. From this perspective, positive and negative partisanship have different psychological antecedents.

Applied to partisanship, these insights suggest that negative and positive partisanship are not the same construct. Indeed, in prior work, I provide empirical support for the notion that positive and negative partisanship – while undoubtedly related – are two relatively distinct constructs (Bankert 2020). I also find that positive and negative partisan identities differentially influence political behavior. Using the example of US partisans during the 2016 election season, I demonstrate that positive partisanship is strongly related to higher levels of political engagement while negative partisanship does not exert any significant effects. From a normative perspective, this is encouraging since it suggests that people are motivated to support their party because of their genuine connection to it. At the same time, the belief that the goals of Democrats and Republicans are incompatible is exclusively driven by negative, rather than positive, partisanship. Thus, positive partisan attachments are not the main obstacle to productive bipartisanship; it is

---

[4] I would like to thank an anonymous reviewer for making me aware of this example.

negative partisanship that is more likely linked to partisan gridlock. Similarly, the chance of voting for the in-party is much more strongly related to positive partisanship, suggesting that the vote indeed reflects partisans' support, rather than opposition, for a political party. However, these findings diverge when examining the 2016 vote for Democrats and Republicans separately. Democrats' vote for Clinton was strongly driven by their positive party attachments while negative partisanship did not impact their vote. In contrast, Republicans' vote for Trump was influenced by both negative and positive partisanship. These results support the idea that positive and negative partisanship are independent constructs that impact political behavior in different ways, based on the political context. The core of democratic citizenship – voting and political engagement – is strongly linked to positive partisanship while hostility toward the out-party is mainly driven by negative partisanship. These results substantially change how we evaluate partisanship and its contribution to a functioning democracy.

Despite the possibility of its independence, most contemporary work on negative partisanship (NPID) analyzes self-declared partisans who – by definition – already have a positive party identification. These prior party attachments make it challenging to disentangle the effects of positive and negative partisanship. One way to address this empirical challenge is to isolate negative partisanship by surveying self-identified independent voters who lack a positive party attachment. Utilizing independents, thus, provides substantial empirical leverage to examine negative partisanship in the absence of positive partisanship and advance our understanding of the relationship between positive and negative partisanship. My recent work has followed this promising path and demonstrated that negative partisanship among American independents not only exists but that it also predicts a range of political behaviors, including turnout, political engagement, and strong emotional responses to the 2020 US presidential election outcome (Bankert 2022). In other words, the strong rejection of one of the two major parties boosts the political involvement of independents. From a normative standpoint, this could be good news since negative partisanship offers even independents an impetus to engage with the political system. At the same time, however, independent voters with high levels of negative partisanship are more critical of bipartisan legislation and less likely to think that Democrats and Republicans should work together. Thus, it is once again negative partisanship that has troubling consequences for democratic representation and accountability, even in the absence of positive party attachments.

4.5 THE DEVELOPMENT OF NEGATIVE PARTISANSHIP

Currently, political scientists know little about the mechanisms that lead to the development of negative partisanship independently of or in conjunction with positive partisanship. Past scholarship appears to have assumed that negative partisanship is born out of positive partisanship, but we have yet to find conclusive evidence in support of that argument. While positive partisanship might provide fertile ground for the development of negative partisanship under certain conditions, it is not clear to what extent the reverse can be true. In other words, can negative partisanship promote the development of positive partisanship? Prior evidence suggests that negative partisanship does little to support positive party attachments. For example, Rose and Mishler (1980) argue that many negative partisans in post-Communist countries failed to develop a positive partisanship toward any party and instead have become skeptical of political parties in general without becoming apathetic or apolitical (p. 231). Similarly, Mudde and Kaltwasser (2018) explain that in many Western European democracies, populist parties are the targets of negative partisanship while levels of positive partisanship are on the decline. More work is needed to examine whether this opposition to populist parties eventually translates into stronger attachment to mainstream parties. Despite the inconclusive evidence, examining multi-party systems provides the opportunity to test if and how negative partisanship can eventually foster the growth of its positive counterpart.

Rather than fostering a distinct positive identity, negative identities can also develop as a superordinate identity that unites a diverse coalition of groups and thereby temporarily facilitates political mobilization. Employing the example of negational racial identities (i.e., "I am not White"), Zhong and colleagues (2008) show that "negational identity leads people to differentiate from a common out-group, making the out-group the central focus and psychologically primary. By drawing attention away from one's own group, negational categorization may offer a route for coalition building among groups that share the same non-membership" (p. 1564). In the context of race, whiteness constitutes the common out-group for racial and ethnic minorities. By drawing attention away from their own positive racial identity such as being Black or being Asian, the focus on the shared non-White membership can facilitate coalition building among racial minority groups that otherwise might not feel like they have much in common. Other real-world examples of such superordinate, negative identities include *Occupy Wall Street* and the *Never Trumpers* movement that highlight non-membership – the exclusion from a particular group – to unite groups and recategorize them as one in-group – even if just temporarily. Temporary coalitions are also a common feature of multi-party systems in which political parties might form coalition blocs either before or after elections. Yet it remains unclear if and how negative partisanship responds to these coalitions. Does negative partisanship develop anew in response to any political party outside the in-party's coalition or does it remain centered on the in-party's strongest competitor, either within or outside the coalition? Variation in a coalition's stability might further complicate this question.

In countries with common but unstable political alliances, in- and out-party demarcations might constantly be shifting, thereby making it more difficult to develop negative partisanship toward a particular party (Gonzalez et al. 2008; Hagevi 2015; Meffert et al. 2011). For example, the party that was a competitor during the elections might feasibly turn into a coalition partner after the election. This fluid political environment might weaken negative partisanship over time. On the other hand, in countries with stable coalitions that run and govern sometimes over the course of several election cycles, positive and negative partisanship could even develop toward coalitions in addition to individual parties. Indeed, in some countries like Sweden, coalition blocs of ideologically similar parties even have their own names and logos, such as *The Alliance* and *Red-Greens*, which promotes the image of an entity that is somewhat decoupled from the individual parties the bloc consists of. Within this context, Huddy, Bankert, and Davis (2018) examine the role of (positive) partisan identity in shaping affect toward parties of the in-group coalition and the opposing coalition (i.e., out-coalition). The authors demonstrate that Swedes' partisan identity predicts more positive affect for their own party over other parties, even within the coalition that their party is embedded in. This finding suggests a preference hierarchy involving the in-party, the in-group coalition that includes the in-party, the other individual parties in the in-group coalition, and the out-group coalition and its constituent parties. It remains unclear but worth investigating to what extent negative partisanship is related to similar gradations in affect toward out-parties and the out-group coalition.

Similarly, González and colleagues (2008) show, using the example of Chile, that coalitions create their own partisan dynamics: "The more party members identified with their coalition, the more they exhibited positive affect toward their own-coalition party members. This social identity seems to have created a superordinate category that redefined attitudes toward parties included in the inclusive category, adding a protecting boundary for intra-coalition dynamics (Gaertner and Dovidio 2000). . . . In addition, identification with the coalition helped to overcome the negative consequences associated with previous political conflicts among parties that belong to the coalition" (p. 112). Here, the evidence strongly suggests that partisans can develop an identification with a coalition that their in-party is part of and that this superordinate identity fosters positive affect toward the other members of that coalition, even when they used to be considered political opponents. At the same time, González and colleagues find that affect toward Chilean partisans' own party was not associated with negative feelings toward parties that are members of the opposing coalition. This lack of out-coalition hostility is consistent with the core idea proposed in this chapter, namely that an affirmative identity like positive partisanship does not necessarily lead to the derogation of opposing parties. I would argue that these dynamics, crucially, depend on how an identity is defined – is it affirmative of the group's core valuesand fosters a sense of belonging among group members? Or is it negational and purely defined by its rejection of an out-group's values, norms, and goals? Real-world identities most likely fall somewhere in between, combining both affirmational and negational elements in the construction of their group's identity.

4.6 NORMATIVE ASSESSMENT OF POSITIVE AND NEGATIVE PARTISANSHIP

Overall, prior scholarship on negative partisanship leaves us with two important insights: First, positive and negative partisanship do not have to occur together – partisans are able to strongly identify with their party without automatically vilifying the out-party. Put simply, in-party love without out-party hate is possible. Second, positive partisans is linked to various forms of political engagement that are considered desirable in a healthy democratic society: Strong positive partisans are more likely to turn out, to vote for their in-party, and to engage in even effortful forms of political participation. Negative partisanship, on the other hand, is strongly related to partisan gridlock and out-party hostility.

From a normative perspective, these findings are vital since they challenge the narrative that partisanship is at the root of most problems in American politics and beyond. Instead of condemning positive partisanship altogether, it seems more constructive to identify conditions that disentangle positive and negative partisanship and promote the former without the latter. Following this logic, partisans could be categorized based on their levels of positive and negative partisanship, whereby the ideal partisan shows high levels of positive partisanship to benefit from its participatory impetus while displaying low levels of negative partisanship.

This might require a drastic change in the rhetoric employed by politicians and political pundits who regularly portray their political opponents in cynical and hostile terms, possibly for both strategic benefits and entertainment value. Indeed, this elite-driven hostility might promote the alignment of positive and negative partisanship, ultimately creating partisans that score high on both positive *and* negative partisanship or even partisans with solely high levels of negative partisanship.

Indeed, there are reasons to assume that negative partisanship is a more readily available identity than its positive counterpart. Since negative identities do not provide a psychological sense of belonging, it is possible that negative partisanship is less stable than positive partisanship and therefore more prone to activation for political gains. Zhong and colleagues (2008) support this notion, suggesting that "negational identification can be a cause and not just a consequence of having a common enemy that unifies warring factions . . .. Thus, to some extent activating negational identification can also 'create' the common enemy" (p. 1565).

In most cases, such a strategy would be considered manipulative, unscrupulous, and dishonest, and yet it has become a more common phenomenon in contemporary politics where attack ads and partisan rancor are no longer the exception. Thus, it is up to ordinary party supporters to hold their leaders accountable when their actions sow discord rather than mutual trust and respect across the political aisle. However, in other contexts, highlighting negative identities can mobilize groups that might normally be less inclined to participate in politics and thus lack political representation. Zhong and colleagues illustrate that notion with the example of racial minorities whereby negative racial identities (e.g., not being White) can lessen divisions among racial minority groups and foster collaboration between them. From this vantage point, negative identities can be a powerful tool to promote more equal access to political power for all.

Last, negative and positive partisanship can also be used to examine independent or unaffiliated voters who receive much less scholarly attention than their partisan counterparts. For a long time, independents in the United States were perceived as either being torn equally between the Democratic and Republican side of the political spectrum (see also Weisberg 1980) or as unwilling or unable to identify with any party. However, independent voters might develop negative partisanship toward one or even multiple political parties. From this perspective, an independent identity might be negative in the sense that it develops in opposition to one or multiple established political parties (see Klar and Krupnikov 2018). However, it is also possible that being an independent voter is a positive identity that is grounded in voters' self-image as unbiased and objective observers of politics. The distinction between positive and negative identities is thus not just relevant for the study of partisanship but also for the political involvement of independents who often engage with the political world much less than their partisan peers. While independents admittedly comprise a very small share of the US electorate – indeed, only 11% – some European multi-party systems feature significantly higher shares of these unaffiliated or floating voters, ranging between 15% in the United Kingdom to up to 40% in the Netherlands and Italy. No matter how small independent voters' impact might be, proponents of democracy should be interested in promoting the inclusion of all eligible voters in the political process.

4.7 SUMMARY

The distinction between positive and negative partisanship provides a more comprehensive understanding of how citizens identify with political parties.

Most fundamentally, positive and negative partisanship can operate independently of each other. In a series of prior studies, researchers have found that strong positive partisanship encourages political participation while negative partisanship promotes gridlock and more hostile relations between partisan groups. These preliminary findings challenge the notion that strong party attachments are inherently problematic. Instead, it appears that negative partisanship poses a bigger challenge to civil relationships between partisans. It is thus imperative to investigate the development of positive and negative partisanship as well as the conditions under which the two align. Beyond that, negative partisanship also provides a useful template to examine the formation of party coalitions which are a regular feature in multi-party systems. Last, negative partisanship can also be utilized to study independent voters and the factors that drive their political engagement in the absence of a positive party identification.

5

The Measurement of Positive Partisan Identity

5.1 WHAT IS IN THIS CHAPTER?

This chapter focuses on the measurement of positive partisanship. If partisanship can be conceptualized as a social identity – as argued in previous chapters – then survey instruments need to reflect that. For that purpose, I introduce the reader to the (positive) partisan identity scale that captures crucial components of partisan identity such as partisans' sense of belonging to the in-party, feeling connected to other in-party members, and the emotional significance of the party membership. Notably, and in contrast to prior work on partisanship, this scale does not gauge political attitudes, policy preferences, or ideological convictions. Utilizing data from the United States and four European multi-party systems, I examine the scale's measurement properties and assess the magnitude of positive partisanship among the electorate in each of these five countries.

5.2 WHY DOES IT MATTER?

Precise measurement of partisan identity matters for two reasons: First, it allows researchers to conceptually and empirically distinguish between instrumental and expressive partisanship. Second, it enables researchers to accurately estimate the impact of partisanship on various political behaviors such as turnout, voting, and political engagement. With a unified measure, it is also possible to compare the effects of partisanship across different political systems, which adds to our understanding of how generalizable the concept of expressive partisanship is beyond the United States. While this chapter might be most useful to researchers, it also provides readers outside of academia with a more concrete understanding of the term "partisan identity" and its manifestations.

***

Research on partisanship has evolved and expanded dramatically since the *The American Voter*. There is an abundance of research providing empirical support for the impact of partisanship on various key political outcomes such as vote choice (Brader and Tucker 2009; Green et al. 2002; Lewis-Beck et al. 2008), political attitudes (Cohen 2003; Gerber et al. 2010; Goren et al. 2009), political participation (Bankert et al. 2017; Huddy et al. 2015), and action-oriented emotions like anger and enthusiasm (Groenendyk and Banks 2013; Valentino et al. 2011). It is thus not a novel idea that partisanship matters. However, the idea of partisanship as an identity has only recently gained traction among political scientists – a development that also challenges traditional measurements of partisanship that mostly rely on two survey items: one item asks partisans about the political party they identify with and one follow-up item that gauges the strength of that identification. In combination, these two items capture the direction and the strength of partisan identification.

The partisanship measure follows somewhat different phrasings across national election surveys. For example, while the *American National Election Study* asks respondents whether they are "strong" or "not so strong" Democrats/Republicans, the *British National Election Study* asks whether respondents are "very strong," "fairly strong," or "not so strong" partisans. In general, though, the partisan strength item tends to categorize partisans into weak and strong partisans – with either two or three response categories[1] – and is included in most election studies around the world, including countries in North and South America, Europe, and Africa. Yet, despite its seemingly universal use, there are a few significant shortcomings, especially for studying the nature and origins of partisan attachments: It is unclear whether this traditional partisanship measure reflects instrumental or expressive partisanship or both. For example, respondents might call themselves "strong Republicans" because they identify with that party and feel a deep sense of belonging to it (i.e., expressive) or because they hold conservative beliefs and strongly support the policies put forth by the Republican Party (i.e., instrumental), or – as suggested in prior chapters – because of a mix of both factors. The partisan strength item cannot distinguish between these different motivations. Thus, while many prior studies on partisanship are successful at documenting the effects of partisanship on political behavior, they are mostly unable to speak to the *nature* of partisanship. From that perspective, a precise measure of partisanship – either in its expressive or instrumental form – is useful not just for empirical reasons but also for

---

[1] Indeed, there is a lot of variation across European countries. For example, in the Netherlands, partisans are asked whether they would call themselves a "very convinced adherent," "convinced adherent," or "not so convinced adherent" while in Sweden, party identifiers are asked whether they felt "very close,, "rather close," or "not very close" to their in-party. Overall, in most European election studies, the partisan strength item has at least three categories.

advancing our understanding of the factors that shape expressive and instrumental party attachments. In the remainder of this chapter, I cover three different aspects of the measurement debate. First, I distinguish between an expressive and instrumental measure of partisanship; second, I introduce the positive partisan identity scale that has been utilized by a growing number of scholars to gauge expressive partisanship; and third, I examine the measurement properties of the scale, using data from the United States and four European multi-party systems. I conclude this first empirical chapter with implications for future survey research on partisanship.

5.3 INSTRUMENTAL AND EXPRESSIVE MEASUREMENT OF PARTISANSHIP

In its instrumental version, partisanship is grounded in issue preferences, a reasoned and informed understanding of the parties' positions, ideological convictions, or even contemporary leadership evaluations. Thus, as a test of instrumental partisanship, researchers have utilized measures of ideology, support for the in-party's policies (i.e., issue proximity), assessments of the economy, approval ratings, and leader evaluations (Dalton and Weldon 2007; Garzia 2013). Garzia (2013), for example, demonstrates that leadership evaluations are an important factor in shaping partisanship in the United Kingdom, Germany, Italy, and the Netherlands, providing evidence in support of instrumental partisanship. While this instrumental approach is quite straightforward, measuring expressive partisanship or partisan identity is bit more complicated. After all, how can we measure partisanship without references to ideology, policies, and prominent party leaders? Recall that the expressive approach to partisanship rests on the assumption that strong party identifiers defend their party even in the face of poor leadership and changing policy positions. From this vantage point, a measure of expressive partisanship needs to acknowledge partisans' resistance to the instrumental factors that past conceptualizations of partisanship built on.

Another necessary feature of an expressive partisanship measure is its ability to gauge fine-grained variations in identity strength. Indeed, Social Identity Theory would predict that the effects of partisan identity are most pronounced among strong identifiers (see Huddy 2001; 2013). That is why psychologists typically measure social identities with multiple items to create a continuum of identity strength that spans from weak to strong partisan identifiers. The traditional item with its simple distinction between weak and strong partisans can hardly capture these gradations.

These considerations led to the development of a multi-item scale that gauges partisanship as a social identity, rather than the sum of instrumental concerns. The scale, in its earliest form, originated in the Identification with a Psychological Group (IDPG) scale by psychologists Mael and Tetrick (1992)

TABLE 5.1 Measures of expressive versus instrumental partisanship

Expressive partisanship	Instrumental partisanship
When I speak about this party, I usually say "we" instead of "they."	Leadership evaluations on a 0–100 feeling thermometer scale
I am interested in what other people think about this party.	Approval ratings of the in-party leadership, as well as the president, and congress
When people criticize this party, it feels like a personal insult.	Evaluations of the economy and other key policies
I have a lot in common with other supporters of this party.	Personal stances on key policies and their importance
If this party does badly in opinion polls, my day is ruined.	Ideological placement of the in-party
When I meet someone who supports this party, I feel connected with this person.	Ideological self-placement and intensity
When people praise this party, it makes me feel good.	Satisfaction with government performance
When I speak about this party, I refer to them as "my party."	Increase/decrease in household income

Note: The partisan identity scale's response options include "Never/Rarely," "Sometimes," "Often," and "Always." The list of instrumental measures is not exhaustive.

and was adapted by political scientist Steven Greene (2002) to measure identification with one's preferred party (i.e., in-party). My own work (Bankert et al. 2017) has built on and further developed this scale, whereby my colleagues and I adapted a few items from the original scale and added three new items. The result is the partisan identity scale displayed in the first column of Table 5.1. Of the five items adapted from the IDPG scale, the first three items are taken almost verbatim from the scale, but we completely reworded the fourth and fifth items. The original item "I have a number of qualities typical of members" was reworded to "I have a lot in common with other supporters of the party" and "If a story in the media criticized this group, I would feel embarrassed" was rephrased to "If this party does badly in opinion polls, my day is ruined." The last three items were newly added to the scale.

The partisan identity scale draws strongly from Social Identity Theory (SIT), which defines a social identity as "that part of an individual's self-concept which derives from his knowledge of his membership in a social group (or groups) together with the value and emotional significance attached to that membership" (Tajfel 1978). Items such as "When people criticize this party, it feels like a personal insult" and "When I speak about this party, I usually say 'we' instead of 'they'" are meant to capture the importance of the in-party to an individual's self-image as well as the emotional significance of the party membership. For each of the eight scale items, respondents are asked how frequently they encounter these thoughts and feeling when thinking about their in-party, with response options that include "never/rarely," "sometimes," "often," and "always." Combining these eight items into one scale yields a continuum that can account for fine gradations in partisan identity strength and that has been shown to be a better predictor of political outcomes such as vote choice and political participation than the single partisan strength item in the United States (see Huddy et al. 2015 for a shorter version of the scale) and even in European multi-party systems (Bankert et al. 2017).

The expressive measure differs quite drastically from the instrumental measures of partisanship, which can include, among others, partisans' evaluations and approval of their leaders, the economy, personal stances on important key policies, and ideological self-placement (see column 2, Table 5.1). Despite their different facets, both expressive and instrumental partisanship measures include a strength component that either gauges the strength of partisan identity or the strength of ideological convictions and policy preferences. This commonality is crucial for examining the link between expressive and instrumental components of partisanship: Citizens' ideology – whether they place themselves on the left/liberal or the right/conservative side of the ideological spectrum – and their policy preferences are linked to the *direction* of partisanship, that is, the initial decision to support a particular party over another. However, the *intensity* of their ideological self-placement – that is, whether respondents consider themselves slightly, somewhat, or extremely liberal/conservative – is only weakly linked to the strength of their partisan identity (see Bankert et al. 2017). This weak correlation indicates that strong policy preferences or ideological convictions are not necessarily linked to a strong partisan identity. Expressive and instrumental factors can but do not have to operate in a joint and synchronous fashion.

With the focus on measuring partisan *strength*, researchers can also examine the origin of its variations, which constitutes a somewhat unexplored territory. As Johnston (2006) put it: "It is surprising that we know very little about the sources that drive the intensity of partisan attachments. In fact, most research on partisanship has remained focused on investigating the direction of partisanship and its sources even though ... it seems fairly clear ... that [partisan] intensity varies more than direction does" (p. 339). Recently, however, there has been more interest in the subject, producing interesting work that shows that personality predispositions such as the Big 5 personality traits (Gerber et al. 2011, see also Bakker et al. 2021 for a reconsidered relationship between personality traits and political preferences) or authoritarianism (Luttig 2017) impact the intensity of partisan attachments. Since strong partisans are at the forefront of partisan conflict (Cassesse 2021; Kalmoe and Mason 2019; Martherus et al. 2021), it seems vital to investigate why and how these attachments strengthen over time, especially when they are not grounded in stronger political preferences. The partisan identity scale with its ability to gauge identity strength can be useful for this endeavor.

To illustrate this point, I next apply the scale to a sample of partisans in the United States, the United Kingdom, Sweden, the Netherlands, and Italy. Utilizing that cross-country data, I compare the levels and distributions of partisan identity in these five different countries. In the following analyses, partisan identity is an affirmational identity as it describes partisans' attachment to their party. I thus refer to that type of partisanship as positive partisanship or positive partisan identity (PPID).

5.4 PARTISAN IDENTITY IN THE UNITED STATES AND EUROPE

Utilizing a uniform measure of partisan identity offers a comparison of PPID's distribution across five vastly different countries and invites inferences about the role of institutional differences in shaping party attachments. For this endeavor, I utilize survey data that was collected between 2021 and 2022 by the survey firm Bovitz Inc.[2] While the samples are not nationally representative, they do reflect their respective country's population along key demographics such as gender, race, and religion. A comparison of each country's population and the corresponding sample composition can be found in the Appendix (see Tables A1–A5).

I combine all eight items of the partisan identity scale to obtain one overall PPID score. For improved comparability across countries, this PPID score and all other relevant variables in subsequent analyses are scaled to range from 0 (minimum value) to 1 (maximum value) with 0 representing the weakest partisans and 1 representing the strongest partisans. I also examine the PPID scale's correlation to instrumental facets of partisanship, namely the intensity of partisans' political and ideological preferences. For this purpose, I select eight political issues that are relatively salient in each country's political discourse, such as environmental regulations, the European Union, taxes, income inequality, affordable housing, and abortion. With these eight items, I create an issue intensity scale that resembles the PPID scale in terms of the number of constituent survey items, which allows for a fair comparison between both. For a more comprehensive account of instrumental partisanship, I also utilize the strength of partisans' ideological beliefs whereby partisans who identify themselves as moderates/middle of the road have the weakest ideological convictions (value of 0) and partisans who identify themselves as strong liberals/conservatives in the United States or far right/left in Europe have the strongest ideological convictions (value of 1).

---

[2] Bovitz Inc. provides an online panel of approximately one million respondents who participate in multiple surveys over time and receive compensation for their participation. Bovitz Inc. has been used extensively in other political science research (e.g., Druckman and Levendusky 2019). For more information, see http://bovitzinc.com/index.php.

Starting with Italy (Figure 5.1), positive partisanship somewhat follows a normal distribution with most partisans being located around the midpoint of the partisan identity scale (N = 936), a mean of 0.47 and a standard deviation of 0.22. With an alpha coefficient of 0.86, the scale is highly reliable. A closer look reveals that all eight items contribute equally to that high reliability. A couple of items stand out for their high levels of endorsement. For example, 18% of Italian partisans report that they are "always" interested in what other people think about their party, and 22% admit that it "always" makes them feel good when people praise their party, followed by 35% who "often" feel this way. Last, 16% report that when they meet someone who supports their party, they feel connected, followed by a substantial 33% who "often" experience this scenario. Partisan identity strength only weakly correlates with the intensity of political preferences (e.g., taxes, income inequality, affordable housing, and abortion) at 0.11 among Italian partisans, which aligns with the notion that expressive and instrumental components of partisanship are relatively independent of one another. This correlation is even lower when measuring instrumental partisanship with the strength of partisans' ideological self-placement rather than the strength of concrete political opinions.

In the Netherlands (Figure 5.2), positive partisanship is strongly skewed, where a substantial share of partisans is located at the lower end of the PPID

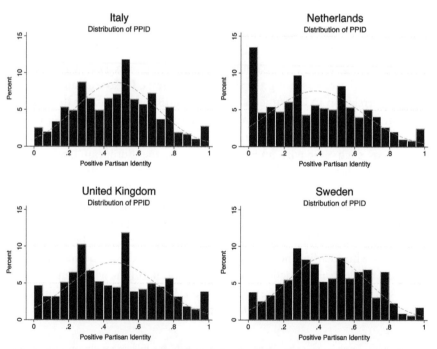

FIGURES 5.1–5.4 Distribution of PPID in Italy, the Netherlands, the United Kingdom, and Sweden
Note: In Italy, N = 936. In the Netherlands, N = 976. In the United Kingdom, N = 741. In Sweden, N = 968. Positive partisan identity is rescaled to range from 0 to 1.

scale's continuum (N = 976). The PPID scale in the Netherlands yields a standard deviation of 0.26 and an average value of 0.38, which is significantly lower than its European counterparts and indicates a larger share of weak partisans. The scale has good reliability across all eight items with an alpha coefficient of 0.84. Among self-identified Dutch partisans, 35% report that they "always" feel good when other people praise their party while 22% "always" believe that they have a lot in common with other supporters of their party, followed by a whopping 50% of Dutch partisans who "often" believe this to be true. Once again, I examine the correlation between the partisan identity scale and a political issue intensity scale. The latter gauges partisans' opinions on a few key political issues, including environmental regulations, euthanasia, income inequality, the European Union, and refugees. The correlation is miniscule (-0.002), suggesting that strong partisan identities are not necessarily accompanied by strong political preferences among Dutch partisans. Yet the correlation between positive partisan identity and the strength of partisans' ideological self-placement is significantly higher at 0.22.

Moving on to the United Kingdom (Figure 5.3), PPID appears to be slightly skewed toward the lower half of the partisan identity continuum, though the largest share of partisans is still located around the midpoint (N = 741), resulting in an average value of 0.46 and a standard deviation of 0.25. The scale has incredibly good reliability among British partisans with an alpha coefficient of 0.90. Among them, 23% and 29% respectively report that they "always" or "often" feel good when people praise their party. Similarly, 32% confess that their day is either "always" or "often" ruined when their party does poorly in opinion polls – a reflection of how important the party's success is to partisans' self-image. Indeed, 35% of surveyed partisans in the United Kingdom "always" or "often" consider it a personal insult when people criticize their party. The instrumental scale in the UK context consists of items that ask about partisans' attitudes on, among others, environmental regulations, funding for the National Health service, affordable housing, and private education. Despite these relatively salient issues, the expressive and instrumental partisanship scales correlate at only 0.05. The critical reader might question the low correlations between the PPID scale and the strength of partisans' political attitudes. These low correlations are at least partially driven by the measure of instrumental partisanship. If I replace the specific policy opinions with the intensity of partisans' general ideological preferences, ranging from far left to far right, the correlation with the PPID scale increases to 0.21 – a substantial jump that suggests that partisans in the United Kingdom are better at matching their party and ideological preferences rather than concrete policy preferences. Yet, even when examining ideological strength, instrumental and expressive partisanship correlate only moderately at best.

In Sweden (Figure 5.4), the highest share of partisans (N = 968) is located in the lower half of the partisan identity continuum, though there is also a substantial share concentrated around the scale's mid-point and the upper half, resulting in an average value of 0.45 and a standard deviation of 0.23 – values that resemble PPID in the United Kingdom and Italy. Like in previous cases, the scale has great reliability among Swedish partisans with an alpha coefficient of 0.86. A staggering 55% of partisans report that they either "always" or "often" feel connected when they meet someone who support their party, corresponding to 57% who think they have a lot in common with other supporters of their party. For the construction of the instrumental scale, I utilize partisans' attitude strength on issues such as taxes, privately run health care, refugees, nuclear power, and social benefits. The expressive and instrumental scales correlate at 0.12, which reiterates the notion that the intensity of partisan identity and the intensity of political attitudes are only weakly related. This assessment also holds when utilizing the strength of partisans' ideological self-placement as an instrumental measure rather than the strength of concrete political issue positions.

Last, in the United States (Figure 5.5), the distribution of positive partisan identity is slightly skewed toward the lower half of the PPID scale's continuum but, similar to Sweden, there are peaks around the mid-point and near the upper quartile (N = 882), with a mean of 0.42 and a standard deviation of 0.25. With a coefficient of 0.90, the scale's reliability in the United States is as high as in the United Kingdom; 43% of US partisans "always" or "often" feel good when other people praise their party, and 42% are interested in what other people think about their party, either "often" or "always." These response

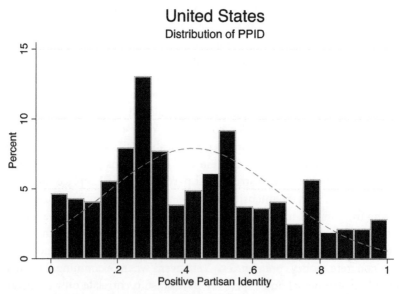

FIGURE 5.5 Distribution of PPID in the United States
Note: N = 882. Positive partisan identity is rescaled to range from 0 to 1.

patterns are quite similar to the ones we observed among European partisans. The instrumental scale in the US data consists of salient political issues such as access to abortion, a pathway to citizenship for undocumented immigrants, gun control regulations, and cuts in government spending. This issue intensity scale correlates with the PPID scale at 0.14, which is higher than in the four European countries but still a negligible correlation. However, this correlation rises to a moderate level of 0.27 if an instrumental scale is used that gauges the intensity of partisans' ideological convictions.

Overall, a simple comparison of PPID's distribution across these five countries reveals four interesting insights: First, the average value of positive partisan identity is relatively similar across countries, hovering around 0.45, with the exception of the Netherlands, where PPID was somewhat lower at 0.38. Second, certain items consistently receive higher levels of endorsement such as "I am interested in what other people think about my party," or "I feel good when other people praise my party," as well as "When I meet someone who supports this party, I feel connected." Third, across all five countries, the correlation between the PPID scale and an instrumental partisanship scale is miniscule, despite the use of salient political issues. When utilizing partisans' ideological self-placement as a measure of instrumental partisanship, the correlation is more substantial and yet remains modest at best, which reiterates the notion that instrumental and expressive components of partisanship can operate relatively independent of each other.

5.5 MEASUREMENT PROPERTIES OF THE PPID SCALE

In addition to theoretical grounding, a new survey instrument must also demonstrate good measurement properties to be useful in a wide range of studies. One of these properties includes the scale's ability to capture fine gradations in partisan identity strength. This measurement property also translates into more accurate predictions of partisan behavior. Recall that strong party identifiers have a greater motivation to defend their party's status, which heightens their likelihood of becoming politically active, especially in time of electoral competition. From this vantage point, the partisan identity scale should ideally be able to identify partisans equally well at low and high levels of identity strength.

I assess the scale's ability to do so, using Item Response Theory, a psychometric method that examines the relationship between a latent trait – that is, partisan identity strength – and its behavioral and attitudinal manifestations (e.g., "When I speak about this party, I usually say 'we' instead of 'they'"). To preserve space, I will present the results from analyzing the PPID scale in only three of the five countries, namely the United States, Sweden, and the United Kingdom. I utilize the same samples from which I drew the distributions of PPID, presented in Figures 5.1–5.5. I start by creating an information function for each item of the partisan identity scale in the United States (see Figure 5.6), Sweden (see Figure 5.7), and the United Kingdom (see Figure 5.8).

An information function illustrates what levels of partisan identity strength are captured particularly well by a specific item. The more

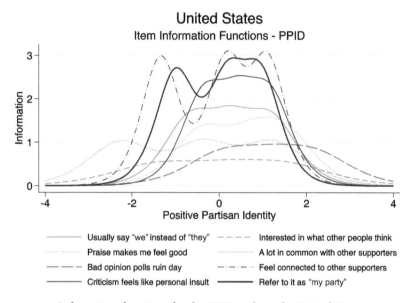

FIGURE 5.6 Information functions for the PPID scale in the United States

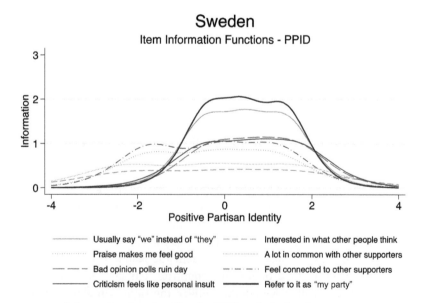

FIGURE 5.7 Information functions for the PPID scale in Sweden

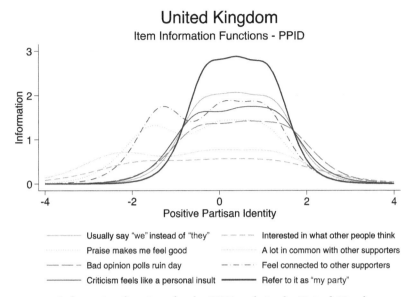

FIGURE 5.8 Information functions for the PPID scale in the United Kingdom

information an item provides, the higher its ability to differentiate between partisans of different strengths levels. The information function that peaks closer to 4 on the partisan identity strength continuum, also referred to as latent trait continuum, provides a considerable amount of information at high levels of partisan identity strength, whereas an information function that peaks closer to -4 better captures lower levels of partisan identity strength.[3] Finally, an information function that peaks in the midpoint of the latent trait suggests an item with considerable ability to distinguish middling from higher and lower levels of identity strength.

While the amount of information provided by an item represents its ability to differentiate between partisans of different strength, the distance between the peaks is suggestive of the range of partisan identity strength that is covered by an item. If the distance between two adjacent peaks is large, the item provides less information about levels of partisan identity in between peaks. When the distance is smaller and the peaks are located more closely together on the latent trait continuum, the item covers a broader range of partisan identity strength. Thus, an ideal scale contains items that cover a wide range of partisan identity strength and, at the same time, can discriminate effectively between different levels of identity strength.

Figures 5.6–5.8 demonstrate that the eight items complement each other well and cover a wide range of partisan identity strength. For example, in the

---

[3] The theoretical range is - ∞ to ∞. However, typical item locations fall within a range of -3 to 3 (de Ayala 2009).

United States (Figure 5.6), the items "When I meet someone who supports this party, I feel connected" and "I have a lot in common with other supporters of this party" display multiple peaks below the midpoint of the partisan identity continuum and thus provide especially good coverage of lower levels of partisan identity. These items display a similar item information function in the United Kingdom (Figure 5.8), where, in addition, the item "If my party does badly in opinion polls, my day is ruined" has its first peak slightly before the midpoint of the latent trait. These three items also cover lower levels of partisan identity in Sweden; yet, given their relatively flat information function, they might not differentiate between them as well as they do in the United States and the United Kingdom. In contrast, the item "When I speak about this party, I refer to them as 'my party'" captures middling to higher levels of partisan identity in all three countries especially well as does the item "When I speak about this party, I usually say 'we' instead of 'they'" as the peak in both items' information functions extends past the midpoint of the latent trait continuum. Admittedly, the item "I am interested in what other people think about this party" is by far the weakest one since it provides little information and fails to discriminate among those at low, middling, and high levels of partisan identity. Yet combining these items into one scale helps to compensate for weaknesses in individual items. For example, in the US sample (Figure 5.6), there is a large gap in the information functions for the item "When I meet someone who supports this party, I feel connected." However, this gap is at least partially covered by the item "When I speak about them, I refer to them as 'my party.'" Overall, the item information functions demonstrate that the partisan identity scale covers a full spectrum of partisan identity strength while effectively distinguishing between its fine variations.

5.6 PREDICTIVE POWER OF THE SCALE AND ITS IMPLICATIONS

Last, a good measurement instrument must also prove its worth by demonstrating that it can predict key outcomes better than prior measures. Indeed, my past work demonstrates that the partisan identity scale has predictive validity and better explains political engagement than the traditional partisan strength item or even instrumental measures of partisanship among partisans in Europe (Bankert et al. 2017). Utilizing a shorter version of the partisan identity scale, Huddy and colleagues (2015) illustrate its predictive power among partisans in the United States. Notably, the scale's better performance compared to the single strength item is not just simply a function of the scale's multiple items.[4] It is the concept of partisan identity itself, rather than

---

[4] My colleagues and I support this argument by replicating their analyses with a shorter version of the partisan identity scale, consisting of four rather than eight items that were chosen based

the number of items in the scale, that drives the strong association with political engagement and vote choice.[5]

These findings have important implications for future research on partisanship. While the traditional partisanship measure might be a satisfactory choice for analyses in which partisan attachment is merely a control variable, researchers who aim to assess the magnitude of partisanship's impact on political behavior might want to consider their measurement choices more carefully. If a researcher is interested in studying the instrumental facets of partisanship, then a multi-item index consisting of issue preferences or ideological considerations might be a better choice. On the other hand, if the researcher is interested in the expressive nature of partisanship, the partisan identity scale presented here is a useful option. While such a distinction might appear trivial, I consider it pivotal: These measurement choices – if made consciously – do not just yield a more accurate estimate of partisanship's impact but they also help delineate the conceptual boundaries between instrumental and expressive partisanship. This is important not just for organizing scholarship on partisanship but also for developing potential solutions to the negative side effects of partisanship in the real world. For example, it is quite conceivable that partisan animosity based on instrumental partisanship requires very different interventions than partisan animosity based on expressive partisanship.

Finally, a multi-item index of partisanship – whether it is instrumental or expressive – creates a fine-grained continuum of partisan strength that enables researchers to examine partisan strength as the dependent variable rather than the independent variable. Indeed, it is easier to detect shifts, especially small ones, in a continuous variable with large variation than in a categorical one that has only two or three values (e.g., "strong" and "not so strong" partisans in the United States or "very strong," "fairly strong," and "not so strong" partisans in the United Kingdom). Capturing more variations in partisan strength promotes new research avenues on the origins of strong party attachments, especially for experimental political scientists. From this perspective, considering the measurement of partisanship is not just an exercise in precision; it also unlocks new ways to study the origins and effects of partisanship.

---

on the amount of information they provided. The items are "When people criticize this party, it feels like a personal insult," "When I meet someone who supports this party, I feel connected with this person," "When I speak about this party, I refer to them as 'my party,'" and "When people praise this party, it makes me feel good."

[5] Indeed, to underscore this notion, we demonstrate that the partisan identity scale significantly predicts vote choice and political engagement among "not so strong," "fairly strong," and "very strong" partisans, which indicates that the scale picks up on variation in partisan identity strength that the 3-point measure fails to account for.

5.7 SUMMARY

A new conceptualization of partisanship requires a new measure. Since the expressive approach to partisanship is grounded in Social Identity Theory, its measurement instrument needs to reflect that by gauging partisans' sense of belonging to members of their party as well as the significance of that group membership to partisans' self-image. The partisan identity scale sets out to do just that. The eight-item index has good and similar measurement properties across several countries, which makes it suitable for comparative work on partisanship. With its ability to capture a wide range of fine gradations in partisan identity strength, the scale enables researchers to assess partisanship's impact on political behavior more accurately. For the same reasons, the scale can feasibly be used as a dependent variable, thereby generating new research avenues on the origins of partisan identity strength. Last, with a strictly expressive measure of partisanship, researchers can disentangle the expressive and instrumental facets of partisanship and their distinct effects on political behavior – an endeavor that is crucial for understanding the origins of political behavior and partisan animosity.

6

The Measurement of Negative Partisan Identity

6.1 WHAT IS IN THIS CHAPTER?

Like its positive counterpart, I conceptualize negative partisanship as a social identity that needs to be reflected in its measurement. In political science, There is no unified measure of negative partisanship. Instead, prior work has relied on a number of different survey items with varying degrees of theoretical grounding and prior assessment of their measurement properties. Many of these items are not comparable to the identity-based multi-item index that captures positive partisanship. These inconsistencies make it hard to examine whether negative partisanship can be expressive too and whether it has similar consequences for political behavior as its positive equivalent. To address these challenges, I introduce a multi-item index that captures negative partisan identity. Utilizing this new scale, I demonstrate the magnitude of negative partisan identity among the electorate in the United States and in four European multi-party systems. After examining the measurement properties of the negative partisan identity scale (NPID), I briefly elaborate on its benefits for research on partisanship and partisan animosity.

6.2 WHY DOES IT MATTER?

While the concept of negative partisanship has recently regained attention among political scientists, reflections on its adequate measurement are still in their infancy. Without a valid measure, however, it is challenging to identify the effects of negative partisanship and to differentiate them from positive partisanship. It thus remains unknown to what extent PPID and NPID align and whether they have similar or different effects on partisans' behavior and attitudes. More broadly, This matters for our understanding of whether partisanship can be a force of good or a force of destruction – as currently presumed in many political narratives – in democratic societies. From this vantage point, an identity-based measure of NPID cannot just validate the concept of negative partisan identity but also provide a more nuanced assessment of partisanship overall.

***

The recent growth in scholarship on negative partisanship is at least partially driven by the rise in affective polarization in the United States and beyond. As partisans have become more polarized, hostility toward the out-party has markedly increased. Yet the notion of negative partisanship surfaced long before that. For example, Weisberg (1980) notes that the one-dimensional partisanship measure that ranges from "strong Democrat" to "strong Republican" is unable to capture the possible distinction between, or a combination of, positive and negative party identification.

Subsequent work on negative partisanship built on this insight and has utilized a variety of measures to capture negative partisanship: Most prominently, scholars have used feeling thermometer ratings to gauge negative affect toward the out-party (Abramowitz and Webster 2015; Iyengar, Sood, and Lelkes 2012; Lelkes and Westwood 2017; Mason 2015; Rogowski and Sutherland 2016). Despite its popularity, the measure has its methodological shortcomings: Differential item functioning is a frequently cited problem with feeling thermometer scales because respondents might use a more nuanced distinction for positive evaluations than for negative ones (see Winter and Berinsky 1999), which ultimately creates an unbalanced measure of positive and negative affect. From a theoretical standpoint, it is also unclear where this negative affect originates from. Social identity researchers have long argued that affective responses to in- and out-groups are largely conditioned by social identities whereby the strongest group identifiers are most likely to report strong affective reactions when their group's status is threatened or bolstered (Greene 1999; Huddy et al. 2015; Rydell et al. 2008; van Zomeren, Spears, and Leach 2008). Thus, affect can be a product of positive or negative partisan identity or even a combination of both. At the same time, a negative identity is not a necessary condition for negative affect. For example, voters can hold strong negative affect toward political objects that they do not identify with. These nuances are hard to detect with feeling thermometer values.

A handful of researchers have suggested measuring negative partisanship more explicitly: Medeiros and Noel (2014) use the question "Is there any party you would never vote for?" to gauge negative partisanship in multi-party systems (see Rose and Mishler 1998). The authors find that negative and positive partisanship significantly impact vote choice whereby positive partisanship had a much stronger effect than its negative counterpart. These results are intuitive for multi-party systems, in which vote choice can be seen as a more affirmative act than in a two-party system where a vote for one party could feasibly be interpreted as a vote against the other. While Medeiros and Noel's study is one of the first to compare and contrast the predictive power of negative and positive partisanship, the authors do not elaborate on potential measurement concerns. For example, the measure of positive partisanship might not be equivalent to the measure of negative partisanship. Similarly, it is unclear whether the "never vote" item captures negative affect or thoughts, or maybe even a strategic decision not to vote for a party that has low chances of winning in the first place. Caruana and colleagues (2015) try to address these questions to a certain extent by expanding the measure of negative partisanship: In their work, the party for which the respondent would never vote, and which received a feeling thermometer value below 50 is considered the target of negative partisanship. While this measure entails an affective component, it does not account for variations in the intensity of negative partisanship. Just like variations in the strength of positive partisanship matter for predicting political behavior (see Huddy et al. 2015), so might variations in the intensity of negative partisanship. While the authors find a unique influence of negative partisanship on Canadian political behavior, it is possible that their measurement strategy underestimates the effect of negative partisanship.

Finally, many prior measurements of negative partisanship cannot distinguish between its expressive and instrumental facets. For example, it is possible that partisans assign a low feeling thermometer score to the out-party because of opposite policy views (i.e., instrumental) or because of their strong rejection of the out-party and its supporters (i.e., expressive). Feeling thermometer values as well as the "never vote" item cannot distinguish between these two dimensions.

6.3 THE NEGATIVE PARTISAN IDENTITY SCALE

I address these measurement challenges by developing a scale of negative partisan *identity* that aims to explicitly capture expressive components of negative partisanship and that closely resembles the positive partisan identity scale. This measurement equivalency allows for a fair test of positive and negative partisanship's impact on political behavior. Following Zhong and colleagues' measurement approach,[1] I flip the items of the positive partisan identity scale to capture the importance and emotional significance respondents associate with their rejection of the out-party. For example, one of the items in the positive partisan identity scale states: "When I meet someone who supports this party, I feel connected." In the negative partisan identity version, this item is phrased: "When I meet someone who supports this party, I feel *dis*connected." Thus, the focus of each item turns from belonging to the

---

[1] Zhong and colleagues flip the items of the identity subscale designed by Luhtanen and Crocker (1992) who also rely on Social Identity Theory to create their scale.

TABLE 6.1 Measure of negative partisan identity

Negative partisan identity scale
When I speak about this party, I say "they" rather than "we."
When people criticize this party, it makes me feel good.
When I meet someone who supports this party, I feel disconnected from that person.
If this party does well in opinion polls, my day is ruined.
I do not have much in common with supporters of this party.
I get angry with people who praise this party.
I am relieved when this party loses an election.
When I speak about this party and its supporters, I refer to it as "their party."

Note: The negative partisan identity's items' response options include "Never/Rarely," "Sometimes," "Often," and "Always."

in-party to the rejection of the out-party. Each of the eight scale items are included in Table 6.1.

I utilize this scale in my prior scholarship (Bankert 2020) and provide evidence for the distinct nature and effects of positive and negative partisan identity among US partisans in the 2016 US presidential election. In a first step, I calculate the percentage of respondents with high and low levels of both negative and positive partisanship as well as high levels on one type of partisanship but low on the other (i.e., high negative partisanship and low positive partisanship and vice versa). While the majority of US partisans in that study (64%) display high levels of positive and negative partisanship, there is a significant share of 22% that score high on one type of partisanship but not the other. Equally noteworthy is the asymmetry in the share of partisans who score high on PPID and NPID versus the share of partisans that scores low on PPID and NPID: While 64% of partisans in the United States display both high levels of negative and positive partisanship, only 15% exhibit both low levels of negative and positive partisanship. These initial findings affirm that negative and positive partisanship are not interchangeable. In Bankert (2020), I further test that notion by conducting a confirmatory factor analysis, which reveals that every fit index significantly improves when negative and positive partisanship are conceptualized as two separate latent factors rather than one. Last, the study also shows that political participation and the vote[2] are driven by positive partisanship, while opposition to bipartisanship in Congress is strongly related to negative partisanship. These prior findings illustrate the

---

[2] There is one notable nuance: Democrats' vote for Clinton in 2016 was driven by positive partisanship, whereas Republicans' vote for Trump was related to both positive and negative partisanship. These results suggest that the disdain felt toward the Democrats, and especially Hillary Clinton, might have motivated even reluctant members of the Republican Party to vote for Donald Trump, while it was Democrats' attachment to their own party that strongly predicted a vote for Clinton.

utility of the negative partisan identity scale for distinguishing between the effects of positive and negative partisanship in the United States. Yet we know little about the applicability of the NPID scale to other political systems beyond the US two-party system. Thus, in the remainder of this chapter, I compare the distribution of negative partisan identity (NPID) as well as the NPID scale's measurement properties across partisans in the United States, United Kingdom, Sweden, the Netherlands, and Italy.

6.4 DISTRIBUTION OF NEGATIVE PARTISAN IDENTITY IN THE USA AND EUROPE

The comparison of NPID across five vastly different countries provides an assessment of how widespread negative partisanship is beyond the United States. For this endeavor, I utilize the same survey data that was collected between 2021 and 2022 by Bovitz Inc. The NPID scale is included in each sample and was presented either before or after the PPID scale in a randomized order. While the samples are not nationally representative, they do reflect their respective country's population along key demographics such as gender, religion, and education. A comparison of each country's population and the corresponding sample composition can be found in the Appendix (see Tables A1–A5). In the United States, the NPID scale was assigned based on respondents' partisanship. For example, a self-identified Democratic respondent received the NPID scale that targets the Republican Party (e.g., "When the Republican Party does well in opinion polls, my day is ruined"). In the context of European multi-party systems, this approach does not work since there is no obvious out-party. Thus, the NPID scale is assigned based on the party that respondents would never vote for. If there are multiple such parties for a respondent, then the party with the lowest feeling thermometer score is the object of the NPID scale. For improved comparability across countries, NPID and all other relevant variables are scaled to range from 0 to 1 with 0 representing weakest levels of negative partisanship and 1 representing the strongest levels of negative partisanship. Similar to Chapter 5, I also examine the correlation of the NPID scale with an instrumental partisanship measure that relies on the same set of political issues and the ideological self-placement item used in prior analyses.

Starting once again with Italy (Figure 6.1), the NPID's distribution is remarkably skewed toward the high end of the scale, with a large share of partisans being located around the mid-point as well as in the upper half of the continuum (N = 1,024). Not surprisingly, the average NPID value is quite high with a mean of 0.57, a standard deviation of 0.26, and a high reliability coefficient of 0.87; 47% of Italian partisans either "always" or "often" feel angry when people praise the out-party, 57% feel good when people criticize it, and 70% are relieved when the out-party loses an election. Yet the NPID

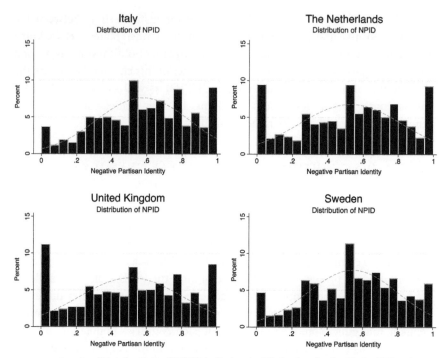

FIGURES 6.1–6.4 Distribution of NPID in Italy, the Netherlands, the United Kingdom, and Sweden

Note: In Italy, N = 1,024. In the Netherlands, N = 971. In the United Kingdom, N = 947. In Sweden, N = 975. Negative partisan identity is rescaled to range from 0 to 1.

scale is only weakly (0.07) related to the strength of Italian partisans' attitudes on political issues such as abortion, immigration, and taxes, as well as their ideological strength (0.09). Thus, the strength of both positive and negative expressive partisanship is quite distinct from Italians' policy preferences.

In the Netherlands (Figure 6.2), the first half of the negative partisan identity's distribution is a mirror image of its second half, with the highest share of partisans being located at the low, high, and mid-point of the scale (N = 971). With a mean of 0.53 and a standard deviation of 0.29, the average NPID value in the Netherlands is significantly higher than its PPID value of 0.38, suggesting a more dominant role of NPID among the Dutch electorate. The scale has equally good reliability with an alpha coefficient of 0.87; 75% of Dutch partisans either "always" or "often" think that they do not have much in common with supporters of the out-party, 66% feel disconnected from them, and 73% are relieved when the out-party loses an election. Negative partisanship correlates with partisans' attitude strength at only 0.09, similar to positive partisanship's low correlation with its instrumental counterpart in the Netherlands. An alternative measure of instrumental partisanship – partisans' ideological strength – fares somewhat better with a correlation of 0.18.

Moving on to the United Kingdom (Figure 6.3), the distribution of negative partisan identity closely resembles the one in the Netherlands, showing multiple peaks at the lowest and highest end of the continuum as well as at its midpoint (N = 947). This results in a mean value of 0.51 and a standard deviation of 0.30, slightly higher values than for positive partisan identity among British partisans. Similar to its positive equivalent, the NPID scale has a high reliability of 0.89 across all items. A staggering 62% of partisans report that they either "always" or "often" feel that they do not have much in common with supporters from the out-party, similar to 54% who say "they" when talking about the out-party, and 65% who are "always" or "often" relieved when the out-party loses an election. These are impressively high levels of endorsement. At 0.05, the correlation between British partisans' policy preferences and their NPID levels is once again very small, though it increases to 0.22 when utilizing a folded ideology measure that gauges the intensity of partisans' ideological self-placement.

In Sweden (Figure 6.4), the distribution of negative partisan identity follows a normal distribution, with a substantial peak around the midpoint of the scale. Yet more partisans are located in the upper half of the continuum than in the lower half (N = 975), resulting in a mean value of 0.54 and a standard deviation of 0.25. In Sweden too, NPID's average value is slightly higher than its PPID's average (0.54 versus 0.45). The scale's reliability is equally high (alpha = 0.85) and many items are strongly endorsed by Swedish partisans; 66% "always" or "often" think that they do not have much in common with supporters from the out-party, 64% say "they" when they speak about the out-party, and 68% are relieved when the out-party loses an election. The strength of Dutch negative partisan identity correlates with an instrumental partisanship measure at 0.06 – similar to other European countries – but increases to 0.21 when using ideological strength as a measure of instrumental partisanship.

Last, in the United States (Figure 6.5), NPID's distribution looks remarkably different from its European peers with a slight skew toward the lower half of the negative partisan identity scale. Indeed, the highest share of partisans centers around a relatively low value of 0.3 (N = 876), resulting in a mean value of 0.42 and a standard deviation of 0.25; notably, NPID's average is lower in the United States than in any of the four European countries included in this study. This is an interesting finding that contradicts the common narrative that partisan animosity is mainly limited to the US two-party system. The scale has a similarly good reliability with an alpha coefficient of 0.88; 48% of US partisans either "always" or "often" think that they do not have much in common with supporters of the out-party, 57% are relieved when the out-party loses an election, and 47% say "their party" when they speak about the out-party and its supporters. With a correlation of 0.18, the relationship between negative partisan identity and the intensity of partisans' attitudes is

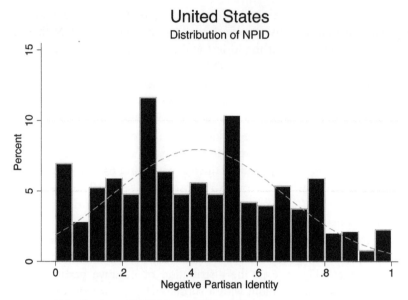

FIGURE 6.5 Distribution of NPID in the United States
Note: N = 876. Negative partisan identity is rescaled to range from 0 to 1.

somewhat more pronounced in the United States than in Europe. Interestingly, at 0.34, negative partisanship correlates more highly with the strength of American partisans' ideological convictions than its positive counterpart.

Overall, this simple comparison of distributions and mean values has provided three important insights: First, levels of negative partisan identity are higher than levels of positive partisan identity in all four European countries. This was not the case for NPID in the United States where NPID is as strong as its positive equivalent. Second, NPID is lower in the United States than in all four European countries, contradicting the notion that strong partisan animosity is limited to the two-party system. Third, across all five countries, NPID was only weakly related to the strength of political attitudes and moderately correlated with the strength of partisans' ideological self-placement, which further speaks to the distinction between expressive and instrumental components of partisanship as well as the significance of measurement choices when capturing instrumental partisanship.

6.5 MEASUREMENT PROPERTIES OF THE NEGATIVE PARTISAN IDENTITY SCALE

Next, I examine the scale's ability to capture fine gradations in the strength of negative partisan identity. Ideally, the NPID scale satisfies the same standards of a good measurement instrument as the PPID scale in Chapter 5, including its ability to identify negative partisans equally well at the low and high ends

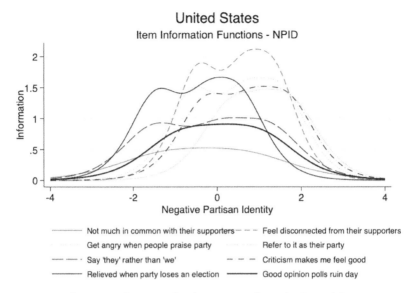

FIGURE 6.6 Information functions for the NPID scale in the United States

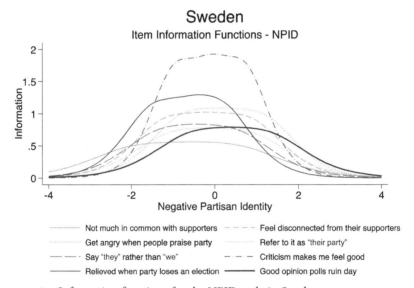

FIGURE 6.7 Information functions for the NPID scale in Sweden

of the continuum. To test this notion, I once again apply Item Response Theory (explained in more detail in Chapter 5) to three select countries that vary the most in their NPID values. I start by creating an information function for each item of the NPID scale in the U.S. (see Figure 6.6), Sweden (see Figure 6.7), and Italy (see Figure 6.8).

Across all three countries, lower to middling levels of negative partisan identity are especially well covered by the items "I am relieved when this party

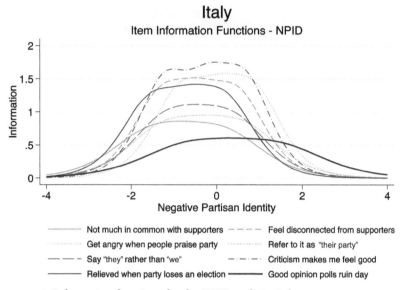

FIGURE 6.8 Information functions for the NPID scale in Italy

loses an election" and "When I meet someone who supports this party, I feel disconnected" as these items peak around −3 to 0 on the latent trait continuum. The same applies to the item "When I speak about this party, I say 'they' rather than 'we'" – though the item provides significantly less information, as its shallow curve suggests. The items "I get angry when people praise this party" and "When people criticize this party, it makes me feel good" perform equally well across all three countries, covering and distinguishing well between middling to high levels of negative partisan identity.

Additionally, high levels of negative partisan identity in the United States are captured by the item "When I speak about this party and its supporters, I refer to it as 'their party'" while, in Italy, the item "If this party does well in opinion polls, my day is ruined" covers the strongest levels of NPID, albeit at a lower information value as the item's flat function suggests. Other items' functions such as "When I speak about this party and its supporters, I refer to it as 'their party'" and "I don't have much in common with supporters of that party" cover a wider area from low to middling to high levels of NPID with moderately high amount of information. The weakest items with little information differ across countries. In the United States and Sweden, the item "I do not have much in common with supporters of this party" covers a wide range of negative partisan identity but it does not seem to differentiate well between strength levels as its relatively wide and flat function suggests. In Italy, the item "If this party does well in opinion polls, my day is ruined" has similar shortcomings though at somewhat higher levels of negative partisan identity.

Overall, the NPID scale performs similarly to the PPID scale; it covers a wide range of negative partisan identity and differentiates well between low and high levels of strength. For scholars who are concerned about the scale's length, I propose a shorter version of it, including the items "I am relieved when this party loses an election," "When I meet someone who supports this party, I feel disconnected," "I get angry when people praise this party," and "When people criticize this party, it makes me feel good." The IRT analyses suggests that these four items perform similarly well across all countries, with the former two covering low to middling levels of negative partisan identity and the latter two items covering and distinguishing well between middling to high levels of negative partisan identity.

6.6 NEGATIVE PARTISAN IDENTITY AMONG INDEPENDENTS

Prior work on negative partisanship in the United States has almost exclusively examined partisans – a reasonable choice since the two-party system allows for a clear identification of the party that can serve as the object of positive and negative partisanship. However, the focus on partisans also makes it difficult to fully distinguish between negative and positive partisanship since partisans – by definition – already have a positive partisanship. One solution to this empirical difficulty is to examine the extent of negative partisanship among unaffiliated voters who lack a positive party identification. By examining these independent or floating voters, it is possible to provide a clean test of the prediction that negative partisanship can exist without any prior positive partisanship. For this purpose, I utilize a sample of 630 US citizens who identify as pure independents without any partisan affiliation or leaning. The data was collected in August 2020 by Bovitz Inc. The sample composition mirrors the demographic profile of the independent voter population in the United States[3] (see Table A6 for more details): 53% of the sample is male, 69% is White, 72% has some college-level education, and the median age is 48 years. The NPID scale is assigned based on respondents' evaluation of the Democratic and the Republican Party. For example, if a respondent evaluates the Democratic Party more negatively than the Republican Party, then the Democratic Party is the object of the NPID scale.[4] Once again, for better comparability, all relevant variables are scaled to range from 0 to 1.

---

[3] Pew Research Center, Political independents: Who they are, what they think, www.pewresearch.org/politics/2019/03/14/political-independents-who-they-are-what-they-think/ (last accessed, May 4, 2021)

[4] This also means that respondents who evaluate both parties equally are excluded from the analysis. I reflect on the implications of this analytical choice as well as possible alternatives in the discussion section of this chapter.

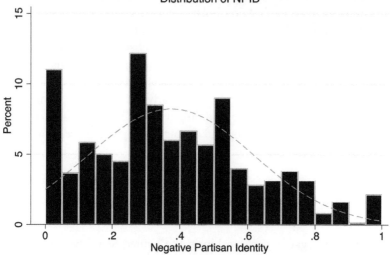

FIGURE 6.9 Distribution of NPID among US independents
Note: N = 630. Negative partisan identity is rescaled to range from 0 to 1.

The distribution of NPID among these independents (Figure 6.9) is skewed toward the lower half of the continuum, with a significant share of respondents located at the scale's minimum 0, at 0.3, and around its mid-point at 0.5. Accordingly, with an average value of 0.36 and a standard deviation of 0.24, levels of NPID are somewhat lower among independents than among partisans who scored a mean value of 0.42. Yet this is a surprisingly small difference given that independent voters do not have a team that they need to defend against a competitor – another piece of evidence in favor of the distinction between positive and negative partisanship. The scale also has equally good reliability with an alpha coefficient of 0.87

There are a few interesting asymmetries between independents with negative partisanship toward the Democratic and the Republican Party: Among the former, only 22% report "often" or "always" feeling good when people criticize the Democratic Party while among the latter, a staggering 43% reported the same reaction when people criticize the Republican Party. Similarly, 43% of independents with NPID toward Democrats think that they do not have much in common with supporters of the Democratic Party, compared to 59% of independents with NPID toward Republicans who "always" or "often" think this way.[5] Yet there is no statistically significant difference between the two groups (p = 0.31).

---

[5] The complete distribution of NPID toward Democrats and Republicans can be found in Tables A7 and A8 in the Appendix.

Similar to their partisan peers, the correlation between the strength of respondents' political attitudes (e.g., abortion, immigration, and gun control) and their negative partisan identity is low with a value of 0.06, though this relationship increases to 0.21 when using the strength of respondents' ideological self-placement. Overall, these preliminary findings show that negative partisanship can exist *without* any prior positive party attachments. These results are encouraging: Positive and negative partisanship are two separate constructs that do not have to go hand in hand. Partisans may be able to strongly support their in-party without feeling deep disdain for their opponents.

6.7 PREDICTIVE POWER OF THE SCALE, ITS IMPLICATIONS, AND FUTURE RESEARCH

The NPID scale strongly predicts a range of political behaviors and attitudes that one could consider problematic in a functioning democratic society, such as a general opposition to bipartisanship in Congress – a finding that applies both to partisans as well as independents in the United States (Bankert 2020, 2022). Indeed, independent voters with strong negative partisanship are more likely to be critical of bipartisan legislation and less likely to agree with the notion that Democrats and Republicans should work together. From this perspective, negative partisanship might have a troubling impact on democratic representation and accountability if it contributes to the partisan gridlock and animosity that has been ailing American politics. At the same time, my work shows that NPID among independents boosts their political participation – a desirable effect especially among unaffiliated voters who tend to turnout at lower rates than their partisan counterparts. However, we know little about the impact of negative partisan *identity* in multi-party systems – a gap that I will address in Chapters 8 and 9 of this book.

Future research can also expand our understanding of NPID among independent voters. The current analyses are limited to independents with negative partisanship toward *one* political party. As mentioned before, it is possible though that independents develop negative partisanship toward both parties or, in the multi-party context, to several political parties of the same ideological bloc or even parties on the fringe of the political spectrum. It is further worth investigating whether citizens with multiple NPIDs are empirically different from those with only one. On the one hand, multiple NPIDs might reinforce each other and, cumulatively, boost political engagement even more so than NPID toward one single political party. On the other hand, there might also be a ceiling effect at which NPID toward too many political parties is related to lower levels of political trust and efficacy, thereby diminishing political participation rather than encouraging it.

Last, critics might wonder whether pure independents – despite their self-identification – can still have a positive partisan identity. From a practical standpoint, this is somewhat challenging to test since the positive partisan identity scale is normally assigned to respondents who identify as partisans or, at least, lean toward a party. One possible way to address this concern is to assign both the negative and positive partisan identity scale in a randomized order to respondents who consider themselves pure independents. This might require more space on researchers' surveys, but it might be worth the costs since it could provide clarity on the independent nature of NPID as well as the ability of the traditional party identification measure to capture even weak partisan leanings.

It is also imaginable that being an independent can be a positive identity on its own, whereby unaffiliated voters consider themselves unbiased and objective arbiters of politics. Future research can examine this prediction by adapting the partisan identity scale accordingly with items such as "I have a lot in common with other independents" or "When I speak about independents, I say 'we' versus 'them.'" With this independent identity scale, it would be possible to distinguish between "independent" as a negative identity, on the one hand, and "independent" as a positive identity, on the other, and to see which of the two keeps independents anchored in the political system long term.

Equally interesting is the development of negative partisanship in multi-party systems. With declining levels of positive attachment to mainstream parties in Western European democracies and rising levels of negative partisanship toward populist parties (Mudde and Kaltwasser 2018), European multi-party systems enable researchers to examine to what extent negative partisan identity can serve as a superordinate identity that draws in partisans from across the ideological spectrum in opposition to a populist challenger. Future work could also assess if, and under what conditions, this opposition eventually translates into stronger attachment to mainstream parties.

Last, more attention needs to be paid to the instrumental aspects of negative partisanship. These efforts include designing and testing the predictive power of an instrumental measure that is explicitly based on the strength of partisans' opposition to the out-party's leadership, disagreement on key policy issues, and ideological dissimilarity. The addition of such a measure would allow researchers to detect and compare the effect of expressive and instrumental negative partisanship on political behavior but it would also permit a closer look at the positive and negative dimensions of instrumental partisanship. Given the well-documented negativity bias (e.g., Ito et al. 1998) in human information processing, it might be reasonable to expect stronger effects for the opposition to concrete policies and ideologies (i.e., negative instrumental) rather than for their strong support (i.e., positive instrumental).

6.8 SUMMARY

A conceptualization of negative partisanship as an identity requires a measure that reflects its psychological nature. Like its positive counterpart, the expressive approach to negative partisanship is grounded in Social Identity Theory, which requires its measurement instrument to gauge the strong rejection of the out-party and its members as well as the personal offense that negative partisans feel when the out-party succeeds. The negative partisan identity scale aims to capture these identity components. The eight-item index has good and similar measurement properties across several countries, which makes it suitable for comparative work on negative partisanship. Indeed, utilizing the NPID scale in this chapter reveals lower NPID values in the United States than in Italy, Sweden, the Netherlands, and the United Kingdom. With its ability to capture a wide range of negative partisan identity strength, the scale enables researchers to assess negative partisanship's impact on political behavior more accurately and to distinguish it from its positive counterpart. For the same reasons, the scale can feasibly be used as a dependent variable, thereby generating new research avenues on the origins of negative partisan identity among partisans and independent voters alike.

7

The Psychological Origins of Positive and Negative
Partisan Identity

7.1 WHAT IS IN THIS CHAPTER?

Despite the extensive prior literature on their effects, we know relatively little about the psychological origins of negative and positive partisanship: Which personality traits are associated with high levels of negative partisanship, and do they differ from the ones that have been linked to positive partisanship? With the help of the PPID and NPID scales, this chapter provides an answer to these questions. Utilizing a sample of US partisans and a sample of Swedish partisans, I examine the link between prominent personality traits – including Authoritarianism, Social Dominance Orientation, the Need for Closure, and the Big Five – and strong negative and positive partisanship. I demonstrate that the personality origins of positive and negative partisanship differ not just across American and Swedish partisans but also across partisans on the left and on the right of the ideological spectrum. I conclude the chapter with implications for future research on political behavior and polarization.

7.2 WHY DOES IT MATTER?

This chapter creates a psychological profile of those partisans that are most likely to develop strong positive and/or negative partisanship, thereby testing the notion that some people might be more susceptible to becoming strong partisans than others. This is an important inquiry: If positive and negative partisanship have different personality origins, then this is one more piece of evidence in support of their independent and distinct nature. Moreover, we can learn who is more likely to develop strong positive partisanship in combination with negative partisanship and who is more likely to be either a strong positive or negative partisan. Last, the cross-country comparison reveals whether these personality predictors are the same among American and Swedish partisans. Overall, this chapter makes the important point that strong partisan identities are a product of personality and the political context it operates in.

***

Throughout this book so far, I have argued and provided evidence that partisanship – both positive and negative – can be conceptualized as a social identity that operates quite independently of concrete political issue positions and ideological beliefs. At the same time, positive and negative partisanship can operate independently of each other: Strong positive partisans might be deeply protective of their party loyalties but care little about the partisan rancor and disdain for the opposing party. Strong negative partisans on the other hand, might be more motivated by their opposition of the out-party rather than their embrace of the in-party. Given their conceptual difference, it is reasonable to expect that PPID and NPID have not only different effects on political behavior but also different psychological origins.

To address this possibility, I examine a range of prominent personality traits, including the Need for Closure (NfC), Authoritarianism, Social Dominance Orientation (SDO), and the Big Five. I focus on these traits because of prior scholarship that has provided evidence for their association with strong partisan attachments. Yet there is little systematic evidence that examines more than just one personality trait at a time or that compares their impact on both PPID and NPID. Moreover, there is little prior comparative work on the relationship between personality and partisanship despite the concern that personality traits' influence might vary across countries due to cultural as well as political differences. I thus examine a sample of American and Swedish partisans. Sweden's political system is not just characterized by proportional representation but also by a "fundamentally consensual political culture" and much lower levels of affective polarization across partisans (Oscarsson et al. 2021, p. 5). These features stand in sharp contrast to the American two-party system, thereby allowing for a comparison of the personality origins of positive and negative partisan identity across two vastly different political systems.

With two separate measures to capture PPID and NPID, it is possible to create a typology of partisans that can be distinguished by their different PPID and NPID levels. Early work by Rose and Mishler (1998) has already done so with the example of post-communist countries, whereby the authors examine four different types of partisans: (a) open partisans with PPID toward their in-party and without NPID toward another party, (b) negative partisans with NPID and without PPID, (c) closed partisans with both NPID and PPID, and (d) apathetic partisans with no identification. Rose and Mishler find that in the four countries they studied, namely Hungary, Poland, Romania, and Slovenia, more than half of respondents held NPID toward at least one party but PPID toward none. Similarly, Mudde and

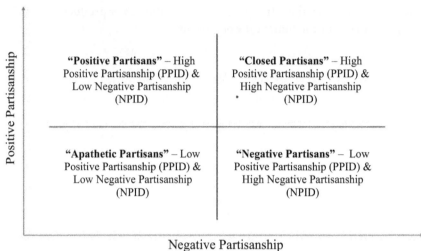

FIGURE 7.1 Typology of partisans

Kaltwasser (2018) note that in many Western European democracies, populist parties are the targets of NPID despite declining levels of PPID. These findings reiterate that NPID and PPID do not always occur together.

While I partly rely on Rose and Mishler's terminology in this study, I slightly alter their typology. Rather than examining the mere existence of positive and/or negative identification with a political party, I examine the intensity or strength of that positive and/or negative identification. This leads to four different types of partisans: Positive partisans with high levels of PPID and low levels of NPID, negative partisans with high levels of NPID and low levels of PPID, closed partisans with high levels of both PPID and NPID, and apathetic partisans with low levels of both PPID and NPID (see Figure 7.1). I will utilize this typology to make predictions about the distinct personality traits that are associated with each partisan type in the United States and in Sweden.

7.3 PERSONALITY AND PARTISANSHIP

Researchers have long been interested in the personality origins of political attitudes and behavior (Adorno et al. 1950; Eysenck 1954; McClosky 1958). Personality traits are defined as "relatively enduring patterns of thoughts, feelings, and behaviors that distinguish individuals from one another" (Roberts and Mroczek 2008, p. 31) and that are exogenous to their political socialization (McCourt et al. 1999). From this perspective, the focus on personality traits as determinants of partisan attachments offers two distinct advantages: First, despite some developmental changes in dispositional traits during early adulthood, personality traits are relatively stable, which allows for a more generalizable interpretation of their effects on partisanship throughout an individual's life cycle. Second, personality traits temporally precede the development of many political values, attitudes, and behavior, including party attachments. Thus, despite the observational nature of the following analyses, personality traits intuitively are more likely to be a determinant of partisanship rather than vice versa (see Luttig 2021, for an exception).

Within the large and diverse share of scholarship on the relationship between personality and politics, there are a few select and distinct traits that are featured quite prominently. These traits include Authoritarianism, SDO, the Need for Closure, and the Big Five. Prior scholarship has focused much more extensively on the personality origins of PPID (Cooper et al. 2013; Gerber et al. 2012; Schoen and Schumann 2007) than NPID (see Webster 2018 for an exception). From this perspective, my predictions for positive partisans are most firmly grounded in prior scholarship, while the determinants of negative, apathetic, and closed partisans constitute mostly uncharted territory. In the following, I will briefly elaborate on each trait and articulate my expectations for their effect on PPID and NPID.

7.3.1 Need for Closure

The NfC is a psychological predisposition that has been used extensively in psychology to describe individuals with a "desire for a firm answer to a question, any firm answer as compared to confusion and/or ambiguity" (Kruglanski 2004, p. 6). Like other psychological constructs, NfC can be conceptualized as a continuum. From this perspective, people with high levels of NfC tend to prefer firm and unequivocal assessments of the world and avoid ambiguity and nuance that could negate their need for order and structure (Kruglanski and Webster 1996), while people with low levels of NfC are more comfortable with more fluid and ambiguous perceptions of the world.

Accordingly, NfC has been associated with heightened in-party favoritism and out-party hostility as well as partisan identity strength. As Luttig (2018, p. 240) explains: "Group identification, ingroup bias, and outgroup prejudice are motivated partly by the need for certainty and closure because groups provide members with a social identity and prescribe beliefs about who one is and what they should believe and think. Furthermore . . . uncertainty as a motivation for group membership can foster extremism, as extreme groups are more distinct and unambiguous." From this vantage point, NfC might strongly predict high levels of PPID and NPID since they facilitate the rigid categorization of political parties into "good" and "bad," "us" versus "them."

In the following analyses, NfC is measured with six items including "I dislike questions, which could be answered in many different ways," "I enjoy having a clear and structured mode of life," and "I do not usually consult many different opinions before forming my own view." Respondents were asked to indicate how much they agree with each statement, ranging from "strongly agree" to "strongly disagree." The scale is somewhat reliable in the United States as well as in the Swedish sample (alpha = 0.62 in the United States with a mean of 0.51 on a 0-1 scale; alpha = 0.67 with a mean of 0.55 on a 0-1 scale in the Sweden sample).

7.3.2 Authoritarianism

Authoritarianism is a psychological predisposition that reflects a general preference for social conformity over individual autonomy (Feldman 2003; Feldman and Stenner 1997; Stenner 2005). This preference is driven by a strong dispositional need for order, certainty, and security as well as a general commitment to conventions and norms (Hetherington and Weiler 2009; Jost et al. 2003). Given these tendencies, it is not surprising that authoritarianism has been linked to ideological conservatism (Federico and Tagar 2014), right-wing policy preferences (Hetherington and Suhay 2011), and traditionalism (Federico, Fisher, and Deason 2011). Yet authoritarianism is also related to intra-group preferences – regardless of their ideological direction – whereby authoritarians prefer in-group compositions that "enhance sameness and minimize diversity of people, beliefs, and behaviors" (Stenner 2005, p. 16). For example, among Democratic voters, authoritarianism predicts voting for establishment candidates such as Clinton over Sanders (Wronski et al. 2018). This illustrates the nature of authoritarianism: Rather than a trait "on the right" of the ideological spectrum, authoritarianism is a general predisposition toward compliance with norms and conventions – regardless of their ideological association.

To disentangle authoritarianism from conservatism, it is measured with questions about child-rearing preferences. Respondents are asked to judge which of two desirable traits is more important for a child to have: "respect for elders"* versus "independence," "curiosity" versus "good manners"*, "obedience"* versus "self-reliance," and "being considerate" versus "being well-behaved"*. Authoritarian choices are marked with an asterisk and coded as 1 while the other choices are coded as 0. I combine all items into one scale that ranges from 0 (minimum) to 1 (maximum). The scale is more reliable in the United States (alpha = 0.64) than in Sweden (alpha = 0.47) with a mean of 0.47 and 0.39, respectively.

As Feldman (2003) notes, this measure "captures authoritarians' emphasis on order and control, conformity, and obedience" without explicit references to ideology or social norms and conventions. The measure is thus less subject to social desirability biases and is unlikely to be confounded with measures of social conservatism – one of the major critique points of prior measures of authoritarianism such as Altemeyer's right-wing authoritarianism (RWA) scale (1988) and Adorno's F-scale (1950).

I expect that authoritarianism is positively linked to strong positive partisan identities since they provide a sense of belonging, prescribe group norms to comply with, and a simplified understanding of who is a friend or foe in a complex political world (see also Luttig 2017). Negative partisan identities, on the other hand, do not satisfy the need for inclusion as easily as positive partisan identities do (see Zhong et al. 2008a, 2008b for a similar argument). Instead, NPID turns the exclusion from a group – the "not being one of them" – into a meaningful social identity while it provides little affirmational guidance on who we are. I thus expect authoritarianism to be negatively related to negative partisanship.

While I treat authoritarianism as a determinant of PPID and NPID, some prior work has challenged this causal order. In the example of the United States, Luttig (2021, p. 786) notes: "As the GOP became more conservative on social issues, embraced the religious right, advocated being tough on crime ... they communicated that their party sees the world as a dangerous place and that they value obedience, respect, good manners, and good behavior. Inferring the associations of the parties with these values, people change either their psychological worldview or the way that they answer survey questions about these topics to reduce cognitive dissonance." This is an important nuance that underlines the power of identities in shaping partisans' worldviews. One way to address this issue of causality is to compare the effect of authoritarianism among American partisans to their Swedish counterparts who are embedded in a much less polarized political system. If authoritarianism has a similar effect across these two vastly different systems, then we can be more confident that authoritarianism precedes strong party attachments. Most likely, though, there is a feedback loop between the two that, over time, leads to a reinforcement of both personality and partisanship.

7.3.3 Social Dominance Orientation

Social dominance orientation (SDO) (Pratto et al. 1994) is another prominent predisposition that has gained traction in political psychology, often in combination with authoritarianism (e.g., Crawford and Pilanski 2014; Henry et al. 2005; Sibley et al. 2006; Wilson and Sibley 2013). Like authoritarianism and NfC, SDO is measured on a continuum: People on the low end of SDO tend to endorse group equality and oppose societal hierarchies, while people on the high end of the scale seek power and high status for their group as well as dominance over others (Satherley et al. 2020).

While authoritarianism and SDO are empirically related, they are conceptually different: Authoritarians cherish traditional norms and values and show hostility toward those who deviate from them. People who score highly on SDO, on the other hand, cherish their group's dominance and power and show hostility toward those who challenge the group hierarchy. SDO thus draws people toward political parties (and policies) that bolster group-based inequalities (Duckitt and Sibley 2009) and that rationalize them as a natural outcome of different groups' abilities and their meritocratic efforts (e.g., Azevedo et al. 2019; Choma and Hanoch, 2017; Crawford and Pilanski, 2014; Duckitt and Sibley 2016; Dunwoody and Plane 2019; Van Assche, Dhont, and Pettigrew 2019). Consistent with these expectations, prior research has shown SDO to be strongly related to conservative or right-wing policies and party preferences in the United States as well as beyond (e.g., Van Assche et al., 2019), which hints at the importance of accounting for ideological differences. However, it remains unclear how SDO relates to PPID and NPID overall.

To measure SDO, respondents are asked to indicate their level of agreement, ranging from "strongly oppose" to "strongly favor," with multiple statements related to intergroup hierarchies such as "An ideal society requires some groups to be on top and others to be on the bottom," "Some groups of people are simply inferior to other groups," "No one group should dominate in society," "We should work to give all groups an equal chance to succeed," and "Some groups of people must be kept in their place." The scale has moderately high reliability in the US sample (alpha = 0.76; mean = 0.29) as well as in the Swedish sample (alpha = 0.64; mean = 0.42).

7.3.4 The Big Five

The Big Five traits are a well-known and established framework for studying personality that specifies a small set of core traits, including Extraversion, Conscientiousness, Agreeableness, Emotional Stability, and Openness to Experience (see McCrae and Costa 2008). Each of these traits is measured on a continuum: People who score low on Openness to Experience tend to be less curious and more conventional, while people on the high end tend to be creative and imaginative. People who score low on Extraversion tend to be quiet and more reserved, while the people on the high end tend to be talkative and active. Expressions of low Conscientiousness include being disorganized and negligent, whereas people on the high end tend to be the opposite – well-organized, punctual, and detail oriented. Agreeableness is characterized by critical and irritable behavior on the low end and trusting and patient behavior toward others on the high end. Last, Emotional Stability (commonly coded in the reverse as Neuroticism) expresses itself as emotional and temperamental on the low end and calm and even-tempered on the high end of the spectrum (see Eysenck 1967 for a review). Prior scholarship has demonstrated the impact of these traits on party preferences on the ideological left and right, albeit with somewhat mixed results (e.g., Alford and Hibbing 2007;

Barbaranelli et al. 2007; Caprara et al. 1999; Mondak 2010; Mondak and Halperin 2008). When it comes to the strength of positive party attachments, Gerber and colleagues (2011) find that Extraversion, Agreeableness, and Openness are significant predictors of partisan identification even when controlling for ideology and a variety of issue positions.

Research is less plentiful regarding the psychological origins of NPID, though there is some evidence that Extraversion, Agreeableness, and Emotional Stability are *negatively* related to strong NPID (Abramowitz and Webster 2018). Indeed, Extraversion and Agreeableness describe a person who is willing to hear the other side in a polite and trusting manner, while Emotional Stability reduces the chance of experiencing strong negative emotions such as anger and disdain in the first place. Webster (2018) further distinguishes between simply being a negative partisan and the intensity of negative partisanship. The author shows that higher levels of Extraversion are associated with a lower probability of being a negative partisan (Webster 2018). This finding has high face validity since, as Webster (2018) notes, extraverted individuals are more likely to be exposed to a vast array of different political viewpoints which moderates their negativity toward the out-party and its members. Webster (2018) also demonstrates that higher levels of Agreeableness lessen the degree to which an individual exhibits negative affect toward the out-party and its members since the trait is associated with friendliness, fairness, and decency – even toward their political opponent. From this perspective, these three traits – Extraversion, Agreeableness, and Emotional Stability – should be negatively related to strong NPID.

I follow conventions and measure the Big Five traits with a list of adjectives. Respondents then rate how well each adjective describes themselves with response options ranging from "strongly disagree" to "strongly agree." In the following analyses, each trait is captured with two items (following Gosling et al. 2003). For example, Openness to Experience is gauged with the item "I see myself as open to new experiences, complex" as well as "I see myself conventional, uncreative" (reverse coded) while Conscientiousness consists of the items "I see myself as dependable, self-disciplined" and "I see myself as disorganized, careless" (reverse coded). There are certainly drawbacks in using only two items per trait, especially regarding internal reliability (see Gerber et al. 2011 for a critique), but I prioritize the inclusion of many prominent personality traits – albeit in short form – over an in-depth examination of only one trait.

7.4 DATA

For the analysis of partisanship in the United States, I utilize the same original survey data that I introduced in prior chapters on the measurement of partisan identity. While the sample is not nationally representative, it does reflect the US population on key demographics. The sample includes 1,007 respondents, 882 of them completed the positive partisanship (PPID) scale, while 876 of them completed the negative partisanship (NPID) scale. Respondents who identified as a Democrat (or Republican) received the PPID for the Democratic (or Republican) Party and the NPID scale for the Republican (or Democratic) Party. The sample included 456 Republicans and 447 Democrats.

For the analysis of partisanship in Sweden, I analyze the same original survey data that I used to examine the measurement properties of the PPID and NPID scale in Chapters 5 and 6. While the sample is not nationally representative either, it does reflect key demographics of the Swedish population. The sample includes 1,208 Swedish respondents, 968 of them completed the PPID scale, while 975 completed the NPID scale. Respondents received the PPID scale if there was a party that they considered "best" or if they indicated feeling closer to a particular party. Most commonly, that applied to the Social Democrats (28%), the Sweden Democrats (29%), and the Moderate Party (13%). The NPID scale was administered based on the question of whether there is a political party that the respondent would never vote for. If so, this party was the target of the NPID scale, which most frequently applied to the Left Party (N = 265), the Green Party (N = 298), the Sweden Democrats (N = 447), and the Feminist Initiative (N = 334).

In the following analyses, I treat the PPID and NPID values as dependent variables. The correlation between the two in the United States is much higher than in Sweden (0.65 versus 0.36), highlighting their overlapping nature in the two-party system. From this perspective, simply regressing the personality predictors onto the PPID and NPID values would make it challenging to disentangle the distinct psychological origins of these two types of partisanship. Following Rose and Mishler's typology, I thus create four different types of partisans based on their values on the NPID and PPID scales. For analytical purposes, "low" is defined as below the sample's mean value on the PPID/NPID scale, while "high" is defined as above the sample's mean value.

The percentage shares for each type of partisan are included in Table 7.1. Both in the United States and in Sweden, the overwhelming share of partisans

TABLE 7.1 Percentage shares of partisan types

	US sample	Swedish sample
Positive Partisans	10%	16%
Negative Partisans	11%	17%
Closed Partisans	42%	43%
Apathetic Partisans	37%	24%

Notes: Percentages are derived from the sample of respondents who completed both the PPID and NPID scales; N = 1,007 in the US sample and N = 1,208 in the Swedish sample.

fall into the categories of closed partisans and apathetic partisans; 42% of all American and 43% of Swedish partisans in the sample score highly on both the PPID and NPID scale, while 37% and 24% of American and Swedish partisans respectively are characterized by low scores on both the PPID and NPID scale. Only 10% of American partisans and 16% of Swedish partisans score highly on the PPID scale in conjunction with low values on the NPID scale. Similarly, 11% of American partisans and 17% of Swedish partisans fall on the high end of the NPID scale while also scoring low on the PPID scale. These comparisons reveal an interesting asymmetry: While NPID and PPID can certainly occur independently, the two types of partisanship much more commonly occur together.

In the next step, I examine whether these partisan types are related to distinct personality traits. For this purpose, I regress each partisan type onto the set of select personality traits as well as several relevant demographic variables such as ideology (coded to range from 0 "very liberal" to 1 "very conservative"), gender (coded 0 for male and 1 for female respondents), race (coded 0 for US respondents of Color and 1 for White US respondents), education (coded to range from 0 "no high school degree" to 1 for "post-graduate degree"), the type of place the respondent lives in (coded to range from 0 for rural to 1 for urban), and religiosity, which measures the frequency of attending religious services (coded to range from 0 "never" to 1 "more than once a week.") Since race is not a common measure in European surveys, I instead include a variable that measures whether the respondent grew up or has spent most of their life in Europe. This variable is called "European."

7.5 AMERICAN PARTISANS AND PERSONALITY

Starting with positive partisans in the United States, SDO, Agreeableness, and Openness to Experience emerge as strong and positive predictors (see Table 7.2). The effects of SDO and Openness are quite sizable. Across the range of SDO, PPID increases from 0.04 to 0.17, while keeping all other variables at their mean. In other words, strong positive partisans in the United States seek power and high status for their in-party and cherish their in-party's norms and conventions There is a similarly steep increase in PPID from 0.02 to 0.1 as Openness increases from 0 to 1. At the same time, NfC is negatively related to being a positive partisans. As NfC increases, the probability of being a positive partisan significantly decreases from 0.12 to 0.03.

Moving on to negative partisans, NfC and Emotional Stability emerge as positive predictors, with similar increases in its predicted probability from 0.05 to 0.17 across the range of these two personality traits. Conscientiousness and Extraversion are uniquely and negatively related to NPID. In combination, these findings suggest that PPID and NPID do have distinct personality origins, in support of the notion that these two are independent constructs. Indeed,

TABLE 7.2 *Personality predictors of partisan types, US sample*

	(1) Positive Partisans	(2) Negative Partisans	(3) Closed Partisans	(4) Apathetic Partisans
Need for Closure	−1.30**	1.30**	0.74	−0.83**
	(0.76)	(0.73)	(0.46)	(0.48)
SDO	1.50**	−0.31	1.70***	−2.20***
	(0.61)	(0.60)	(0.38)	(0.40)
Authoritarianism	0.54	−0.56	0.00	0.06
	(0.36)	(0.34)	(0.22)	(0.22)
Conscientiousness	0.94	−1.08**	−0.47	0.66**
	(0.69)	(0.54)	(0.36)	(0.37)
Agreeableness	1.17**	−0.20	−0.22	−0.12
	(0.68)	(0.61)	(0.39)	(0.41)
Emotional Stability	−0.12	0.94**	0.02	−0.38
	(0.61)	(0.54)	(0.35)	(0.35)
Openness	1.41**	0.88	−0.54	−0.31
	(0.68)	(0.59)	(0.38)	(0.39)
Extraversion	0.50	−1.14***	0.94***	−0.61**
	(0.47)	(0.43)	(0.28)	(0.28)
Ideology	0.40	−0.28	−0.62**	0.72***
	(0.43)	(0.40)	(0.26)	(0.27)
Age	−0.07	0.023	0.08**	−0.07
	(0.07)	(0.07)	(0.04)	(0.04)
Female	−0.24	−0.06	−0.19	0.30**
	(0.23)	(0.21)	(0.13)	(0.14)
White	−0.04	0.35	−0.25**	0.12
	(0.25)	(0.24)	(0.15)	(0.15)
Religiosity	0.96***	−0.90**	0.36**	−0.40**
	(0.33)	(0.35)	(0.20)	(0.21)
Education	−0.08	0.80**	−0.44**	0.12
	(0.41)	(0.38)	(0.25)	(0.25)
Constant	−5.11***	−2.62***	−0.48	0.59
	(0.89)	(0.79)	(0.50)	(0.51)
Observations	994	994	994	994

Note: Entries are coefficients from a logistic regression. All variables range from 0 to 1 for better comparability. Standard errors in parentheses, *** $p < 0.01$, ** $p < 0.05$, * $p < 0.1$.

only NfC appears as a significant predictor in both analyses of positive and negative partisans but with oppositional effects.

Closed partisans are characterized by high levels of SDO as well as Extraversion. The coefficient for NfC is positive and quite substantial. The predicted probability of being a closed partisan increases from 0.26 to 0.67 along the range of SDO – an effect that is similar to Extraversion, which is associated with a growth from 0.28 to 0.51, while holding all other personality variables constant. Last, apathetic partisans are characterized by higher levels of Conscientiousness and lower levels of NfC, SDO, and Extraversion. The effects are particularly strong for SDO. Across its range, the predicted probability of being an apathetic partisan shrinks from 0.56 to 0.12. Taken together, these analyses suggest that all four types of partisanship have distinct personality profiles. Yet three personality traits – NfC, SDO, and Extraversion – emerge frequently as significant predictors. When adjusted for multiple comparisons using Bonferroni correction, several relationships persist, such as the positive relationship between negative partisans and Extraversion, closed partisans and SDO and Extraversion, as well as apathetic partisans and SDO.

7.6 SWEDISH PARTISANS AND PERSONALITY

The prior results can only speak to American partisans, which limits their generalizability given the idiosyncratic nature of the US political system. Thus, I replicate the preceding analyses with a sample of Swedish partisans, which illuminates the nature of partisanship in multi-party systems (see Table 7.3). For the prediction of positive partisans, none of the included personality variables appear to exert an impact, which is an interesting departure from the US model. However, religiosity emerges as a positive predictor of positive partisanship among both Americans and Swedes. Moving on to negative partisans, only Authoritarianism emerges as a negative and significant predictor – which, once again, stands in sharp contrast to the results from the US sample. Indeed, as Authoritarianism increases from 0 to 1, the probability of being a negative partisan in Sweden decreases from 0.22 to 0.13. These partisans tend to be more conventional, traditional, and more rigid in their political outlook.

Among closed partisans, SDO (like in the United States) and Authoritarianism exert significant effects. As these two traits increase from 0 to 1, closed partisanship's likelihood grows from 0.28 to 0.51. Remarkably, these two traits are negative predictors of being an apathetic partisan, with a decline in its predicted probability from 0.31 to 0.17 and 0.35 to 0.14 across the range of Authoritarianism and SDO, respectively. SDO was also negatively related to being apathetic partisan in the United States – an interesting similarity across these vastly different samples.

Additionally, Need for Closure and Conscientiousness are positively associated with being an apathetic partisan in Sweden. The positive effects of Conscientiousness also surfaced among apathetic partisans in the United States, while the Need for Closure had a negative effect on the likelihood of being an apathetic partisan in the United States. This is an interesting departure that might be due to the difference between the two-party system and the multi-party system. In the former, choosing a team is much easier and more definitive than in the latter. A partisan with a need for firm answers and

TABLE 7.3 *Personality predictors of partisan types, Sweden sample*

	(1) Positive Partisans	(2) Negative Partisans	(3) Closed Partisans	(4) Apathetic Partisans
Need for Closure	−0.08	−0.85	−0.04	0.90**
	(0.54)	(0.52)	(0.43)	(0.46)
SDO	0.45	0.01	0.84**	−1.18***
	(0.43)	(0.41)	(0.35)	(0.36)
Authoritarianism	0.20	−0.60**	0.97***	−0.75***
	(0.32)	(0.32)	(0.26)	(0.28)
Conscientiousness	−0.04	−0.59	−0.50	1.03***
	(0.43)	(0.41)	(0.35)	(0.37)
Agreeableness	0.26	0.50	−0.52	0.03
	(0.48)	(0.47)	(0.39)	(0.42)
Emotional Stability	0.09	0.20	−0.58**	0.37
	(0.41)	(0.40)	(0.34)	(0.35)
Openness	−0.11	0.12	−0.27	0.28
	(0.47)	(0.45)	(0.39)	(0.40)
Extraversion	0.047	−0.16	0.29	−0.20
	(0.35)	(0.34)	(0.29)	(0.29)
Ideology	−0.87***	−0.09	0.30	0.42
	(0.33)	(0.33)	(0.27)	(0.28)
Age	−0.01	0.09**	−0.090**	0.03
	(0.05)	(0.05)	(0.046)	(0.04)
Female	−0.03	0.05	0.20	−0.23
	(0.17)	(0.17)	(0.14)	(0.15)
European	−1.28***	0.02	0.76	0.54
	(0.47)	(0.64)	(0.53)	(0.64)
Religiosity	0.71**	−1.19***	0.60**	−0.59**
	(0.28)	(0.34)	(0.24)	(0.27)
Education	−0.56**	0.50	0.49**	−0.56**
	(0.33)	(0.34)	(0.27)	(0.29)
Constant	−0.08	−1.21	−1.61**	−1.80**
	(0.82)	(0.91)	(0.76)	(0.86)
Observations	1,015	1,015	1,015	1,015

Note: Entries are coefficients from a logistic regression. All variables range from 0 to 1 for better comparability. Standard errors in parentheses, *** $p < 0.01$, ** $p < 0.05$, * $p < 0.1$.

clear structures might prefer the rigid categorization of the two-party system and avoid the more fluid and temporary political arrangements of the multi-party system. When using Bonferroni-adjusted p-values, the relationship between closed partisans and Authoritarianism remains as well as the effect of SDO and Conscientiousness on apathetic partisans.

Overall, these results provide two novel insights: First, the four types of partisanship are related to distinct personality profiles both in the United

States and in Sweden. Second, the four types of partisanship in the United States and in Sweden are related to different personality profiles. This variation might speak to the role of institutional features such as the number of political parties (two-party versus multi-party system), the electoral rules (proportional versus majoritarian), the ideological space of the political system, and the country's political culture. Yet a few similarities emerged across partisan types in both samples. Closed partisans in both countries display higher levels of SDO; apathetic partisans in the United States and Sweden display lower levels of SDO and higher levels of Conscientiousness, while Need for Closure increases the chance of being an apathetic partisan in Sweden but decreased that chance in the United States.

7.7 IDEOLOGICAL DIFFERENCES AMONG POSITIVE AND NEGATIVE PARTISANS

The preceding analyses revealed distinct personality profiles for each of the four partisan types. Yet it is possible that there are additional personality differences between positive and negative partisans on the left and right of the ideological spectrum. Prior scholarship on personality supports that notion. For example, Need for Closure (NfC) has been linked to political conservatism as well as more right-wing political party preferences (Kossowska and Hiel 2003), which leads to the expectation that NfC is more strongly related to PPID on the ideological right. The same prediction applies to Authoritarianism, which, as prior evidence demonstrates, is also strongly related to ideological conservatism (Federico and Reifen Tagar 2014) and right-wing policy preferences (Hetherington and Suhay 2011).

Similarly, Social Dominance Orientation (SDO) is strongly related to conservative or right-wing policies and party preferences in the United States and beyond (e.g., Van Assche et al. 2019). It is thus likely that SDO too is more predictive of strong PPID on the right. At the same time, there might also be a strong connection between SDO and NPID toward the ideological left since many left-wing policies aim to eradicate intergroup inequalities (e.g., affirmative action, access to social services, and universal healthcare) and promote awareness of systemic discrimination and privilege.

Last, prior scholarship has also demonstrated the impact of the Big Five traits on party preferences on the ideological left and right, albeit with somewhat mixed results. The most consistent finding is the relationship between Openness to Experience and liberalism, on the one hand, and between Conscientiousness and conservatism, on the other (e.g., Alford and Hibbing 2007; Mondak 2010; Mondak and Halperin 2008). There is also some evidence that Emotional Stability is linked to support for conservative candidates and parties and that Agreeableness is connected to support for liberal candidates and parties (Barbaranelli et al. 2007; Caprara et al. 1999; Mondak 2010). This abundance of prior scholarship provides the foundation for a couple of concrete expectations regarding the relationship between the Big Five and partisan identities on the left and on the right. First, and in alignment with prior findings, Openness to Experience should be related to a strong PPID on the left, while Conscientiousness should be related to a strong PPID on the right.

To assess these possibilities, I first examine the strength of PPID on the right in combination with low levels of NPID toward the left. In the US sample, this involves respondents who identify with the Republican Party but display low levels of NPID toward the Democratic Party. In the Swedish sample, this includes respondents who feel closer to the Moderate Party, the Sweden Democrats, or the Christian Democrats with weak NPID toward the left. Starting with the United States (see Table 7.4, column 1), strong positive Republican partisanship is positively related to multiple personality traits, including SDO, Agreeableness, and Extraversion. The significant effects for SDO and Agreeableness remain even when using Bonferroni-adjusted p-values. These results indicate that strong Republican identifiers seek power and high status for their in-party. At the same time, they also tend to be less concerned with whether they are being perceived as pleasant and amicable by others. In contrast, positive partisans on the right in Sweden (see Table 7.5, column 1) feature lower levels of Agreeableness while also, similarly to Republicans in the United States, scoring more highly on Extraversion. Sweden's political culture is much more progressive than the United States, which might explain why Agreeableness is negatively related to strong party attachments on the right in Sweden. Indeed, we would expect agreeable partisans to align with the more dominant ideological beliefs of their country. For PPID on the left, I examine Democrats in the United States. In Sweden, I include respondents who feel closer to the Left Party, the Green Party, the Feminist Initiative, or the Social Democrats. In both cases (see Tables 7.4 and 7.5, column 2), strong PPID on the left is not related to any personality traits. Only religiosity is a positive determinant in both countries, which is a noteworthy similarity.

Last, I replicate the same analyses for negative partisans who disdain certain political parties on the left or the right while being only weakly attached to a political party. In the US sample, this approach includes respondents with NPID toward either the Democratic (ideological left) or the Republican Party (ideological right). In Sweden, as exemplars of NPID toward the left, I include respondents who would never vote for the Left Party, the Green Party, the Feminist Initiative, or the Social Democrats. For NPID toward the right, I examine respondents who report never voting for the Moderate Party, the Sweden Democrats, or the Christian Democrats.

In the United States (see Table 7.4, column 3), NPID toward the Republican Party is positively related to NfC and Emotional Stability but negatively related to Authoritarianism. The latter finding suggests that

TABLE 7.4 Personality predictors of PPID and NPID among Democrats and Republicans, US sample

	(1)	(2)	(3)	(4)
	PPID Republicans	PPID Democrats	NPID Republicans	NPID Democrats
Need for Closure	−0.01	−0.07	0.20**	0.26***
	(0.08)	(0.08)	(0.08)	(0.08)
SDO	0.31***	0.11	−0.05	0.15**
	(0.06)	(0.07)	(0.07)	(0.06)
Authoritarianism	0.01	0.03	−0.09**	−0.00
	(0.03)	(0.03)	(0.04)	(0.03)
Conscientiousness	0.08	0.08	0.00	−0.16**
	(0.07)	(0.07)	(0.07)	(0.06)
Agreeableness	0.20***	−0.01	−0.09	−0.03
	(0.07)	(0.07)	(0.07)	(0.07)
Emotional Stability	−0.08	0.02	0.10**	−0.00
	(0.06)	(0.06)	(0.06)	(0.06)
Openness	0.10	0.12	−0.00	0.12**
	(0.06)	(0.07)	(0.07)	(0.06)
Extraversion	0.10**	0.05	−0.01	−0.01
	(0.04)	(0.05)	(0.05)	(0.04)
Ideology	0.04	−0.10	−0.35***	0.33***
	(0.06)	(0.06)	(0.07)	(0.07)
Age	−0.00	0.00	−0.00	0.00
	(0.00)	(0.00)	(0.00)	(0.00)
Female	0.00	−0.01	0.01	−0.04**
	(0.02)	(0.02)	(0.02)	(0.02)
White	0.02	−0.02	−0.00	0.02
	(0.03)	(0.02)	(0.02)	(0.03)
Religiosity	0.09***	0.14***	0.00	−0.02
	(0.03)	(0.04)	(0.04)	(0.03)
Education	0.00	−0.04	0.05	0.02
	(0.04)	(0.04)	(0.04)	(0.04)
Constant	−0.13	0.12	0.37***	−0.05
	(0.10)	(0.09)	(0.09)	(0.10)
Observations	238	213	220	244
R-squared	0.188	0.168	0.246	0.203

Note: Entries are coefficients from an OLS regression. All variables range from 0 to 1 for better comparability. Standard errors in parentheses, *** $p < 0.01$, ** $p < 0.05$, * $p < 0.1$.

partisans who value individualism and autonomy are more likely to develop a strong opposition to the Republican Party. In contrast, NPID toward the right in Sweden (see Table 7.5, column 3) is associated with lower levels of Emotional Stability. Thus, the impact of Emotional Stability is radically different across the United States and Sweden. NPID toward the left – that

TABLE 7.5 Personality predictors of PPID and NPID among partisans on the Left and the Right, Sweden sample

	(1) PPID Right	(2) PPID Left	(3) NPID Right	(4) NPID Left
Need for Closure	−0.21	0.02	0.24	−0.01
	(0.15)	(0.15)	(0.20)	(0.16)
SDO	−0.03	−0.03	−0.12	0.36***
	(0.12)	(0.12)	(0.13)	(0.12)
Authoritarianism	0.07	0.09	−0.17	−0.00
	(0.08)	(0.10)	(0.11)	(0.10)
Conscientiousness	0.01	0.02	0.06	0.05
	(0.13)	(0.12)	(0.14)	(0.14)
Agreeableness	−0.30**	0.07	0.10	−0.11
	(0.16)	(0.16)	(0.18)	(0.14)
Emotional Stability	0.02	−0.10	−0.23**	0.21
	(0.13)	(0.12)	(0.14)	(0.13)
Openness	−0.07	0.11	0.23	−0.13
	(0.14)	(0.15)	(0.18)	(0.14)
Extraversion	0.21**	0.01	0.12	0.08
	(0.10)	(0.10)	(0.10)	(0.10)
Ideology	0.07	−0.16	−0.23**	0.02
	(0.12)	(0.10)	(0.12)	(0.12)
Age	−0.01	0.00	0.00	0.00
	(0.01)	(0.01)	(0.02)	(0.02)
Female	0.00	−0.05	0.02	−0.01
	(0.05)	(0.05)	(0.05)	(0.06)
European	−0.10	−0.26	(-)	(-)
	(0.16)	(0.16)		
Religiosity	0.21**	0.20**	−0.03	0.10
	(0.10)	(0.08)	(0.11)	(0.11)
Education	0.04	0.01	0.10	0.04
	(0.10)	(0.10)	(0.12)	(0.11)
Constant	0.63**	0.57**	0.33	0.25
	(0.25)	(0.23)	(0.25)	(0.20)
Observations	88	81	110	123
R-squared	0.20	0.16	0.19	0.14

Note: Entries are coefficients from an OLS regression. All variables range from 0 to 1 for better comparability. Standard errors in parentheses, *** $p < 0.01$, ** $p < 0.05$, * $p < 0.1$.

is, the Democratic Party (see Table 7.4, column 4) – is positively related to NfC, SDO, and Openness to Experience and negatively related to Conscientiousness. The effects are particularly powerful across the range of NfC, whereby strong NPID toward Democrats intensifies from 0.13 to 0.40. Thus, Republicans with strong negative partisanship toward the Democrats tend to accept and reinforce clear intergroup hierarchies and prefer a more rigid categorization of the world into "us" versus "them." The impact of NfC and Conscientiousness is robust to Bonferroni adjustments. In Sweden (see Table 7.5, column 4), NPID toward the left is characterized by high levels of SDO (like in the United States) which is associated with an increase in NPID toward the left from 0.34 to 0.70. This effect also remains valid when Bonferroni-adjusted p-values are used.

Overall, these analyses reveal a few interesting patterns: NfC is positively related to NPID in the United States but not in Sweden. Authoritarianism is negatively related to NPID toward the right in the United States but not in Sweden. Among negative partisans toward a left-wing party, SDO emerges as a common predictor in both the United States and in Sweden; consistent with expectations, a preference for inter-group hierarchies is associated with higher levels of NPID toward the left. Extraversion was positively related to strong PPID on the right in both the United States and Sweden, while Agreeableness was a negative determinant of right-wing PPID in Sweden but a positive one in the United States. This disparity might be reflective of the different political cultures in these two countries, whereby conservatism is a much more dominant *leitkultur* in the United States than in Sweden. Last, in both countries, PPID on the left was associated with religiosity but not with any of the included personality traits. The lack of consistent findings for positive partisanship on the left for both American and Swedish partisans might be related to the different compositions of left- and right-wing parties in general. Right-wing parties tend to attract a demographically more homogenous bloc of supporters, while left-wing parties rely much more heavily on a diverse coalition of voters. This is especially true for the Democratic Party in the United States, which is oftentimes described as a "big tent."

Critics might be concerned about the covariance between the personality traits. Indeed, among US partisans, most of the included traits correlate at a statistically significant level, with the exception of Extraversion and Authoritarianism as well as Extraversion and Agreeableness. Among Swedish partisans, there are three pairs of traits that do not correlate at a significant level, including SDO and Need for Closure, Conscientiousness and Authoritarianism, as well as Extraversion and Authoritarianism. Yet most of these correlations are relatively low or modest at best, ranging from 0.1 to 0.3 (see Tables A9 and A10 in the Appendix). Furthermore, most of the results presented in this chapter remain significant when Need for Closure, SDO, Authoritarianism, and the Big Five are included individually in separate analyses.

7.8 IMPLICATIONS FOR POLITICAL BEHAVIOR AND FUTURE RESEARCH

The partisan typology also has implications for political behavior. Positive partisans are significantly more likely to vote than negative partisans, while closed partisans are significantly more likely to vote than apathetic partisans. At the same time, closed partisans are also significantly more likely to agree that "violence might sometimes be necessary to fight against parties and candidates that are bad for this country" and to believe that their "party's opponents are not just worse for politics – they are downright evil." From this perspective, it is especially vital to recognize these distinct types of partisans and to understand their different psychological origins.

The partisan typology can also be useful to study polarization. Closed partisans are most likely to be polarized since they score highly both on their positive attachment to the in-party as well as negative partisanship toward the out-party. Thus, what we define as polarization – the increasing distance between in-party and out-party evaluations – might be strongly driven by closed partisans. At the same time, we can also think of polarization as asymmetrical, in the sense that in-party evaluations remain modestly positive while out-party evaluations are increasingly negative. This type of polarization might be more strongly related to negative partisans who display low levels of positive partisanship but high levels of negative partisanship. These nuances are important to consider when developing an antidote to polarization.

We can also examine the share of partisan types across the ideological spectrum. For example, among liberals in the United States, 8% are positive partisans, 16% are negative partisans, 45% are closed partisans, and 31% are apathetic partisans. In contrast, among conservative partisans, 12% are positive partisans, 11% are negative partisans, 40% are closed partisans, and 38% are apathetic partisans. These numbers slightly vary among the Swedish left where 22% are positive partisans, 22% are negative partisans, 32% are closed partisans, and 25% are apathetic partisans. Among Swedish partisans on the right, there is a much lower share of positive partisans – only 10% – 15% negative partisans, a whopping 53% of closed partisans, and 22% apathetic partisans. Since certain political behaviors are more strongly related to specific partisan types it is important to acknowledge their uneven distribution across the left and the right side of the ideological spectrum.

Finally, this chapter also sheds light on the scope of each partisan type in the electorate; only about 40% of partisans in both samples constitute closed partisans, while less than 20% comprise negative partisans. That still leaves about 40% of all partisans who are either apathetic or purely positive. This should spur more research into how we can expand the share of positive partisans by, for example, turning apathetic partisans into positive ones.

7.9 SUMMARY

Not all partisans are equally likely to develop strong positive or negative partisanship, and not all partisans are equally likely to develop both. In the United States and in Sweden, closed partisans – who display high levels of both PPID and NPID – tend to score more highly on Social Dominance Orientation, suggesting that this partisan type is more concerned with the in-party's status and therefore inclined to impose and endorse inter-party hierarchies that can bolster the in-party's status. Interestingly, apathetic partisans with neither high levels of PPID nor NPID exhibit the opposite: In both the United States and Sweden, they tend to have *lower* SDO values and higher levels of Conscientiousness. Need for Closure (NfC) also emerges as a significant predictor, but its effects varied across the two countries. While NfC was negatively related to the chance of being an apathetic partisan in the United States, it was positively related to being an apathetic partisan in Sweden. The only trait that emerged among both positive and negative partisans in both the United States and Sweden is religiosity. Religious partisans are much more likely to be positive partisans while negative partisans tend to be less religious.

Examining PPID and NPID on the left and right sides of the ideological spectrum in the United States and Sweden revealed a few similarities such as the role of SDO in shaping NPID toward left-wing parties and the impact of Extraversion on PPID among right-wing party supporters. Emotional Stability increases the chance of strong negative partisanship toward the left in the United States, while it exerts the exact opposite effect in Sweden. There were also many noteworthy differences such as the positive relationship between NPID and Need for Closure in the United States and the negative relationship between Authoritarianism and NPID toward the Republicans (i.e., a right-wing party); neither one of these relationships held among Swedish partisans.

8

The Impact of Partisan Identities on Democratic Behavior in the United States and Europe

8.1 WHAT IS IN THIS CHAPTER?

This chapter demonstrates the political consequences of strong positive and negative partisan identity, including their effect on turnout, vote choice, and various other forms of political participation, among partisans in the United States, the United Kingdom, Sweden, the Netherlands, and Italy. With such a comprehensive cross-country assessment, this chapter builds on but also extends prior scholarship in two ways. First, the wide selection of countries with vastly different electoral systems and political cultures allows for a more generalizable assessment of the impact of positive and negative partisan identity. Second, the inclusion of the full PPID and NPID scales in all five samples allows for a clean test of the differential effects of positive and negative partisan identities, unaffected by measurement discrepancies. Last, this chapter also provides a brief excursion into the role of NPID in shaping the political behavior of self-declared independents – a crucial addition that empirically supports the argument that negative partisanship can exist independently of positive partisanship. I conclude the chapter with a normative assessment of partisanship's role in promoting democratic citizenship.

8.2 WHY DOES THIS MATTER?

Strong partisan identities are often portrayed in a negative light. Yet they do more than just provoke partisan animosity: They provide citizens with a team to root for (or one to root against), which, over time, fosters a habit of political interest and engagement. From this perspective, partisan identities *promote* citizens' political involvement; they motivate them to care about politics, to turn out, and to become active on behalf of their in-party (i.e., PPID) or in opposition to one (i.e., NPID). In other words, partisanship keeps partisans anchored in the political world. Thus, despite their contemporary vilification, strong partisan ties can also foster the kind of democratic citizenship that healthy democracies are built and thrive on. This change in perspective matters for our normative assessment of partisanship.

***

In Chapter 3, I reviewed the extensive prior scholarship on partisanship and its effects on key political behaviors, such as vote choice, turnout, and other forms of more active and effortful political engagement (e.g., volunteering for a campaign). Yet a large share of that existing research either examines the effect of partisanship in a single country or utilizes different measures of partisanship across countries, which makes a clean assessment of partisanship's effects more difficult. Moreover, there is little comparative work on negative partisanship that employs an identity-based measure such as the NPID scale and that is comparable to the PPID scale – a measure that is used increasingly in studies of European political behavior and beyond (Bankert et al. 2017). Currently, Common measures for NPID include feeling thermometer ratings to gauge negative affect toward the out-party (Abramowitz and Webster 2015; Iyengar, Sood, and Lelkes 2012; Lelkes and Westwood 2017; Mason 2015; Rogowski and Sutherland 2016) as well as a survey item that asks respondents which party they would never vote for (Caruana et al. 2015; Medeiros and Noel 2014). As discussed in Chapters 5 and 6, these measurement differences challenge researchers' ability to disentangle and compare the effects of positive and negative partisanship.

Given these challenges, the following analyses offer multiple advantages: First, they provide a comparative perspective on the effects of positive and negative partisanship across a range of different electoral systems. Second, they compare the effects of positive and negative partisan *identities* on core forms of democratic engagement such as turnout and vote choice. Third, they demonstrate the predictive validity of the NPID scale in European multi-party systems. Last, they compare the effects of expressive and instrumental partisanship by including both the partisan identity scales and instrumental measures of partisanship such as partisans' ideology and the intensity of their political attitudes.

In the remainder of this chapter, I will describe a few new aspects of each country's sample to re-familiarize the reader with the data. I will then examine the impact of PPID and NPID on key political outcomes across all countries. To preview the results: Positive and negative partisanship exert different influences on political behavior, whereby the former is a strong promoter of democratic practices like voting. I conclude the chapter with a brief analysis of negative partisanship among independent voters. The results further bolster the notion that negative and positive partisanship are distinct concepts with divergent influences.

8.3 DATA

In the following analyses, I examine the partisans in the US two-party system as well as in four European multi-party systems, including Sweden, the Netherlands, the United Kingdom, and Italy. Each sample reflects the national population on key characteristics such as gender, religiosity, and education (see Tables A1–A5 in the Appendix). In Chapter 5 and 6, I demonstrated the distribution of positive and negative partisanship in each country. In the following sections, I provide more details on the variability of PPID and NPID in each country, as well as their relationship to other political key variables. For better comparability, all variables are scaled to range from 0 (minimum value) to 1 (maximum value).

8.3.1 United States

For the analysis of partisanship in the United States, I utilize a sample of 1,130 respondents, 882 of them completed the PPID scale, while 876 of them completed the NPID scale. In the survey, respondents were given the PPID scale if they identified with either the Democratic or the Republican Party. The NPID scale was distributed based on that positive identification so that, for example, a respondent who identified as a Democrat received the PPID for the Democratic Party and the NPID scale that targets the Republican Party. Respondents who indicated no positive party identification (i.e. pure independents with no partisan leaning) were asked whether there was a political party they would never vote for. If that party was either the Democratic or the Republican Party, these independent voters were considered "negative partisans" and thus given the NPID scale based on the party they would never vote for. Negative partisanship toward the Republican Party is slightly higher than negative partisanship toward the Democratic Party (0.44 versus 0.40 respectively). At the same time, Republicans' and Democrats' positive party attachments are similar at an average strength of 0.41. As Figure 8.1 shows, PPID and NPID are distributed very similarly in the United States. Both have identical values for the minimum (0), the maximum (1), and for the first quartile (0.21), but NPID's third quartile (0.62) is slightly higher than PPID's (0.58). Similarly, the median for NPID is slightly higher than for PPID (0.42 versus 0.38) but the means are identical (0.42). Given this similar distribution, it is not surprising that PPID and NPID in the United States correlate at 0.65.

8.3.2 Netherlands

For the analysis of partisanship in the Netherlands, I utilize a sample of 1,011 respondents, 976 of them completed the PPID scale, while 971 completed the NPID scale. The PPID scale was administered to respondents who identified

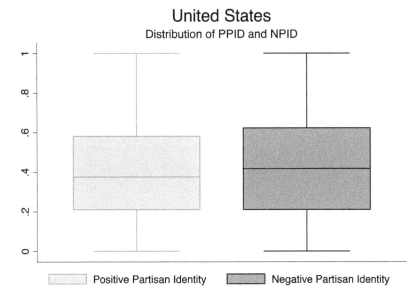

FIGURE 8.1 Distribution of PPID and NPID in the United States

themselves as supporters of a particular party or indicated that they felt closer to a party. The selected party was the target of the PPID scale. Most commonly, Dutch respondents supported the VVD (Liberal Party; 24% of the sample), the PVV (Wilders Freedom Party, 18% of the sample), or the SP (Socialist Party; 9% of the sample). PPID was strongest among supporters of the Christian Democratic Party (CDA) with an average value of 0.59.

The NPID scale was administered based on the question of whether there is a political party that the respondent would never vote for. If so, this party was the target of the NPID scale. If there were multiple political parties that respondents would never vote for – as is possible in multi-party systems – then respondents were asked to rate these parties on a feeling thermometer scale from 0 to 100. In this scenario, the party with the lowest rating was selected as the target for the NPID scale. Dutch respondents most frequently reported they would never vote for the PVV (Wilders Freedom Party, 42%), the SGP (Reformed Political Party, 37%), the DENK (THINK Party, 48%), and FVD (Forum For Democracy, 45%). NPID values for most political parties range between 0.55 and 0.61, with the Christian Democratic Party (CDA) invoking the strongest negative partisanship. As Figure 8.2 shows, negative partisanship is somewhat more common among Dutch partisans than positive partisanship: While both scales' dispersion is similar, their quartile values are quite different. The PPID's scale first quartile value is 0.17, the median is 0.37, the third quartile is located at 0.58. For the NPID scale, these values are 0.33, 0.56, and 0.75 respectively, suggesting higher levels of NPID than PPID among Dutch respondents. Indeed, the mean of NPID is

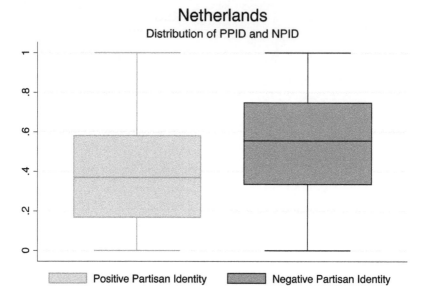

FIGURE 8.2 Distribution of PPID and NPID in the Netherlands

significantly higher than the mean of PPID (0.52 vs. 0.38, p < 0.001). These different distributions are also reflected in the low correlation between PPID and NPID: At 0.43, the two types of partisanship are related to each other at a much lower level than in the United States. Notably, The median for NPID, when paired with low levels of PPID, is almost twice as high as the median for PPID, when paired with low levels of NPID (0.42 versus 0.23 respectively). This is an interesting finding and a meaningful departure from the US two-party system.

8.3.3 Sweden

For the analysis of partisanship and political behavior in Sweden, I utilize a sample of 1,065 Swedish respondents, 968 of them completed the PPID scale, while 975 completed the NPID scale. Respondents received the PPID scale if there was a party that they considered "best" or if they indicated feeling closer to a particular party. Most commonly, that applied to the Social Democrats (28%), the Sweden Democrats (29%), and the Moderate Party (13%). PPID is strongest among supporters of the Sweden Democrats (0.50) and the Moderate Party (0.52). The NPID scale was distributed in the same way as in the Dutch survey, namely by relying on a combination of the "never vote" question as well as the feeling thermometer values. Among Swedish respondents, the Left Party (N = 265), the Green Party (N = 298), the Sweden Democrats (N = 447), and the Feminist Initiative (N = 334) are most common

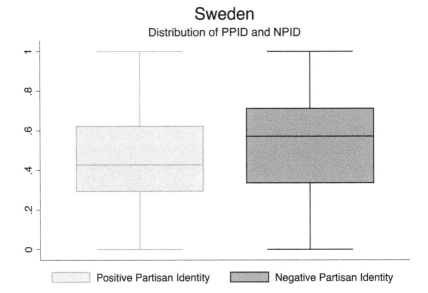

FIGURE 8.3 Distribution of PPID and NPID in Sweden

targets of negative partisanship and yet, negative partisanship is strongest toward the Liberal People's Party with an average NPID value of 0.64. NPID values for most parties range quite highly between 0.55 and 0.64. As illustrated in Figure 8.3, PPID and NPID's distributions look somewhat similar, but there are substantial differences: The first quartile of the PPID scale is located at 0.29, the median at 0.43, and the third quartile at 0.62, while these values are slightly higher for the NPID scale, namely 0.33, 0.57, and 0.71 respectively. Indeed, the mean value of NPID is significantly higher than the mean for PPID (0.54 versus 0.44, $p < 0.001$), suggesting that NPID is stronger among Swedes than PPID, similar to the Netherlands. With a correlation of 0.36, the relationship between PPID and NPID in Sweden is weaker than in the Netherlands or in the United States and shrinks even further to 0.11 when examining partisans with high values of PPID and NPID but low values of NPID and PPID respectively, whereby NPID with low levels of PPID is much more common than PPID with low levels of NPID (mean differences of 0.48 versus 0.36, $p < 0.001$). These simple summary statistics suggest that PPID and NPID are even more unrelated to each other than in the Netherlands and the United States.

8.3.4 Italy

For the analysis of partisanship in Italy, I utilize a sample of 1,170 Italian respondents, 936 of them completed the PPID scale and 1,024 completed the

NPID scale. Respondents received the PPID scale if they indicated their support for a particular party. Most commonly, respondents identified Partito Democratico (17%), Movimento 5 Stelle (21%), Lega (13%), and Fratelli d'Italia (13%) as the party they support. PPID is generally strong across all partisan groups but positive partisan identity strength stands out for partisans of Movimento 5 Stelle (0.47), Lega (0.47), and Fratelli d'Italia (0.47). For the distribution of the NPID scale, Lega (N = 448), Movimento 5 Stelle (N = 222), and Partito Democratico (N = 243) were selected most frequently as political parties that respondents would never vote for. NPID among Italian partisans ranges between 0.54 and 0.66, whereby negative partisanship is strongest toward Fratelli d'Italia. As Figure 8.4 shows, the distributions for PPID and NPID in Italy are quite different from each other. Starting with PPID, its first quartile is located at 0.29, the median at 0.46, and the third quartile at 0.62. In contrast, NPID's first quartile value is 0.38, its median is 0.58, and its third quartile is located at 0.79, which already hints at stronger levels of negative partisanship in Italy – a notion that is further supported by NPID's significantly higher mean value compared to PPID (0.57 versus 0.46, $p < 0.001$), similar to the Netherlands and Sweden. Like the Netherlands, PPID and NPID correlate only weakly at 0.34. This relationship only slightly decreases to 0.28 when examining PPID and NPID in combination with low values of NPID and PPID respectively. Notably, among these singular partisans, NPID with low levels of PPID is significantly stronger than PPID with low levels of NPID, with mean values of 0.51 versus 0.38 respectively ($p < 0.001$). Overall, these analyses of Italian partisans align with the results from their multi-party system peers: First,

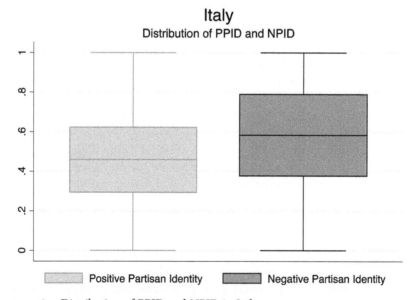

FIGURE 8.4 Distribution of PPID and NPID in Italy

negative and positive partisanship are only weakly to moderately related to each other; second, negative partisanship is stronger than its positive counterpart.

8.3.5 United Kingdom

For the analysis of partisanship in the United Kingdom, I utilize a sample of 1,088 British respondents, 741 of them completed the PPID scale and 947 completed the NPID scale. The PPID scale was administered to those respondents who indicated thinking of themselves as a little closer to a political party. A clear majority (80%) identified this party to be either the Conservatives (41%) or Labour (39%). PPID was strongest among Labour supporters (0.48) and supporters of the Green Party (0.52). PPID was similarly strong among supporters of the United Kingdom Independence Party (UKIP) but the number of UKIP partisans was a bit too low in the sample for reliable inferences (N = 26). At the same time, the Conservatives (N = 325) and Labour (N = 317) were also among the political parties that respondents would never vote for, as was the British National Party (N = 355) and the United Kingdom Independence Party (N = 261). NPID toward most parties ranges between 0.48 and 0.56 but it is highest toward the British National Party and the United Kingdom Independence Party.

Figure 8.5 reveals that the distributions of PPID and NPID look similar, with a few notable exceptions: The median and the third quartile for PPID are located at 0.46 and 0.67 respectively while, for NPID, these values are somewhat higher, with a median at 0.54 and a third quartile at 0.75. Not surprisingly, NPID's mean value is also significantly higher than PPID's mean value (0.51 versus 0.45 respectively, $p < 0.001$), which adds to the consistent evidence that negative partisanship tends to be stronger in multi-party systems than positive partisanship. Yet with a correlation of 0.45, the relationship between PPID and NPID is substantially stronger in the United Kingdom than in Sweden and Italy. When examining PPID and NPID in combination with low values of NPID and PPID respectively, this correlation is somewhat reduced to 0.37 – a pattern that resembles Dutch partisans. Consistent with evidence from the three other multi-party systems, NPID with low levels of PPID is significantly stronger than PPID with low levels of NPID (0.43 versus 0.36; $p < 0.001$).

8.4 PARTISANSHIP AND TURNOUT

Voting in elections is at the core of democratic citizenship. Yet many citizens abstain from elections. Indeed, voter turnout in Europe has decreased significantly since the 1990s and, in past elections, the United States even trailed most developed countries in voter turnout (Desilver 2020). While there is a myriad of reasons for why people turn out (or decide not to), one factor that

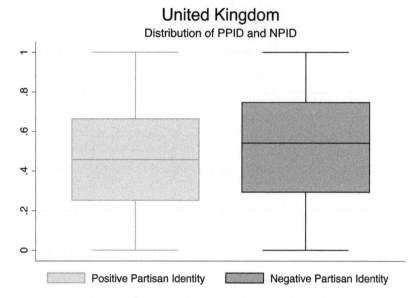

FIGURE 8.5 Distribution of PPID and NPID in the United Kingdom

promotes citizens' turnout is partisanship, especially strong partisanship (Bankert 2021; Campbell et al. 1960; Smets and van Ham 2013).

This notion aligns with the expressive model's expectation that partisans are driven by the desire to see their team succeed, especially the ones who are most strongly attached to their party. From this perspective, I expect that strong partisans across all five countries are more likely to turn out than weak partisans.

Questions remain, however, regarding the role of negative partisanship, especially in the absence of positive partisanship. Can strong opposition to a political party motivate citizens to turn out? My own work on independent voters in the United States suggests that this is indeed the case: Negative partisanship motivated unaffiliated voters to turn out in the 2020 presidential elections (Bankert 2022). Similarly, Caruana and colleagues (2015) find a unique and positive influence of negative partisanship on turnout among Canadians. Mayer (2017) finds very similar results for both partisans and non-partisans across multiple European party systems. Yet it is unclear if these patterns persist when both types of partisanship are measured uniformly as an identity. The following analyses address this question.

For this purpose, I regress the likelihood of turning out (an ordinal variable that ranges from "very unlikely" (coded as 0) to "very likely" (coded as 1)) on to the key independent variables, NPID and PPID, as well as a host of demographic control variables, including ideology (ranging from 0 "far left" to 1 "far right"), age (measured in decades), education (coded to range from 0 "no completed primary school" to 1 "postgraduate degree"), income (coded to range from 0 "low income" to 1 "high income"), union membership (0 indicating "no member" and 1 "member," measured in Europe only), frequency of attending religious services (coded to range from 0 "never" to 1 "more than once week"), place of residence (coded to range from 0 "countryside" to 1 "large town or city"), and gender (0 indicating male and 1 indicating female respondents). In the United States, the analyses include a variable that captures respondents' race (coded 0 for respondents of Color and 1 for White respondents), while, in the analysis of the European data, I utilize a variable that gauges whether respondents have spent most of their life in Europe or whether they recently immigrated (coded as 0 "Europe" and 1 "outside of Europe"). I also include a variable that measures the intensity of respondents' attitudes on a range of prominent policies (see Chapters 5 and 6 for details on each country's policy items).

8.5 ANALYSES

In the United States (column 1 in Table 8.1), positive partisanship strongly promotes turnout. Indeed, the predicted levels of turnout significantly increase from 0.74 to 0.97 as positive partisan identity strength increases from its weakest to its strongest values. No other variable in the model is as strongly related to turnout as positive partisan identity. Yet issue intensity also exerts a noticeable, albeit much more muted, effect that raises the chance of turning out from 0.81 among partisan with the weakest political attitudes to 0.87 among partisans with the strongest ones. Equally noteworthy are the positive effects of age, education, and income: Older, more educated, and wealthier partisans are more likely to turn out.

Moving on to the United Kingdom (see column 2 in Table 8.1), neither positive nor negative partisan identity appear to impact turnout; while both coefficients are positive, they remain statistically insignificant. However, other variables emerge as positive influences such as the intensity of partisans' political attitudes. Indeed, the likelihood of turning out on election day increases substantially from 0.87 to 0.98 as partisans' attitudes become stronger. This finding suggests that instrumental facets of partisanship might be more powerful in motivating British partisans to turn out. Older and wealthier partisans also report a higher chance of turning out while more religious and female ones tend to report lower chances of participating in the election.

In Italy (column 3 in Table 8.1), a somewhat different pattern emerges: Negative, rather than positive, partisan identity significantly increases the chance of turnout. As NPID rises from 0 to 1, so does the chance of voting from 0.83 to 0.90. This is a departure from the United States, where only positive partisan identity significantly predicts turnout, and from the United Kingdom, where neither PPID nor NPID impact turnout. Yet, in Italy, as in the United Kingdom, the intensity of partisans' political attitudes fosters

TABLE 8.1 *PPID, NPID, and turnout*

	(1) United States	(2) United Kingdom	(3) Italy	(4) Sweden	(5) Netherlands
Positive partisanship	0.25***	0.01	0.01	0.02	0.09**
	(0.04)	(0.02)	(0.03)	(0.03)	(0.03)
Negative partisanship	−0.06	0.02	0.06**	0.01	0.11***
	(0.04)	(0.02)	(0.03)	(0.03)	(0.03)
Ideology	0.01	0.04**	0.02	0.03	0.02
	(0.03)	(0.02)	(0.02)	(0.02)	(0.03)
Issue intensity	0.05***	0.15***	0.10***	0.09**	0.10***
	(0.01)	(0.02)	(0.03)	(0.03)	(0.03)
Religiosity	0.00	−0.06***	−0.06**	−0.15***	−0.07**
	(0.02)	(0.02)	(0.02)	(0.02)	(0.03)
Age	0.03***	0.02***	0.01***	0.02***	0.02***
	(0.00)	(0.00)	(0.00)	(0.00)	(0.00)
Education	0.11***	0.00	0.05**	0.07**	0.13***
	(0.03)	(0.00)	(0.03)	(0.03)	(0.03)
Income	0.13***	0.05**	−0.04	0.03	0.01
	(0.04)	(0.02)	(0.03)	(0.03)	(0.04)
White/European	0.02	0.01	0.14**	0.04	0.12***
	(0.01)	(0.01)	(0.07)	(0.05)	(0.03)
Union	(–)	−0.00	−0.02	0.04***	0.03**
		(0.01)	(0.01)	(0.01)	(0.01)
Urban	−0.01	0.01	0.05**	0.04**	−0.04**
	(0.02)	(0.02)	(0.02)	(0.02)	(0.02)
Female	−0.01	0.02**	−0.01	0.0256	−0.01
	(0.01)	(0.01)	(0.01)	(0.0156)	(0.01)
Constant	0.44***	0.65***	0.57***	0.632***	0.47***
	(0.04)	(0.03)	(0.08)	(0.0698)	(0.05)
Observations	843	701	757	774	810
R-squared	0.166	0.168	0.064	0.134	0.139

Note: Results are obtained from an OLS regression on the entire sample of partisans. All variables are scaled to range from 0 to 1, except for age, which is measured in decades. Standard errors in parentheses
*** $p < 0.01$, ** $p < 0.05$, * $p < 0.1$

higher turnout, at a notably higher rate than NPID. The likelihood of turning out on election day grows from 0.83 to 0.95 among partisans who feel strongly about several salient policies. This result reiterates the role of instrumental partisanship in driving turnout. Other notable factors include age, education, religiosity, having lived in Europe for most of one's life, and living in more urban areas. Among these variables, only religiosity reduces, rather than increases, the chance of turnout.

The analysis of Swedish partisans (column 4 in Table 8.1) yields results that strongly resemble their British peers: Neither PPID nor NPID promote Swedes' turnout as both their coefficients remain statistically insignificant. While the strength of positive and negative partisanship might not have any significant effect on turnout, having either type of partisanship does. Having any level of positive or negative partisanship increases the predicted levels of turning out among Dutch voters from 0.51 to 0.86. Thus, having any type of partisanship – positive or negative – is more important for turnout than its strength. Other variables are influential as well, such as age, religiosity, union membership, education, residing in a more urban area, and the strength of partisans' issue preferences. Indeed, as political attitudes intensify, the chance of turning out increase from 0.84 to 0.94 – a substantial growth that was also detectable among partisans in the United States, the United Kingdom, and Italy.

In the Netherlands (column 5 in Table 8.1), the decision to turnout is related to both positive and negative partisanship with effects that are quite similar in magnitude. The predicted level of turning out increases from 0.83 to 0.93 as PPID increases from 0 to 1 (while holding NPID constant at its mean). Similarly, as NPID gets stronger, the chance of voting increases from 0.81 to 0.93. Thus, both positive and negative partisanship are equal partners in driving turnout among Dutch partisans. The effect of instrumental partisanship can compete with these effects: Turnout likelihood increases from 0.83 to 0.94 across the spectrum of political attitude strength. There is also a host of other variables that foster voting such as age, education, religiosity, having spent most of one's life in Europe, and being a union member as well as living in more urban environments.

While the coefficient for PPID is much more substantial in the United States than in the Netherlands, strong positive partisan identity increases the chance of turning out in both countries. From a normative standpoint, this is good news since it suggests that citizens are motivated to partake in a core activity of democratic citizenship to support their political party. In contrast, negative partisan identity on its own boosts turnout rates among citizens only in Italy, which suggests that the strong disdain for a particular party propels Italians to show up on election day. This is an interesting departure from the United States and from the Netherlands. Last, in the United Kingdom and in Sweden, neither PPID nor NPID promote people's turnout as their coefficients remain statistically insignificant. Instead, other variables appear to be more influential such as the strength of citizens' political issue preferences and age, whereby older people are more likely to turn out – an established finding in the literature on electoral behavior. Indeed, the intensity of citizens' political positions and age are significant predictors of turnout among partisans in all five countries. Interestingly, the frequency of attending religious services is negatively related to turnout in all four European multi-party systems while there is no effect in the United States. Other variables that boost turnout in some countries but not in others are the level of educational attainment (no effect in the United Kingdom), income (positive effect in the United States and the United Kingdom), union membership (positive effect in Sweden and the Netherlands), and being European whereby respondents who have been living in Europe most of their lives are more likely to turnout in Italy and the Netherlands.

8.6 PARTISANSHIP AND VOTE CHOICE

Partisanship is highly predictive of people's vote choices (see Chapter 3). This close association is exacerbated in the US two-party system where a vote for the in-party is not just an expression of party loyalties but also of voters' ideological convictions. But does this connection also emerge in multi-party systems? Indeed, there are reasons to believe that party affiliations are only weakly related to vote choice in these systems. First, voters can switch between political parties of the same or similar ideology, which allows a vote for a different party without crossing over to a different ideological camp. This flexibility might weaken party ties. Moreover, multi-party systems often generate coalitional governments aligned along ideological lines that can also blur loyalty to a single party (Gonzalez et al. 2008; Hagevi 2015; Meffert et al. 2009). While we thus might expect partisanship to be a weaker predictor of vote choice in multi-party systems, recent scholarship has provided evidence to the contrary: Bankert, Huddy, and Rosema (2017) show that levels of in-party voting – that is voting for the party voters identify with – is quite high across several European countries, with 88% in Sweden, 76% in the United Kingdom, and 61% in the Netherlands and that, even in these multi-party systems, partisan identity has a strong impact on vote choice.

Yet questions remain regarding the role of negative partisanship in shaping vote choice, both on its own as well as in combination with positive partisanship. Some prior work shows that positive partisanship is a stronger predictor of voting for the in-party than negative partisanship, when measured with the "never vote" item, both in the US two-party system as well as in Anglo-American multi-party systems such as Canada, New Zealand, and Australia (see Caruana et al. 2015; Medeiros and Noel 2014). In my own work, I found similar patterns for vote choice in the United States: While both positive and negative partisan identity were significant predictors of voting for the in-party candidate in the 2016 US presidential elections, positive partisanship exerted a significantly stronger impact than its negative counterpart. Given these prior findings, I expect that positive partisanship is a more powerful predictor of vote choice than negative partisanship in both the US two-party system and in the select four European multi-party systems.

8.7 ANALYSES

Starting with the United States (see column 1 in Table 8.2) – where 72% of respondents voted for the in-party – I find that both negative and positive

TABLE 8.2 PPID, NPID, and in-party vote

	(1)	(2)	(3)	(4)	(5)
	United States	United Kingdom	Italy	Sweden	Netherlands
Positive partisanship	4.22***	1.82***	1.03**	1.56***	1.14
	(0.56)	(0.52)	(0.44)	(0.51)	(0.69)
Negative partisanship	2.01***	0.19	−0.33	−0.48	0.38
	(0.50)	(0.42)	(0.37)	(0.42)	(0.55)
Ideology	0.84**	−0.04	−0.73**	0.25	0.14
	(0.37)	(0.46)	(0.34)	(0.35)	(0.57)
Issue intensity	−0.00	1.09**	1.11***	0.08	0.80
	(0.22)	(0.45)	(0.42)	(0.46)	(0.63)
Religiosity	−0.43	−0.77**	−0.49**	−1.94***	−1.44***
	(0.28)	(0.34)	(0.28)	(0.32)	(0.41)
Age	0.19***	0.27***	0.36***	0.28***	0.17**
	(0.05)	(0.07)	(0.065)	(0.07)	(0.08)
Education	0.53	−0.07	0.75**	0.52	0.81
	(0.37)	(0.07)	(0.37)	(0.40)	(0.54)
Income	0.13	0.04	−0.82**	0.48	0.07
	(0.45)	(0.50)	(0.34)	(0.39)	(0.59)
White/European	−0.37**	−0.41	0.05	0.62	0.33
	(0.20)	(0.31)	(0.76)	(0.65)	(0.42)
Union	(–)	−0.61**	−0.04	0.11	−0.33
		(0.26)	(0.20)	(0.20)	(0.28)
Urban	−0.24	0.78**	0.33	0.14	−0.51
	(0.26)	(0.38)	(0.33)	(0.29)	(0.44)
Female	−0.17	0.17	−0.16	−0.13	−0.07
	(0.18)	(0.21)	(0.17)	(0.20)	(0.28)
Constant	−2.35***	−0.34	−0.52	−0.36	−0.08
	(0.47)	(0.64)	(0.85)	(0.80)	(0.88)
Pseudo R-squared	0.22	0.07	0.07	0.10	0.09
Observations	844	698	698	762	548

Note: Results are obtained from a logistic regression on the entire sample of partisans. All variables are scaled to range from 0 to 1, except for age, which is measured in decades. Standard errors in parentheses

*** $p < 0.01$, ** $p < 0.05$, * $p < 0.1$

partisanship promote voting for the in-party, as the significant and positive coefficients for both PPID and NPID indicate. These results are intuitive since, in the US two-party system, a vote for the in-party can, simultaneously, be a vote against the out-party. Thus, both PPID and NPID mutually influence vote choice among US partisans. Yet it is noteworthy that PPID's impact is much more powerful than NPID's. To illustrate this point, I calculate the predicted probabilities of the in-party vote along the levels of PPID and NPID: In-party vote's probabilities increase from 0.36 to 0.97 along the continuum of PPID while keeping NPID constant at its mean. In contrast, that effect is much more muted for NPID, which increases in-party vote probabilities from 0.59 to 0.90. Thus, PPID is a more powerful predictor of in-party vote in the United States. Notably, and in contrast to the analysis of turnout, the intensity of partisans' political attitudes fails to yield a significant influence, while other factors, such as being an older and White American, as well as being more conservative, significantly promote the decision to vote for the in-party.

In the United Kingdom (see column 2 in Table 8.2), in-party voting is high with 80% of British respondents voting for the party they identify with. Yet, positive partisan identity significantly increases the chance of voting for the in-party, starting at a predicted probability of 0.76 at the low end of PPID to a probability of 0.95 at the high end of PPID. This is a significant increase in in-party voting, driven by strong positive party attachments. At the same time, negative partisanship did not exert any influence on the voting decision of British partisans. Other demographic factors are more relevant such as age, employment status, religiosity, union membership, and the place of residence. Instrumental partisanship also fosters the decision to vote for the in-party, which rises from 0.83 to 0.93 across the range of partisans' political attitude strength.

In Italy (see column 3 in Table 8.2), 67% of partisans voted for their in-party in the last election. Once again, positive partisan identity is a substantial and positive driver of that decision. As PPID increases from its lowest to highest levels, the probability of voting for the in-party rises from 0.57 to 0.79. At the same time, the intensity of partisans' policy attitudes rivals that effect with an increase in in-party voting from 0.59 at the weakest attitudes to 0.81 at the strongest policy attitudes, suggesting that both expressive and instrumental factors are at play. Other relevant partisan characteristics in Italy include identifying with the left, being older, more educated, less religious, and reporting lower income.

Moving on to Sweden (see column 4 in Table 8.2), the rate of in-party vote resembles the United States, with 70% of Swedes voting for the party they identify with. A familiar picture re-emerges: Positive partisanship promotes in-party vote, while negative partisanship remains insignificant, as does the strength of partisans' policy opinions. The impact of positive partisanship cannot be overstated. As PPID increases from 0 to 1, the predicted probability of voting for the in-party surges from 0.68 to 0.91 – an impressive effect. Yet there are other relevant factors. Indeed, the coefficient for religiosity slightly surpasses the one for PPID, suggesting a strong, negative effect on in-party vote. Also noteworthy is the positive effect of age, whereby older Swedes are more likely to vote for their party – a reliable finding in the literature as well as in prior analyses.

Last, results in the Netherlands (see column 5 in Table 8.2), show an entirely different picture. Here, neither positive[1] nor negative partisanship significantly influence in-party vote, even though 84% of Dutch respondents report voting for their party. However, like in Sweden, religiosity plays a substantial role in the voting decision, whereby more religious partisans are less likely to vote for their in-party. Older Swedes are more likely to vote for the in-party – a finding that consistently emerges in all five countries.

Overall, this second set of analyses reveals that positive partisan identity strongly influences the decision to vote for the in-party in four of the five countries surveyed here, while negative partisan identity fails to exert a significant influence in any of the four multi-party countries.

8.8 PARTISANSHIP AND POLITICAL ENGAGEMENT

In addition to voting, citizens can become politically involved in a series of other political actions, ranging from discussing politics on social media or watching a political debate on TV to volunteering time or even money to a political campaign. Political scientists oftentimes study and conceptualize political engagement as a continuum that gauges the number of political activities citizens report participating in, ranging from low to high. Operationalizing political having participated on such a continuum provides a couple of benefits. First, it allows us to examine a more comprehensive range of political behavior that goes beyond the binary choice of voting. Second, it allows testing a key prediction of Social Identity Theory and its application to partisan identity, namely that the strongest partisans, whose self-image is most closely tied to their party, work most actively and ardently on behalf of the in-party (Andreychick and Gill 2009; Ethier and Deaux 1994; Fowler and Kam 2007). From this vantage point, strong partisans should engage in a higher number of political actions than their weakly attached counterparts.

Indeed, prior research has shown that partisan identity in the United States is a strong predictor of campaign involvement such as working for or donating money to a political party or candidate (Huddy et al. 2015), to an even larger extent than strong ideological convictions or issues preferences. In

---

[1] Note though that the coefficient for PPID approaches marginal significance p < 0.1.

my own work, my colleagues and I found similarly strong effects for partisan identity in the three multi-party systems (Huddy and colleagues 2018), showing that political engagement among partisans in Sweden, the Netherlands, and the United Kingdom is driven to a much larger extent by partisan identity than more instrumental concerns such as ideological intensity. Given these consistent findings, I too expect that strong positive partisanship promotes political participation.

There is, however, less clarity on the role of negative partisanship in shaping political engagement. Some evidence demonstrates that positive partisanship is a more powerful driver of political engagement than its negative counterpart in Canada (Caruana et al. 2015) as well as in the United States (Bankert 2021). I expect to find similar patterns in the following analyses. Yet, like positive partisanship, negative partisanship can motivate citizens to become active as well, as an expression of their opposition to a political party and in an attempt to impede its electoral chances. The following analyses thus test the following two predictions: First, strong PPID is related to higher levels of political engagement and, second, NPID is related to higher levels of political engagement, albeit at a smaller magnitude than PPID.

For the analyses, I create a multi-item scale of political participation that includes political activities such as discussing politics, going to political meetings or rallies, wearing a campaign button, placing an election sign in front of the house, and volunteering for or donating money to a political party. I combine these items into one scale, which allows me to treat this political participation scale as a continuous dependent variable. Like in prior analyses, I include the PPID scale, NPID scale, and a set of control variables as predictors.

8.9 ANALYSES

Examining the determinants of political engagement reveals a consistent pattern: Across all five countries, positive partisanship emerges as a strong and positive influence on political engagement. Starting with the United States (column 1 in Table 8.3), the coefficient for PPID is significant and substantial. To illustrate these effects, I once again calculate the predicted levels of political participation across the range of PPID, which shows a steep incline from 0.14 to 0.30. At the same time, negative partisanship promotes political engagement too, albeit at a lower rate than positive partisanship, leading to an increase in predicted levels from 0.17 to 0.26. Notably, the intensity of partisans' political attitudes does not emerge as a significant factor in driving engagement, while being older, more religious, more educated, and identifying as a liberal tend to be associated with higher levels of political participation in the United States.

TABLE 8.3 PPID, NPID, and political participation

	(1)	(2)	(3)	(4)	(5)
	United States	United Kingdom	Italy	Sweden	Netherlands
Positive partisanship	0.14***	0.09***	0.11***	0.18***	0.13***
	(0.03)	(0.02)	(0.03)	(0.02)	(0.01)
Negative partisanship	0.08**	0.09***	0.12***	0.02	0.04***
	(0.03)	(0.02)	(0.02)	(0.02)	(0.01)
Ideology	−0.06**	−0.05**	−0.09***	−0.03**	−0.02
	(0.02)	(0.02)	(0.02)	(0.01)	(0.01)
Issue intensity	0.02	0.08***	0.10***	−0.01	0.01
	(0.01)	(0.02)	(0.03)	(0.02)	(0.02)
Religiosity	0.05**	0.03**	−0.01	0.03**	0.05***
	(0.02)	(0.02)	(0.02)	(0.01)	(0.01)
Age	0.01***	−0.00**	−0.01***	−0.01***	−0.00**
	(0.00)	(0.00)	(0.00)	(0.00)	(0.00)
Education	0.07**	0.01***	0.09***	0.08***	0.06***
	(0.02)	(0.00)	(0.02)	(0.02)	(0.01)
Income	0.04	0.00	−0.07***	0.03	0.03**
	(0.03)	(0.02)	(0.02)	(0.02)	(0.02)
White/European	0.01	0.01	0.03	−0.05	−0.00
	(0.01)	(0.01)	(0.06)	(0.03)	(0.01)
Union	(–)	0.02	0.05***	0.01	0.01
		(0.01)	(0.01)	(0.01)	(0.00)
Urban	0.02	−0.00	−0.00	0.01	−0.01
	(0.02)	(0.02)	(0.02)	(0.01)	(0.01)
Female	−0.04***	−0.00	−0.00	−0.02***	−0.01**
	(0.01)	(0.01)	(0.01)	(0.01)	(0.00)
Constant	−0.01	0.03	0.12**	0.11**	0.02
	(0.03)	(0.03)	(0.07)	(0.04)	(0.03)
Observations	844	70	759	774	810
R-squared	0.141	0.187	0.159	0.179	0.216

Note: Results are obtained from an OLS regression on the entire sample of partisans. All variables are scaled to range from 0 to 1, except for age, which is measured in decades. Standard errors in parentheses

*** $p < 0.01$, ** $p < 0.05$, * $p < 0.1$

In the United Kingdom (column 2 in Table 8.3), both positive and negative partisan identity boost levels of political participation. As PPID and NPID increase from their weakest to their strongest identity strength, the likelihood of being politically involved increases from 0.11 to 0.20. I find a similar growth in the predicted levels of political engagement for partisans with strong political attitudes. Other factors that promote political participation in the United Kingdom include education and religiosity, while age and ideology show a negative association, suggesting that older and more conservative partisans are less likely to participate.

Political participation among partisans in Italy (column 3 in Table 8.3) mirrors its British counterpart. Positive and negative partisanship equally drive political participation with an increase from 0.19 to 0.30 in the predicted levels of political engagement across the range of PPID and NPID; the intensity of partisans' political attitudes has an almost identical effect, boosting political engagement levels from 0.21 to 0.32 as attitudes intensify. More educated partisans and union members tend to be more politically engaged, while older and more conservative partisans show lower levels of political participation.

In Sweden (column 4 in Table 8.3), partisans' engagement is strongly related to positive partisanship while negative partisanship remains insignificant. In this regard, Sweden is the first case in which positive partisanship impacts engagement without any significant influence of negative partisanship. Indeed, levels of political engagement increase from 0.07 at the low end of PPID and rise to an impressive 0.26 at the high end of PPID. Put differently, strong positive partisanship more than triples the chance of being politically active. Interestingly, I detect no effects for the intensity of partisans' attitudes, similar to the United States. In both Sweden and the United States, these instrumental facets of partisanship appear to have less influence in driving partisans' political participation. Other common patterns apply to Sweden: More religious and more educated Swedes are politically active, while older, more conservative, and female Swedes are less politically active.

Last, in the Netherlands (column 5 in Table 8.3), positive and negative partisanship are positively related to political participation but the effects of the former far surpass the effects of the latter. As PPID increases from low levels to high levels of identity strength, the predicted levels of political engagement surge from 0.06 to 0.19; the effect for NPID is much more muted, leading to an increase from 0.08 to 0.13. This asymmetry between the predictive power of PPID and NPID also emerged when examining the political participation of US partisans. Like in the United States and Sweden, the intensity of political attitudes is not related to political engagement but the usual suspects – age, education, and religiosity – reliably predict higher levels of engagement, as does income. Older and female Swedes, on the other hand, tend to participate at lower rates.

Overall, a key prediction of this section holds true: Political participation is driven by both positive and negative partisanship in four out of five cases. However, in two of them – the United States and the Netherlands – the effects of positive partisanship are far greater than the effects of negative partisanship, while in Sweden only positive partisanship promoted political participation. In the other two remaining cases – the United Kingdom and Italy – the two types of partisanship exerted effects of similar magnitude. These findings support the notion that both positive and negative partisanship can significantly boost citizens' political participation. In a democratic political system that depends on an active citizenry, this finding might challenge our normative assessment of partisanship. At the same time, the intensity of political attitudes – which was used as a measure of instrumental partisanship – is positively related to political engagement in only two of the five cases, thus providing only limited evidence that these instrumental components of partisanship encourage political participation. However, as mentioned before, ideology too can be an instrumental facet of partisanship. If we adopt that measurement strategy, then instrumental partisanship fares much better: In four out of five countries, respondents' ideology emerges as a significant factor, albeit with much weaker effects than positive and/or negative partisanship.

8.10 WHAT ABOUT INDEPENDENTS?

The prior analyses demonstrate that positive and negative partisanship in tandem influence partisans' turnout rates as well as their political engagement. While the study of partisans is useful to examine the power of both positive and negative partisanship among a large share of the electorate, it remains challenging to isolate and test negative partisanship's individual impact without any interference from positive partisanship. This is because partisans – by definition – already have a positive partisanship to begin with.

I thus turn to a sample of 630 US citizens who identified as pure independents without any partisan leaning. The data was collected in August 2020 by Bovitz Inc. and mirrors the demographic profile of the independent voter population (see Table A6 for more details). When asked which political party they normally vote for, 51% of respondents report no history of favoring one party over the other in their vote choice, followed by 14% of respondents who report not voting at all in the past. Thus, for the majority of the sample, respondents' identification as independents also matches their voting history. Second, 61% of respondents place themselves at the midpoint of the ideology scale, followed by 20% who are conservative and 19% who are liberal, suggesting that a large share of these independent voters are also ideological moderates.

The NPID scale was assigned to respondents based on the question of which party they would evaluate more negatively, the Democratic Party or the Republican Party. If a respondent chose "both equally," respondents had to indicate their feelings for both political parties with a feeling thermometer scale. The party with the lower value on this 0–100 scale was selected as the target of the NPID scale. Similar to their partisan counterparts, the NPID scale achieves a high reliability of 0.87 even when applied to independent voters. On a scale from 0 (NPID's minimum) to 1 (NPID maximum), the sample's average value on the NPID scale is 0.36, the first quartile is placed at 0.17, the median at 0.33, and the third quartile is located at 0.51. Thus, most respondents are concentrated below or close to the midpoint of the negative partisan identity scale.

I examine two forms of political engagement among these unaffiliated voters: First, the likelihood of turning out, which is an ordinal variable that ranges from "very unlikely" (coded as 0) to "very likely" (coded as 1); second, the levels of political participation, which gauges the number of political activities that respondents have engaged in during the 2020 election season such as wearing a campaign button and volunteering for a campaign. The scale combines seven such items and takes on a value of 0 if the respondent did not engage in any sort of political activity during the 2020 election season and a value of 1 if the respondent participated in all of the seven political activities; 51% of all respondents report no form of political engagement while the remainder of the sample reported at least one political activity during election season.

I regress these dependent variables on the NPID scale and a set of demographic factors that are known to impact political engagement such as gender (coded as 1 for female and 0 for male respondents), education, age (measured in decades), religiosity (coded 1 for "attending religious services more than once a week" and 0 for "never"), race (ranges from low to high, coded as 0–1), ideology (ranges from "very liberal" to "very conservative," coded 0–1), and a political issue scale that measures the strength of respondents' attitudes on a variety of policy issues such as gun control, abortion access, immigration, and the minimum wage (ranges from low to high, coded as 0–1).

Similar to their partisan peers in the United States, independents with strong negative partisanship are more likely to turnout (see column 1 in Table 8.4) with an increase in the chance of voting from 0.79 at the low end of NPID to 0.90 at the high end of NPID. Notably, the intensity of independents' political attitudes does not show any significant relationship with their decision to turn out. Instead, other demographic factors promote turnout among independent voters such as education, being White, being male, and religiosity.

The results are even stronger for political participation. As NPID intensifies, the predicted levels of becoming politically active sizably increase from 0.07 to 0.25. No other variable influences independents' political engagement to such a large extent. Political attitude strength slightly boosts participation as does being more educated and being male. Overall, these results attest to the idea that even in the absence of positive party attachments, negative

TABLE 8.4 NPID and independents

	(1)	(2)
	Turnout	**Political Participation**
Negative partisan identity	0.11**	0.18***
	(0.06)	(0.03)
Issue intensity	0.08	0.05**
	(0.06)	(0.03)
Ideology	−0.07	−0.01
	(0.08)	(0.04)
Religiosity	0.11**	0.01
	(0.04)	(0.02)
Age	0.01	−0.00
	(0.01)	(0.00)
Male	0.08***	0.02**
	(0.03)	(0.01)
White	0.07**	−0.01
	(0.03)	(0.02)
Education	0.28***	0.09***
	(0.06)	(0.03)
Constant	0.43***	0.01
	(0.07)	(0.03)
Observations	565	596
R-squared	0.10	0.11

Note: Results are obtained from an OLS regression on the entire sample of partisans. All variables are scaled to range from 0 to 1, except for age, which is measured in decades. Standard errors in parentheses *** $p < 0.01$, ** $p < 0.05$, * $p < 0.1$

partisanship can encourage political involvement. From a normative stand-point, this is good news since negative partisanship offers even independents an impetus to engage with the political system. On the other hand, this engagement is motivated by the strong opposition to a political party rather than enthusiastic support for a party's policy platform. Thus, negative partisanship might be a double-edged sword for democratic representation and accountability.

8.11 SUMMARY

Positive and negative partisanship significantly influence a range of political behaviors, including turnout, in-party vote, and other forms of political participation. Yet their effects vary across countries. Positive partisanship significantly increases the chance of turnout in the United States and the Netherlands. In the Netherlands, this motivation is also enmeshed with negative partisanship. In Italy, in contrast, NPID boosts turnout rates among citizens without its positive counterpart, which suggests that the strong disdain for a particular party motivates Italians to participate on election day. More consistent results emerged for the analysis of in-party vote, which is strongly related to positive partisanship in the United States, the United Kingdom, Italy, Sweden, and the Netherlands. Last, political participation is driven by both positive and negative partisanship in four of the five countries. However, in two of them – the United States and the Netherlands – the effects of positive partisanship are far greater than the effects of negative partisanship, while Sweden was the only case in which PPID, but not NPID, emerged as a positive driver of political engagement. In the other two remaining cases – the United Kingdom and Italy – the two types of partisanship had similar effects. The analysis of independent voters in the United States further highlighted the independent role of negative partisanship in fostering political engagement. Altogether, these findings support the notion that strong partisanship *promotes* a democratic community by motivating citizens to participate in the political process.

9

The Impact of Partisan Identities on Anti-Democratic Behavior in the United States and Europe

9.1 WHAT IS IN THIS CHAPTER?

As Chapter 8 demonstrated, strong partisanship promotes citizen's active involvement with their political system. At the same time, partisanship is often portrayed as the root cause of escalating hostility and even violence between partisans in the United States and beyond. How can we reconcile these two conflicting views on partisanship? One answer may lie in the distinction between positive and negative partisanship. Utilizing data from the United States, United Kingdom, Sweden, the Netherlands, and Italy, I examine to what extent positive and negative partisanship promote attitudes that are antithetical to a healthy democratic society, including the support for a ban of political parties as well as the desire to see politicians physically harmed. I find that many of these undesirable expressions are more frequently and more strongly linked to negative partisanship, rather than positive partisanship. I discuss the normative implications of these results for the assessment of partisanship and its vital role in a democratic society.

9.2 WHY IS THIS IMPORTANT?

Partisanship has a range of positive effects on citizens' political behavior: higher turnout, higher political interest, and more active engagement are just a few of them. Yet, the public debate has increasingly focused on a narrative that portrays partisanship as the main reason for erupting partisan hostility, violence, and even democratic erosion. This perspective invites a rather critical, if not even cynical, view on partisanship that might motivate citizens to withdraw from of the political system all together. It is thus important to provide a more balanced assessment of partisanship's effects. For this purpose, I examine to what extent negative partisanship is responsible for the hostility, incivility, and even violence we have indiscriminately been attributing to positive partisanship. This distinction matters because it reveals the possibility of a political world in which partisans are able to feel deeply attached to their own party without feeling deep disdain for their political opponents.

***

Partisanship has been in the news. In the United States, partisan tensions do not only flare up in debates on gun control, abortion, and immigration but have also been linked to the horrendous attack on the Capitol in Washington, DC, on January 6, 2021. Indeed, a new poll by the Southern Poverty Law Center shows that 44% of Americans believe the nation is headed toward another civil war (Southern Poverty Law Center 2022). The attack on Capitol Hill resembles the events in Rome in October 2021, when protesters broke into the building of the left-leaning General Confederation of Labour and ransacked its contents. In the aftermath of the attack, many observers criticized Italy's far-right parties, especially Fratelli d'Italia, for exploiting public anger over COVID-19 restrictions. In the United Kingdom, the conservative Member of Parliament (MP) Sir David Amess died in 2021 after being stabbed multiple times at his constituency office in Essex, following a similarly tragic death of Jo Cox, a member of the Labour Party, in 2016. In the Netherlands, threats and harassment toward politicians are on the rise, leading the Dutch Parliament to contemplate a proposal that would increase the maximum penalty for threatening public officeholders (Nan 2022). Sweden is not unfamiliar with these challenges either, following the assassination of their foreign minister Anna Lindh in 2003 and an assault on a politician from the Left Party in 2017.

Explanations for these incidences of politically motivated violence are oftentimes linked to increasing polarization and extreme party loyalties, leaving the impression that citizens' strong attachments to political parties are an unfortunate development in mass democracies. Recent public opinion polls show a reflection of that sentiment: Most Americans "agree that partisanship has made it more difficult to conduct elections and deal with the economic and health impacts of the pandemic. Half of Americans also say partisan divisiveness has made solving problems in their community more difficult and one-third say it has strained personal relationships" (Public Agenda 2021). This negative perception of partisanship also aligns with contemporary research on independents in the United States and their motivation to stay out of the partisan conflict. According to Klar and Krupnikov (2016), many Americans are becoming embarrassed of their political party and tired of the partisan bickering, which leads them to deny, or at least hide, their partisan ties. The authors label this group of citizens "undercover independents" who intentionally mask their partisan preferences in social situations to escape the seemingly inevitable partisan conflict. Unfortunately, this motivation also diminishes their willingness to become politically active. The decision to opt out of politics instigates a vicious cycle, whereby the clamorous and most convinced partisans are more likely to shape and participate in the political process, which further alienates citizens who feel dismayed by the hostility between the political parties and their supporters.

The decision to abstain from politics and the partisan rancor becomes even more understandable when examining the contemporary work on some of partisanship's worst effects, such as the dehumanization of the out-party and its members. Cassese (2021) demonstrates that dehumanizing the members of the opposing party was a common element in the political rhetoric of the 2016 US presidential election campaigns. The author notes that "candidates were characterized explicitly as inhuman monsters (e.g., 'Trump is the GOP's Frankenstein monster,' Kludt 2016), or more implicitly as aberrant, deviant, or warped. Their supporters were also cast as lacking in basic humanity (e.g., as a 'basket of deplorables,' Reilly 2016)" (p. 30). the author goes on to show worrying results: Strong partisans are more likely to assign animalistic traits (e.g., uncivilized, stupid, and inarticulate) and mechanistic traits (e.g., robotic, object-like, and unemotional) to members of the opposing party and to classify them as subhuman. Perceiving people as "subhuman" is a form of "blatant dehumanization," which is measured using the so-called Ascent of Man scale. The use of this scale is simple: Respondents are asked to rate which stage in the evolution of men the opposing party and its members belong to, ranging from subhuman to human (see Haslam 2006; Haslam and Loughan 2014). Naturally, if we think of someone as subhuman, then we do not want to personally interact with them. Thus, this form of blatant dehumanization also promotes the desire to avoid any social exchanges with the out-party, which, in turn, creates a dangerous feedback loop: Dehumanizing the out-party leads to fewer social interactions with members of the out-party, which creates fewer chances to foster empathy and civility across the political aisle. Put simply, distance reinforces disdain between partisans.

Other contemporary work not only confirms the troubling trend of dehumanization but also tries to investigate its origins. One might assume that partisans with strong party attachments are most likely to depict their opponents as subhuman. However, Matherus and colleagues (2021) show that not all strong partisans inevitably dehumanize the opposing party. Instead, dehumanization is particularly pronounced among partisans with very high levels of affective polarization as well as partisans with more fixed worldviews that make them more critical of change and more sensitive to perceived threats (see Hetherington and Weiler 2018). While strong partisans were somewhat more likely to dehumanize out-party members, the authors themselves admit that the relationship is "underwhelming" (p. 525). The difference in the feeling thermometer scores that partisans assigned to their own party *and* the opposing party (i.e., affective polarization) was much more strongly related to levels of blatant dehumanization. These are interesting findings since they line up with the main argument of this chapter: Strong positive partisanship alone is not the main driver of partisan-motivated dehumanization and violence.

Sadly, there is no shortage of other examples: Kalmoe and Mason (2019) provide evidence for what they refer to as "lethal partisanship." These lethal partisans condone physical harm to members of the opposing party, they lack sympathy over their possible deaths, and they feel less restraint about violence toward the out-party. The authors find that "15 percent of Republicans and 20 percent of Democrats agreed that the country would be better off if large numbers of opposing partisans in the public today 'just died' . . . 17 percent of Democrats and 7 percent of Republicans report ever 'wishing that someone would injure one or more politicians from the outparty' . . . [and] 12 percent of Republicans and 11 percent of Democrats believe that it is at least occasionally acceptable to send threatening messages to public officials" (p. 22–23).

There is a bigger picture to consider: Dehumanization of political opponents as well as partisan hostility are only a couple of the many symptoms that are oftentimes associated with democratic erosion – the gradual chipping away of democracy's foundations. These foundations include fair elections, civil and open discourse, a free press, and the peaceful transition of power after an election. The attacks on the US Capitol in January 2021 present a haunting example of how unconditional political loyalties can weaken the commitment to these democratic norms and values.

In the remainder of this chapter, I will empirically test whether negative – rather than positive – partisanship is the primary culprit behind these anti-democratic attitudes and behaviors. Indeed, there are many open questions. Do positive and negative partisanship carry equal responsibility for partisan animosity? If strong positive partisanship has been linked to lethal partisanship, then does this relationship persist when taking into account the independent effects of negative partisanship? From a normative standpoint, these are important considerations. If we cannot be strong partisans without abandoning the responsibilities and duties of democratic citizenship, then this poses a challenge to representative mass democracies, which, after all, depend on political parties and their ability to represent and mobilize voters. On the other hand, if negative, rather than positive, partisanship diminishes our commitment to democratic norms and values, then it is important to reassess the role of positive partisanship and to develop strategies that can foster positive partisan ties without promoting their negative counterparts.

The following analyses aim to provide a first step in that direction. Utilizing data from the United States, the United Kingdom, Sweden, the

TABLE 9.1 Commitment to democratic norms

(1) Some parties and candidates should be barred because of their beliefs and ideologies

	Strongly disagree	Disagree	Neither agree nor disagree	Agree	Strongly agree
United States	25%	22%	31%	16%	5%
United Kingdom	10%	18%	38%	23%	11%
Sweden	21%	18%	35%	18%	8%
Netherlands	7%	22%	35%	27%	9%
Italy	9%	15%	34%	27%	15%

(2) My party's political opponents have their heart in the right place but just come to different conclusions about what is best.

	Strongly disagree	Disagree	Neither agree nor disagree	Agree	Strongly agree
United States	8%	18%	35%	32%	7%
United Kingdom	7%	11%	40%	33%	9%
Sweden	8%	13%	45%	24%	9%
Netherlands	5%	11%	43%	35%	6%
Italy	5%	14%	44%	31%	6%

(3) Have you ever wished that someone would physically injure one or more politicians?

	Yes	No	Not sure
United States	14%	79%	7%
United Kingdom	14%	69%	17%
Sweden	18%	64%	18%
Netherlands	18%	64%	18%
Italy	18%	74%	9%

Netherlands, and Italy, I examine if and how positive and negative partisanship are related to several anti-democratic attitudes such as (1) "Some parties and candidates should be barred because of their beliefs and ideologies" and (2) "My party's political opponents have their heart in the right place but just come to different conclusions about what is best," which is a reverse-coded item so that *lower* levels of agreement indicate stronger anti-democratic attitudes. Respondents in all five countries also indicate whether they (3) had ever wished that someone would physically injure one or more politicians from the out-party. The level of endorsement for each of the three attitudes is presented in Table 9.1.

A cursory look at the levels of support for each item reveals a substantial degree of variation across countries: 21% of US partisans endorse a ban, which is almost a quarter of partisans in the sample. The levels of support are even higher in the United Kingdom, where 34% agree with a ban on certain political parties, as do 26% of partisans in Sweden, 36% in the Netherlands, and a staggering 42% in Italy.

The perceptions of the out-party are more positive. Here, a large share of partisans in all five countries agree that their party's political opponents have their heart in the right place but just come to different conclusions about what is best. This sentiment reflects the confidence that the out-party and its members are not evil or mean-spirited despite their different political vision for the country. Such trust in the other side is crucial for collaboration between parties in governance as well as for civil and respectful social interactions with members of the out-party; 39% of partisans in the United States share this sentiment, as do 43% of partisans in the United Kingdom, 33% of partisans in Sweden, 41% of partisans in the Netherlands, and 37% of partisans in Italy. Despite these seemingly high numbers, it is important to note that over half of the partisans in each country are either ambivalent or distrustful about the out-party's character.

The last attitude item explicitly measures the endorsement of violence by asking partisans if they have ever wished that someone would physically injure one or more politicians of the out-party. Reassuringly, a clear majority of partisans in each of the five countries negate that statement. Yet, 14%–18% of surveyed partisans do respond in the affirmative, suggesting that the desire to see the out-party harmed is not a rarity among partisans. Moreover, due to social desirability bias, these numbers most likely represent a lower estimate of the true levels of endorsement.

In a next step, I examine if and to what extent positive and negative partisanship affect support for these anti-democratic attitudes. For this purpose, I regress each of the five attitude items on positive and negative partisanship as well as the same set of control variables I used in prior analyses. For better comparability, all variables are scaled to range from 0 to 1.

9.3 ANALYSIS 1: BANNING PARTIES AND CANDIDATES

First, I examine the support for banning certain parties and candidates for their beliefs and ideology. Support for a ban is strongest in the Netherlands and Italy, where 36% and 42% of partisans respectively agree with the idea of barring candidates or parties of a particular ideology. It makes sense that support is higher in multi-party systems where fringe and populist parties are more likely to be the target of negative partisanship and where banning a political party (especially a small one) would not lead to the disappearance of half of all viable parties – as would be the case in the United States. I examine to what extent this support is grounded in positive and negative partisan identity. To account for instrumental partisanship, I also include the intensity of partisans' political attitudes, as well as partisans' demographic features as control variables.

TABLE 9.2 Banning political parties

	(1)	(2)	(3)	(4)	(5)
	United States	United Kingdom	Sweden	Netherlands	Italy
Positive partisan identity	0.01	0.12***	0.11**	0.07	−0.05
	(0.05)	(0.04)	(0.05)	(0.04)	(0.05)
Negative partisan identity	0.28***	0.12***	0.16***	0.13***	0.25***
	(0.05)	(0.04)	(0.04)	(0.04)	(0.04)
Ideology	−0.08**	0.04	−0.12***	−0.01	−0.10**
	(0.03)	(0.04)	(0.04)	(0.04)	(0.04)
Issue intensity	0.00	0.18***	0.05	0.06	0.12**
	(0.02)	(0.04)	(0.05)	(0.05)	(0.05)
Age	−0.02***	−0.02***	−0.04***	−0.00	−0.01
	(0.00)	(0.00)	(0.01)	(0.01)	(0.01)
Female	0.03**	0.02	0.07***	0.03**	0.06***
	(0.01)	(0.02)	(0.02)	(0.02)	(0.02)
White/European	0.01	−0.00	−0.14**	−0.04	0.00
	(0.02)	(0.03)	(0.08)	(0.04)	(0.10)
Religiosity	0.03	−0.03	−0.05	0.06	0.05
	(0.02)	(0.03)	(0.04)	(0.04)	(0.03)
Urban	−0.01	0.02	−0.04	−0.06**	0.03
	(0.02)	(0.03)	(0.03)	(0.03)	(0.04)
Education	−0.10***	−0.00	−0.03	−0.15***	0.03
	(0.03)	(0.00)	(0.04)	(0.04)	(0.04)
Income	−0.00	0.01	−0.07	0.11**	0.06
	(0.04)	(0.04)	(0.04)	(0.05)	(0.04)
Union membership	(−)	−0.02	−0.00	0.03	−0.02
		(0.02)	(0.02)	(0.02)	(0.02)
Constant	0.44***	0.39***	0.64***	0.50***	0.34***
	(0.04)	(0.06)	(0.10)	(0.07)	(0.11)
Observations	844	702	774	810	756
R-squared	0.101	0.091	0.13	0.07	0.09

Note: Results are obtained from an OLS regression on the entire sample of partisans. All variables are scaled to range from 0 to 1, except for age, which is measured in decades. Standard errors in parentheses*** $p < 0.01$, ** $p < 0.05$, * $p < 0.1$

Starting with the United States (see column 1 in Table 9.2), negative partisan identity is strongly related to the desire to ban certain parties and candidates, while positive partisan identity does not seem to have any effect as the statistically insignificant coefficient for PPID suggests. On the other hand, NPID's effect is substantial: Across the range of negative partisan identity, support for a ban increases from 0.28 to 0.56 – a considerable growth. Hardly any other variable can compete with NPID's impact. However, there are few demographic variables that are associated with higher support: More liberal, female, younger, and less educated partisans in the United States tend to be more comfortable with the idea of banning certain parties and candidates.

In the United Kingdom (see column 2 in Table 9.2), a different picture emerges: Both positive and negative partisan identity drive the support for a ban to an almost equal extent. As PPID and NPID rise, the predicted level of support increases from 0.47 to 0.60, not as steep of an increase as seen in the United States but nevertheless considerable. Yet the intensity of partisans' political attitudes slightly surpasses that effect. Those partisans with the strongest political opinions have a predicted support level of 0.65. Interestingly, when examining PPID on its own while keeping NPID below its mean, the coefficient for PPID barely reaches conventional levels of statistical significance. This finding might suggest that positive partisanship on its own is a weaker force in driving support for a ban on political parties, though it could also be driven by the smaller sample size. Similar to prior analyses of British partisans, instrumental facets of partisanship remain a powerful influence. Younger partisans in the United Kingdom are also more likely to endorse a ban – like their American counterparts.

A similar pattern emerges in Sweden (see column 3 in Table 9.2), where both positive and negative partisanship drive support for a ban on certain political parties. Yet NPID's effect is greater, leading to an increase in support from 0.38 at the weakest levels of NPID to 0.55 at its highest, compared to 0.43 to 0.54 along PPID's range. Similar to the supplementary analysis of UK partisans, PPID's coefficient loses its statistical significance when NPID is kept below its mean. Younger and more liberal Swedes tend to be more in favor of a ban than their older and more conservative counterparts.

Partisans in the Netherlands and in Italy (columns 4 and 5 in Table 9.2) strongly resemble US partisans, in that only negative partisan identity is significantly related to supporting a ban of certain political parties, while the coefficient for positive partisan identity remains insubstantial and insignificant. In the Netherlands, support levels rise from 0.45 to 0.58 across the range of NPID – an increase that is even more substantial in Italy where support intensifies from 0.42 at the weakest levels of NPID to 0.68 at its highest. Being more educated decreases support for a ban in the Netherlands, while being more liberal, female, and having strong political attitudes are related to higher levels of support for a ban among partisans in Italy.

Overall, these results demonstrate that, across all five countries, NPID is a strong predictor of support for banning parties and candidates. Admittedly, in the United Kingdom and in Sweden, both NPID and PPID increase support for banning political parties, though the effects for NPID in Sweden were somewhat stronger than for PPID. Notably, among partisans in the United States, in the Netherlands, and in Italy, only NPID is a significant force while PPID does not exert any statistically significant impact. Once again, this analysis supports the notion that strong positive party attachments are not inherently disconcerting for democracy.

9.4 ANALYSIS 2: POLITICAL OPPONENTS HAVE THEIR HEART IN THE RIGHT PLACE

Next, I examine the factors that drive support for the statement: "My party's political opponents have their heart in the right place but just come to different conclusions about what is best." Reassuringly, most partisans across all five countries endorse this rather favorable perception of their political opponents.

When examining its connection to positive and negative partisanship, a few interesting patterns surface. In the United States (see column 1 in Table 9.3), strong positive partisanship increases the chance of partisans viewing their opponents in a positive light, as PPID's positive and significant coefficient suggests. These effects are quite sizable: As positive partisan identity rises from its weakest to its highest levels, partisans' chance of humanizing their opponents increases from 0.43 to 0.65. This is a noteworthy finding because it suggests that strong partisans can be *more* likely to assume good intentions behind their opponents' actions. At the same time, negative partisanship reduces that likelihood quite drastically from 0.64 at its weakest level to 0.36 at its strongest level. Thus, negative partisanship, not positive partisanship, is driving a more hostile view of the out-party among US partisans. There are also a few noteworthy demographic markers: Younger, more liberal, and more religious Americans tend to share that positive perspective on the out-party and its members.

Like in the United States, positive partisanship promotes a favorable view of the opponent among partisans in the United Kingdom (see column 2 in Table 9.3). Here, predicted levels of humanizing the out-party rise from 0.53 at the weakest levels of positive partisan identity to 0.63 at the highest levels. Negative partisanship's coefficient is negative – as expected – but it does not reach statistical significance. Nevertheless, the analysis of British partisans reiterates the point that positive partisanship can promote sympathy for the out-party rather than resentment. In contrast to the United States, conservative partisans are more likely to believe that their opponents have good intentions.

In Sweden (see column 3 in Table 9.3), positive partisanship operates in the same way as it does in Britain; it fosters a more benign attitude toward the opposition, whereby its predicted levels increase 0.46 to 0.57 across the range of positive partisan identity strength. Once again, negative partisanship's effect appears to trend in the opposite direction, and yet its effects do not reach statistical significance, similar to the United Kingdom. When

TABLE 9.3 Good-hearted opponents

	(1)	(2)	(3)	(4)	(5)
	United States	United Kingdom	Sweden	Netherlands	Italy
Positive partisan identity	0.22***	0.08**	0.11**	−0.01	0.19***
	(0.04)	(0.04)	(0.05)	(0.04)	(0.04)
Negative partisan identity	−0.28***	−0.04	−0.01	0.01	−0.08**
	(0.04)	(0.03)	(0.04)	(0.03)	(0.04)
Ideology	−0.06**	0.18***	0.05	0.07**	0.04
	(0.03)	(0.04)	(0.03)	(0.04)	(0.03)
Issue intensity	0.00	0.05	−0.04	0.11***	0.12***
	(0.02)	(0.04)	(0.05)	(0.04)	(0.04)
Age	−0.01***	0.00	0.00	−0.00	0.02***
	(0.00)	(0.00)	(0.01)	(0.01)	(0.01)
Female	−0.00	0.00	0.05**	−0.02	−0.01
	(0.01)	(0.01)	(0.02)	(0.02)	(0.02)
White/European	0.00	−0.01	−0.07	0.05	0.02
	(0.02)	(0.03)	(0.07)	(0.03)	(0.08)
Religiosity	0.06**	0.05	0.03	0.01	0.05**
	(0.02)	(0.03)	(0.03)	(0.03)	(0.03)
Urban	0.00	0.02	−0.04	0.02	−0.00
	(0.02)	(0.03)	(0.03)	(0.03)	(0.03)
Education	−0.05	0.00	0.06	−0.04	0.03
	(0.03)	(0.00)	(0.04)	(0.03)	(0.04)
Income	0.00	0.06	0.02	0.02	0.01
	(0.04)	(0.04)	(0.04)	(0.04)	(0.04)
Union membership	(–)	0.03	−0.01	−0.01	0.01
		(0.02)	(0.02)	(0.02)	(0.02)
Constant	0.67***	0.38***	0.54***	0.48***	0.36***
	(0.04)	(0.06)	(0.09)	(0.06)	(0.09)
Observations	844	701	774	810	757
R-squared	0.074	0.056	0.04	0.02	0.08

Note: Results are obtained from an OLS regression on the entire sample of partisans. All variables are scaled to range from 0 to 1, except for age, which is measured in decades. Standard errors in parentheses*** $p < 0.01$, ** $p < 0.05$, * $p < 0.1$

examining demographic predictors, only gender emerges as significant, whereby women in Sweden are slightly more likely to view their opponents positively.

Among Dutch partisans (see column 4 in Table 9.3), neither positive nor negative partisan identity influence this particular attitude toward the outparty. Both the coefficients for PPID and NPID are insubstantial and insignificant. However, the strength of partisans' political preferences boosts the chance of perceiving the opponent in a positive light from 0.53 at the weakest political attitudes to 0.64 at the strongest. Thus, even partisans with strong political convictions are not condemned to disdain their opponents. This too is an important finding that emphasizes that substantive political disagreement does not necessarily lead to partisan hostility.

Last, in Italy (see column 5 in Table 9.3), positive and negative partisanship operate the same way they do in the United States. Strong positive partisan identity *increases* the chance of partisans' favorable assessment of their out-party, while negative partisan identity *decreases* it. Note, however, that positive partisanship's effects are somewhat greater, driving positive perceptions from 0.46 at its weakest levels to 0.65 at its highest. Across the range of negative partisanship, predicted levels decrease from 0.60 to 0.51, a smaller yet significant magnitude. Older, and religious Italians with strong political opinions tend to be more favorable as well.

Overall, this analysis reveals important nuances to our understanding of positive and negative partisanship. In four out of five countries, positive partisanship fosters an empathetic view of the out-party. Put differently, positive partisanship promotes, rather than impedes, civility toward the other side. In two of the five countries, negative partisanship significantly reduces support for this humanizing view of political opponents. Taken together, these results provide another piece of evidence in defense of positive partisanship.

9.5 ANALYSIS 3: WISHING HARM TO POLITICIANS

Next, I move on to a more disconcerting attitude, namely whether partisans wish that someone would physically injure one or more politicians of the opposition. While a clear majority of respondents in all five countries denied ever having wished harm on a politician, there is nevertheless a substantial share of partisans, ranging from 14% to 18% in each country, that admit to having had these thoughts.

When examining their origins, the effects of positive and negative partisanship vary across countries. In the United States (see column 1 in Table 9.4), positive partisan identity significantly *reduces* the likelihood of partisans' wishing harm on their opponents, as PPID's negative and significant coefficient suggests. Indeed, strong positive partisans show significantly lower predicted probabilities of endorsing harm (0.07) than partisans with weaker attachments (0.18). This is a noteworthy finding that contradicts the notion that strong partisanship drives hostility between party supporters. At the same time, negative partisan identity strongly *increases* that desire from 0.04 at its weakest levels to 0.45 at its strongest – a remarkable surge. As predicted, negative partisanship is the main contributor to partisans' acceptance of violence while positive partisanship reduces it. Beyond positive and negative partisanship, more educated, less religious, and urban partisans in the United States are more likely to report having wished harm on to politicians.

TABLE 9.4 *Physical harm to opponent*

	(1)	(2)	(3)	(4)	(5)
	United States	United Kingdom	Sweden	Netherlands	Italy
Positive partisan identity	−0.98**	0.15	1.44***	1.73***	−0.58
	(0.56)	(0.54)	(0.55)	(0.60)	(0.49)
Negative partisan identity	2.96***	1.11**	1.10**	1.31**	1.10**
	(0.58)	(0.48)	(0.51)	(0.56)	(0.44)
Ideology	−0.54	−0.17	0.33	0.04	−0.16
	(0.36)	(0.47)	(0.39)	(0.56)	(0.38)
Issue intensity	−0.01	0.71	2.58***	−0.48	−0.79
	(0.25)	(0.47)	(0.53)	(0.59)	(0.48)
Age	−0.08	−0.43***	−0.37***	−0.30***	−0.38***
	(0.06)	(0.08)	(0.08)	(0.08)	(0.08)
Female	0.03	−0.63***	−0.22	0.06	0.23
	(0.21)	(0.24)	(0.22)	(0.28)	(0.19)
White/European	0.11	−0.2	−0.41	0.30	(-)
	(0.23)	(0.29)	(0.77)	(0.44)	
Religiosity	−0.60**	1.18***	1.77***	1.19***	−0.25
	(0.33)	(0.35)	(0.34)	(0.38)	(0.32)
Urban	0.86***	0.29	0.73**	1.51***	−0.31
	(0.30)	(0.42)	(0.34)	(0.45)	(0.37)
Education	0.74**	0.11	−0.79**	0.16	−0.48
	(0.42)	(0.08)	(0.46)	(0.57)	(0.42)
Income	−0.77	−0.46	−0.20	−0.26	0.45
	(0.51)	(0.51)	(0.44)	(0.58)	(0.39)
Union membership	(–)	0.49**	−0.02	0.72***	0.89***
		(0.26)	(0.23)	(0.27)	(0.22)
Constant	−2.44***	−1.57**	−2.63***	−3.76***	−0.50
	(0.55)	(0.68)	(0.94)	(0.94)	(0.51)
Observations	790	654	655	722	712
R-squared					

Note: Results are obtained from an OLS regression on the entire sample of partisans. All variables are scaled to range from 0 to 1, except for age, which is measured in decades. Standard errors in parentheses*** $p < 0.01$, ** $p < 0.05$, * $p < 0.1$

In the United Kingdom (see column 2 in Table 9.4), only negative partisanship powerfully promotes the desire for harming the out-party, leading to an increase in its predicted probabilities from 0.04 at NPID's lowest value to 0.13 at its highest, which equals a triple growth in the desire for harm. Remarkably, positive partisanship does not exert any influence, which, once again, reiterates the point that strong positive party attachments can exist without partisan acrimony. A few demographic features appear relevant as well, such as age, gender, and religiosity. Younger and female partisans in the United Kingdom show less intense desire for harming the out-party while, more religious Britons report having wished harm at somewhat higher rates.

In Sweden and the Netherlands (see columns 3 and 4 in Table 9.4), the results paint a somewhat different picture. In these two countries, the coefficients for PPID and NPID are both positive and quite substantial in magnitude suggesting that both positive and negative partisanship significantly increase the desire for out-party harm. In Sweden, a 0 to 1 change in positive partisanship increases the predicted probabilities of wishing harm to politicians from 0.09 to 0.29 – a progression that is only slightly smaller for the range of negative partisanship, from 0.09 to 0.23. These substantial growth rates can also be detected in the Netherlands where predicted probabilities increase from 0.03 to 0.16 along positive partisanship's continuum and 0.03 to 0.11 along negative partisanship's continuum. Yet, when examining PPID on its own while keeping NPID below its mean, positive partisanship no longer promotes the desire for harming politicians, suggesting that truly positive partisans with low levels of NPID might not be more likely to wish harm on their opponents. In Sweden, the intensity of partisans' political attitudes greatly outperforms the effects of partisanship, whereby partisans with strong opinions are significantly more likely to endorse harm. In fact, the rise from 0.09 to 0.57 across the issue intensity continuum is considerable and hints at the role of instrumental components of partisanship in shaping out-party hostility, though this is only the case in Sweden. Once again, more religious, younger, urban, and less educated Swedes are also more likely to express the desire for harm, similar to the Netherlands.

Last, in Italy (see column 5 in Table 9.4), results mirror the ones from British partisans where only negative partisanship impacts the wish for out-party harm. As negative partisanship increases from 0 to 1, wishing harm to politicians jumps from 0.09 to 0.24. This substantial increase highlights negative partisanship's detrimental effects, which are ordinarily attributed to positive partisanship. Younger partisans and union members in Italy show a similarly elevated level of support for out-party harm.

In all five countries, negative partisanship is a strong predictor of wishing harm on politicians. In only two of these countries, Sweden and the Netherlands, both positive and negative partisanship promote that desire for harm. However, in the United States and in Italy, strong positive partisanship *reduces* the chance of partisans wishing harm on to politicians, a finding that contradicts the narrative that strong party loyalties drive hostility between partisans. Consistent with prior analyses, negative partisanship uniquely promotes the disturbing wish of seeing politicians harmed in three of the five countries, namely the United States, the United Kingdom, and Italy. In sum, the majority of these analyses tell a mostly consistent story:

Partisans can feel deeply attached to their party without feeling deep disdain toward the out-party. While positive partisanship emerges as a significant predictor of a couple of disconcerting attitudes, mostly in Sweden and the Netherlands, it never does so on its own, only in combination with negative partisanship. In most cases, though, it is negative partisanship that powerfully drives these anti-democratic attitudes.

9.6 WHAT ABOUT INDEPENDENTS?

The prior analyses investigated the distinct effects of negative and positive partisanship on attitudes that are antithetical to democratic values such as the desire to physically harm political opponents. Yet, similar to analyses in prior chapters, it is challenging to fully isolate the effects of negative partisanship when examining partisans since they already identify with a political party. Thus, in the final analysis of this chapter, I examine independent voters in the United States and their conviction that some political parties or candidates should be banned because of their beliefs. For this purpose, I once again turn to a sample of pure independents in the United States. Among the 630 respondents in that sample, 89% disagree with the idea of banning political parties but, like their partisan counterparts, there is a substantial share of about 21 % who support such a ban.

Examining the origins of these attitudes reveals a few familiar patterns (see Table 9.5): Negative partisan identity significantly fosters support for banning certain political parties, even among independents who lack a positive partisan attachment. The increase is substantial, from 0.18 at the weakest levels of negative partisan identity to 0.37 at its strongest levels. This is an interesting finding that corroborates the results from the United States, the Netherlands, and Italy where only negative partisanship increased support for a ban. Similarly, older independent voters tend to be less in favor of a ban, as do unaffiliated voters with strong political opinions.

In sum, these analyses provide an important insight: Many of the alarming attitudes that we associate with democratic backsliding are exclusively associated with negative partisanship. This should affect how we evaluate positive partisanship and its impact on healthy democratic behavior. Admittedly, some of these attitudes are related to both positive and negative partisanship. However, their combined effects suggest that positive partisanship on its own is not the main driver of out-party hostility and violence. Even in cases where both positive and negative partisanship foster undemocratic attitudes, negative partisanship frequently appeared to be a much stronger influence. Indeed, in some cases, positive partisanship reduces the chance of endorsing an anti-democratic attitude. Thus, it is pivotal to explore strategies that can promote positive partisanship without promoting negative partisanship – a topic that I will investigate in Chapter 10.

TABLE 9.5 *Banning political parties, independents*

	Banning Political Parties
Negative partisan identity	0.19***
	(0.05)
Ideology	−0.12
	(0.07)
Issue intensity	−0.12**
	(0.06)
Religiosity	0.03
	(0.04)
Age	−0.02***
	(0.01)
Gender	−0.01
	(0.03)
White	0.01
	(0.03)
Education	−0.05
	(0.06)
Constant	0.42***
	(0.06)
Observations	592
R-squared	0.05

Note: Results are obtained from an OLS regression. All variables are scaled to range from 0 to 1, except for age, which is measured in decades. Standard errors in parentheses *** $p < 0.01$, ** $p < 0.05$, * $p < 0.1$

9.7 SUMMARY

In this chapter, I provided evidence that positive and negative partisanship have distinctive effects on anti-democratic attitudes. While strong positive partisanship is frequently blamed for disdain and hostility between partisans, my analyses reveal that positive partisanship, in some cases, can strengthen the commitment to democratic norms. Many of the disconcerting attitudes we see in contemporary politics, such as the desire to harm politicians or even ban political parties for their beliefs, are more strongly and more consistently related to negative partisanship while perceiving the opposition as good-hearted – despite political disagreements – is significantly related to strong positive partisanship. Thus, it is the disdain for the opposing party, rather than the fierce embrace of the in-party, that presents a challenge to the core values of democratic society.

10

Reconciling Partisanship and Democracy

10.1 WHAT IS IN THIS CHAPTER?

In this chapter, I aim to repartconcile partisanship with the ideals of democratic citizenship. For this endeavor, I create and test three interventions that aim to dampen negative partisanship without diminishing positive partisanship: First, I investigate the impact of cross-cutting identities that make partisans aware of differences among supporters within their party as well as similarities between parties and their supporters. Second, I examine the impact of shared identities that can unify partisans and decrease inter-partisan hostility. Third, I explore the role of party elites in fostering positive relationships between their supporters and partisans of the opposition. I test these predictions with experimental data collected in the United States. The results emphasize the extraordinary power of party elites in curbing negative partisanship. I conclude the chapter with a reflection on the responsibility of party elites to practice civility in their rhetoric and interactions with their opponents.

10.2 WHY IS THIS IMPORTANT?

Political parties are inevitable in mass democracies. As long as there are political parties, there will be partisanship. Yet partisanship is not just a "necessary evil." As demonstrated throughout this book, positive partisanship promotes a range of healthy democratic behaviors such as voting and even more effortful forms of political engagement. From this perspective, it seems futile to contemplate a future without party loyalties. Instead, I suggest shifting our attention to the development and implementation of strategies that can diminish negative partisanship without sacrificing positive partisanship and its beneficial effects on political participation. As I will show in this chapter, party elites are an integral part of these strategies. For partisans, this means holding those in power accountable when they forego civility for political gains.

***

The previous chapters identified and distinguished the effects of positive and negative partisanship on democratic and anti-democratic political attitudes and behavior. However, ideally, scholarship goes beyond mere assessment of the problem; it must also aim to find solutions for the escalating partisan hostility, animosity, and violence in the United States and beyond. In the following, I will review three approaches that have shown exceptional promise in this endeavor, including priming cross-cutting identities, shared identities, and positive interactions between party elites. The three corresponding experimental interventions I test in this chapter are adapted from preexisting studies; but to each study I add the positive and negative partisan identity scale as dependent variables. By doing so, I can examine if and how PPID and NPID are affected by each intervention. The ideal intervention promotes positive partisanship without intensifying negative partisanship or, alternatively, reduces negative partisanship without diminishing positive partisanship. These two scenarios create partisans that are deeply attached to their political party and are politically active on its behalf without degrading or dehumanizing their opponents.

In the remainder of this chapter, I will introduce the reader to the prior scholarship that developed promising interventions to reduce partisan animus in the United States. I then provide a detailed description of how I adapted each intervention for the experiments presented in this chapter. For each experiment, I critically assess why an intervention did or did not turn out to be successful in promoting positive partisanship and/or reducing negative partisanship.

10.3 REDUCING PARTISAN ANIMUS

One promising strategy includes correcting misperceptions about supporters of the out-party. Despite stereotypical beliefs, the demographic profile of Democrats and Republicans is surprisingly similar: Most supporters of the Democratic and the Republican Party are White, middle-aged Christians, and yet most people think of the two parties' composition as complete opposites: Democrats are young, live in cities, and belong predominantly to racial and ethnic minorities, while the image of Republicans is embodied by older, wealthy, evangelical Christians (Iyengar et al. 2019). Partisans rely on these stereotypes and thus tend to underestimate the share of identities that cut across both partisan groups. Political scientists Ahler and Sood (2018) investigate the pervasiveness of these partisan stereotypes, showing that, on average, respondents overestimate their prevalence by a whopping 342%! These results are important because they suggest that the distorted, rather than real, image of the opposing party's members might be the source of much partisan animus. Indeed, Ahler and Sood find that when these biases are corrected levels of partisan hostility decrease.

Another fruitful approach examines the role of commonly held identities in bridging the affective gap between partisans. In the case of Democrats and Republicans, the one identity that they objectively share is being American. In a natural experiment, which leverages the 4th of July holiday, Levendusky (2018) tests and finds evidence for the prediction that highlighting partisans' shared American identity significantly reduces the disdain between them. Indeed, partisans with a primed American identity were 25% less likely to rate the other party negatively (i.e., at 0 degrees on a 0–100 feeling thermometer scale), and 35% more likely to rate the other party more positively (i.e., at 50 degrees or higher). These results are encouraging because they build on a readily available, common identity. As Iyengar and colleagues (2019) aptly put it: "When we bring forward what unites Democrats and Republicans, rather than emphasizing what divides and differentiates them, partisan animus subsides" (p. 140).

Finally, an emerging string of research investigates the role of party leaders in reducing hostility between their supporters. In the context of Social Identity Theory, Hogg and colleagues, fittingly, coined the term "identity entrepreneurs" to refer to group leaders and their power to define and shape the group's identity, including its relation to out-groups. Applied to political parties, this means that leaders are influential in shaping norms for how partisans are expected to behave toward friends and foes (Hogg and van Knippenberg 2003) through their rhetoric and interactions with opposition leaders. Thus, party leaders have the power to lessen or intensify partisan animosity.

In a recent experimental study, Huddy and Yair (2021) test this prediction, arguing that "negative rhetoric, insults, threats, and hostile actions between leaders of rival parties very likely intensify affective polarization whereas polite rhetoric and warm relations can reduce it ... leaders are especially effective in establishing the tone of intergroup relations because they have the authority to act on behalf of their group. In that sense, the creation of positive relations between leaders is a form of extended contact" (p. 294, see also Hogg et al. 2012). The authors find evidence in support of their prediction, showing that the portrayal of friendly interactions between a Democratic and a Republican party leader significantly reduces Democrats' animosity toward Republicans and vice versa, more so than a policy compromise between the two party leaders. These results relate to other important work (Druckman et al. 2019) that emphasizes the role of civility in partisan media as an effective way to reduce partisan hostility.

Overall, prior scholarship suggests that these three interventions have the potential to reduce partisan animosity.[1] Thus, In the following experiments,

---

[1] Another promising intervention encourages face-to-face conversations between Democrats and Republicans. Based on insights from Intergroup Contact Theory (Pettigrew and Tropp 2011), Santoro and Broockman (2022) test the hypothesis that constructive interpersonal

I will include adaptations of these interventions and examine their direct impact on positive and negative partisanship. First, I consider the role of identities that cut across partisan groups and thus highlight intra-party differences and inter-party similarities. Second, I examine the role of identities that are shared by and thus unite partisan groups. Third, I explore the role of party leaders in setting an example of positive relations with the out-party. I aim to identify the intervention that can either foster positive partisanship without promoting negative partisanship or reduce negative partisanship without diminishing positive partisanship.

10.4 INTERVENTION #1: CROSS-CUTTING IDENTITIES

In the United States, being a Democrat or a Republican conveys more than just ideology and political issue preferences. Partisanship is linked to a number of other social identities such as religion (Layman 1997, 2001), race (Krupnikov and Piston 2014; Mangum 2013), sexual orientation (Kiley and Maniam 2016), and even dietary choices (Mosier and Rimal 2020). When partisanship becomes intertwined with other meaningful social identities, partisans do not just differ in terms of their party affiliation but also in terms of the many other social group memberships that are encompassed by it, turning partisanship into an umbrella identity. This alignment of identities along partisan lines makes Democrats and Republicans appear more similar within their respective party and, at the same time, diametrically opposed to each other – with severe consequences for the relations between partisan groups.

First, partisans overestimate the difference between the two parties, while also overestimating the degree of similarity among members of their own party (Ahler and Sood 2018; see also Brewer and Pierce 2005). These exaggerated inter-party differences and intra-party similarities can lead to more intolerance and hostility across party lines (Mason 2016; Roccas and Brewer 2002). Such effects are plausible: When partisanship encompasses multiple other key identities, then a threat to the party is a threat to all of them, thereby

conversation can humanize members of the opposing party and thus reduce partisan hostility. Notably, the authors emphasize the importance of conversation topics that are more likely to promote agreement rather than disagreement between partisans. Their study finds that "cross-partisan conversations ... can dramatically reduce affective polarization and boost ... the perception that the outparty respects members of the inparty. The reductions in affective polarization we found were substantively quite large, reversing approximately two decades worth of increases" (p. 6). While these improvements are substantial, the authors also show that they are not permanent, and instead, decay within three months without repeated cross-partisan interactions. Given that this intervention involves interpersonal interactions that are difficult to replicate in a survey experiment, I do not test it in this chapter.

Beyond Partisanship

We hear a lot these days about how Democrats and Republicans differ from each other in their values, ideologies, and lifestyle. However, many of these differences are vastly overestimated. In a recent survey, researchers found that American voters misperceive who Democrats and Republicans actually are:

Respondents thought that 39% of Democrats belonged to a labor union—**only 10% do**. Even more egregiously, they estimated that 38% of Republicans earned over $250,000 per year when **just 2% of GOP supporters** do.

Respondents also thought that the share of Democrats who are gay, lesbian, or bisexual was roughly five times greater than it actually is (**it's 6%**). Similarly, respondents assumed that 29% of Democrats are atheists or agnostic when, in fact, **only 9% are.** When it comes to race, respondents thought that 50% of the Democrats identify as Black when, again, **only 24% do**.

On the Republican side, we see similar misperceptions: Respondents overestimated the share of evangelicals among Republicans (**it is 33%**, not - as assumed by respondents - 45%). Only **20% of Republicans** are older than 65; respondents assumed the number was 41%. Last, respondents guessed that 45% of Republicans are Southerners while the number, in reality, is **35%.**

FIGURE 10.1 Experimental treatment to correct partisan biases
Note: Percentages were taken from Ahler and Sood (2018).

intensifying the perceived social distance and animosity between partisan groups. While this might be a relatively new phenomenon in US politics, even early research on American political behavior showed that partisans are only weakly attached to their party if their other social group memberships – such as religion or race – conflict with their party identification (Campbell et al. 1960).

Given these predictions on identity alignment as well as the aforementioned work on partisan stereotypes (Ahler and Sood 2018), I expect that highlighting differences within the in-party and the out-party will decrease negative partisanship since it diminishes the perception that the Democratic and Republican Party are two uniform blocks that diametrically oppose each other. Breaking this perception of "they are all the same and all different from us" makes the opposing party's members feel less distant and less threatening to the in-party. This very same mechanism, however, can also reduce positive partisanship: As partisans learn that they might have less in common with their fellow in-party members – who, in turn, might even share characteristics with the out-party – their party attachments carry less meaning to the self and thus might become weaker.

TABLE 10.1 Levels of PPID and NPID in partisan bias experiment

	Treatment	Control	P-Value of difference
NPID	0.40 (N = 297)	0.44 (N = 314)	0.03
PPID	0.41 (N = 291)	0.44 (N = 304)	0.06

Note: P-values are obtained through a one-tailed significance test.

To test these predictions, I implement an experiment that randomly assigns information about the prevalence of partisan biases and their corrections taken from Ahler and Sood (2018). Ultimately, this experimental intervention is supposed to weaken the perception of uniform demographic profiles among members of the in-party and the out-party (see Figure 10.1). Respondents in the treatment group (T) receive this information and are subsequently asked to answer the items of the PPID and NPID scale. Respondents in the control group (C), skip the information sheet and go directly to the PPID and NPID scales. By comparing the respondents in the control group to the respondents in the treatment group, I can identify the effect of correcting partisan biases on PPID and NPID.

For this first experiment, I utilize a sample of 1,007 American respondents[2] collected in February 2022 by Bovitz, Inc. The sample reflects the US population in terms of age, gender, race, and census region (see Table A1 in the Appendix). For ease of comparability, all variables are scaled to range from 0 to 1.

10.4.1 Analyses

I first examine the overall values of positive and negative partisanship across the treatment and control group (see Table 10.1). As predicted, negative partisanship is significantly lower in the treatment group compared to the control group (p < 0.03). These results are consistent with Ahler and Sood (2018) who find that correcting partisan biases lowers partisan hostility. At the same time, positive partisanship is significantly lower in the treatment group than in the control group (p < 0.06). This aligns with my second prediction that introducing intra-party heterogeneity can also weaken party attachments since they are no longer bolstered and reinforced by other social identities.

To see whether these patterns are identical for Democrats and Republicans, I next examine levels of positive and negative partisanship

---

[2] Only a share of them were assigned to the experiment to avoid contagion effects across studies.

TABLE 10.2 Levels of PPID and NPID in partisan bias experiment, by party

	Treatment	Control	P-Value of Difference
PPID Republicans	0.42 (N = 149)	0.44 (N = 157)	0.77
PPID Democrats	0.38 (N = 142)	0.43 (N = 147)	0.08
NPID Republicans	0.42 (N = 149)	0.44 (N = 157)	0.77
NPID Democrats	0.39 (N = 148)	0.42 (N = 157)	0.09

Note: P-values are obtained through a one-tailed significance test.

separately for these two partisan groups. I indeed find evidence for asymmetrical effects (see Table 10.2): While Republicans' positive party attachments do not differ across treatment and control, positive partisanship among Democrats is significantly lower in the treatment group than in the control group ($p < 0.08$), suggesting that it is the change in PPID among Democrats that drives the differences in overall PPID levels. The opposite pattern applies to NPID levels: While Democrats' negative partisanship toward Republicans remains somewhat unaffected by the treatment, it is Republicans' negative partisanship toward Democrats that is significantly lower ($p < 0.09$) after correcting their partisan biases. In other words, the intervention worked ideally among Republicans: It lowered their levels of negative partisanship toward Democrats while, at the same, time, leaving their levels of positive partisanship unaffected. Among Democrats, the intervention had the exact opposite effects: It lowered their levels of positive partisanship but left their levels of negative partisanship toward the Republican Party unaffected.

The significant reduction in PPID among Democrats suggests that the party's identity might be much more wrapped up in other social identities such as race and sexual orientation than the Republican Party's identity. Thus, disentangling the Democratic Party's identity from these other social groups might affect Democratic partisans more than their Republican counterparts.

From this perspective, the treatment might have been more powerful among Democrats because it affected a higher number of relevant identities. To test this possible explanation, I examine the PPID and NPID values of Black Democrats who might have been particularly affected by the treatment since it emphasized the relatively low number of Democrats who identify as Black. While their sample size is very small ($N = 58$), Black Democrats' positive partisanship is lower in the treatment group (0.39 versus 0.47, $p < 0.09$) compared to the control group – a change that is somewhat more pronounced than among White Democrats. Notably, Black Democrats' negative partisanship toward Republicans is significantly weaker in the treatment group than in the control group (0.35 versus 0.47, $p < 0.02$) while there is no such decline among White Democrats in the treatment group.

Does the same mechanism apply to religious Republicans? Religion is arguably a central identity within the Republican Party. Since the treatment highlighted the relatively low number of evangelicals within the party, we would expect that positive partisanship among respondents who identify as protestant and evangelical Republicans is lower than among their nonreligious counterparts. Effectively, correcting the stereotype about religious Republicans should de-align the evangelical and Republican identity or at least weaken their connection. Indeed, evangelical Republicans' party attachments (i.e. PPID) are significantly lower after the treatment compared to their counterparts in the control group (0.38 versus 0.45, $p < 0.05$). At the same time, nonreligious Republican respondents in the treatment group display significantly higher levels of positive partisanship than their counterparts in the control group (0.49 versus 0.38, $p < 0.08$). Learning about the relatively small number of evangelicals among Republicans might have bolstered PPID among nonreligious Republicans in the treatment group. These heterogeneous treatment effects suggest that correcting partisan stereotypes might weaken the party attachments especially of those partisans whose other identities are wrapped up in their partisanship.

10.4.2 Discussion Study #1

In sum, the first study's results demonstrate that correcting misperceptions about the in- and out-party's demographic composition can have substantial effects on positive and negative partisanship. In this study, respondents in the treatment group learned about the exaggerated and the real share of partisans from different social groups in both their own party as well as the out-party. This process weakened positive attachments to the in-party as well as negative partisanship toward the opposing party, likely because it made both parties appear less aligned, or less sorted (Mason 2018), with partisans' other social groups. Yet the experiment has its limitations: The treatment rectifies stereotypes about both the in-party and the out-party that might explain why we see movements in both positive and negative partisanship. A future iteration of this study might distinguish between in-party and out-party stereotypes and, based on this setup, assign respondents to one of four conditions: correcting stereotypes about the in-party, correcting stereotypes about the out-party, correcting stereotypes about both the in-party and the out-party, and a control condition that can serve as a benchmark to estimate treatment effects on positive and negative partisanship.

Despite the study's inability to disentangle the effects of correcting in-party and out-party biases, its findings still have implications for real-world politics: Partisans are frequently exposed to rhetoric – both from party elites as well as the media – that imposes an "us" versus "them" perception and portrays both partisan groups as antithetical to each other. However, these socioeconomic differences relating to race, religion, and even sexual orientation are oftentimes vastly exaggerated, possibly for political gains. The media as well as party elites are especially equipped to correct these false and oversimplified narratives and to highlight the multitude of different Americans that can be found in both political parties – if they want to.

10.5 INTERVENTION #2: UNIFYING IDENTITIES

The second intervention focuses on the promotion of unifying identities that supporters of both parties have in common. In social psychology, the Common Ingroup Identity Model would predict that emphasizing such a shared identity can reduce partisan hostility by encouraging the recategorization of out-party members (Gaertner and Dovidio 2000; Gaertner et al. 1993) from a member of an out-group to a member of a shared in-group. This logic rests on the assumption that partisans are members of multiple social groups, and the challenge is to find one that unites members of the in- and out-party.

In the case of Democrats and Republicans, a viable candidate for such a common in-group identity is their national identity, being American. As Levendusky eloquently put it in his study: "They are fellow Americans, not members of an opposing political tribe" (2018, p. 61). Note that this mechanism is different from emphasizing cross-cutting identities in the earlier experiment. *Some* partisans might share an identity that cuts across both parties but *all partisans* in the sample share an American identity. By highlighting this unifying identity, partisan out-group members are being recategorized as a national in-group member, which ultimately lessens the hostility between partisans (see Tajfel and Wilkes 1963). I thus expect that priming Democrats and Republicans' shared American identity will reduce their negative partisanship toward each other.

What happens to positive partisanship when this unifying identity is made salient? There are two possible scenarios: First, positive partisanship remains unaffected since partisans' attachments to their party are compatible with their national identity. Making this identity more salient should thus not change anything about partisanship per se. Yet there is a second scenario in which partisans experience what social psychologists call "identity threat" (Branscombe et al. 1999; Ellemers et al. 2002) whereby partisans no longer feel that their own party is sufficiently distinct from the out-party due to the salient common national identity. Identity threat might thus weaken positive partisanship, but it can also lead to a backlash against the other partisan group if their credentials as "true" Americans are being challenged.

To test these predictions, I utilize a sample of 565 undergraduate students from a public university in the South which includes 47% Democrats and 49% Republicans, 60% women, and 74% White respondents. While this sample does not reflect the US adult population, it nevertheless is useful to test my predictions and their underlying causal mechanisms. The experiment includes a randomly assigned intervention that was designed by Levendusky (2018) for a study in which the author successfully demonstrates that priming American identity reduces antipathy toward the opposing side. The intervention includes a series of paragraphs on what makes America great, listing the country's advances in technology, economy, education, entertainment, etc. The following experiment builds on Levendusky's design but, crucially, it adds the measures of negative and positive partisanship. This addition allows me to examine to what extent positive and negative partisanship are differentially affected by priming American identity.

Respondents were randomly assigned to either the American identity prime or a control group in which respondents read an article about a cat library in New Mexico that was unrelated to their national or partisan identities. Figure 10.2 shows the complete treatment text on which respondents had to linger for at least 20 seconds before they could advance to the next page in the survey.

To strengthen the American identity prime, respondents in the treatment group were subsequently asked to express why they are proud to be an American and to state the most important reason they think other people like America. All respondents filled out an American identity scale that served as a manipulation check and included questions such as "How strongly do you identify as an American?," "How important is being an American to you?," and "How well does the term 'American' describe you?." These items were developed based on insights from Social Identity Theory (Tajfel and Turner 1979) and are frequently used to gauge American national identity (see Huddy and Khatib 2007). This manipulation check was followed by the two key variables of interest – the PPID and NPID scales – to see if and how these two types of partisanship are impacted by the American identity prime. For better comparability across analyses, all variables are scaled to range from 0 to 1.

10.5.1 Analyses

The first step in the analysis is to ensure that the treatment successfully primed American identity. To do so, I examine levels of American identity strength between respondents in the treatment and control group. If the intervention worked as expected, we should see significantly higher levels of American identity in the treatment group. The preliminary results align with these expectations: Respondents in the treatment group report significantly stronger attachments to their American identity than respondents in the control group (0.71 versus 0.68, $p < 0.05$).

America: What Makes It Great

The Declaration of Independence, whose signing we celebrate every July 4th, established America as one of the first representative democracies in the world. As we approach America's 246th year, let's reflect on some of the factors that continue to make America a great nation:

INNOVATION — Edison, Gates, Jobs: they and we are known for thinking outside the box. As a people, we create and innovate; we don't wait for others, then appropriate their creations. From search engines to social networks — Google, Yahoo, Twitter and Facebook — it all started here.

TECHNOLOGY — From cotton gin to light bulb, records to movies, rockets to the Internet, the gadgets and discoveries originating from the U.S. have changed the world, and continue to do so today.

DIVERSITY — "Give me your tired, your poor, your huddled masses yearning to breathe free..." So says the inscription on the Statue of Liberty in the middle of New York Harbor. We are a nation of immigrants whose spirit of hard work and desire for a better life have been a hallmark since the first settlers arrived here more than 400 years ago.

ECONOMY — Despite the spotlight on China and other Asian countries, the United States still possesses the world's richest economy and consumer base — larger than Japan, Germany, China and Great Britain combined. The economy of a single U.S. state-- California--would be among the top 10 economies in the world if it were a country.

ENTREPRENEURSHIP — The U.S., by far, has more self-made millionaires and billionaires proportionally than anywhere in the world.

EDUCATION — Over a million of students from everywhere in the world come here for their education, not the opposite.

ENTERTAINMENT — OK, we didn't invent classical music, but we created Dixieland, ragtime, jazz, swing, big band, bluegrass, Hawaiian, pop, rock 'n' roll, hip-hop, rap and even disco; then there's radio, television, movies, video games, hula hoops, Hollywood and Disneyland.

NATURAL BEAUTY — From the California coast, through the Rocky Mountains to the forests of Maine and Vermont, and including our national parks, we are a nation of contrasts, with two oceans, numerous lakes and rivers, gargantuan mountains, vast plains and spacious deserts, all with their individual charm.

GENEROSITY — Americans are the most generous nation in terms of donating to charities, both in total dollars given and total hours. No other nation has America's generosity of spirit and willingness to help their fellow community members.

FIGURE 10.2 Experimental treatment to prime American identity
Note: Treatment text is taken from Levendusky (2018) with slight modifications.

Next, I test whether levels of positive and negative partisanship differ across respondents in the treatment and the control group. A simple t-test reveals that there is no difference in positive partisan identity between respondents in the treatment and the control group (0.41 versus 0.41).

TABLE 10.3 PPID, NPID, and American identity

	(1) PPID	(2) NPID
Treatment	0.01 (0.028)	−0.02 (0.03)
American identity strength	−0.10 (0.04) **	0.10 (0.05) **
Treatment X American identity strength	−0.08 (0.07)	0.06 (0.07)
Constant	0.44 (0.01) ***	0.38 (0.02) ***
R-squared	0.03	0.02
N	537	537

Note: Results are obtained from an OLS regression. All variables are scaled to range from 0 to 1. Standard errors in parentheses*** $p < 0.01$, ** $p < 0.05$, * $p < 0.1$

I find similar null results for negative partisanship: While negative partisanship is slightly lower in the treatment group (0.39 versus 0.42), the difference is not statistically significant ($p < 0.24$). Thus, priming American identity did not affect levels of negative and positive partisanship. It is possible that the treatment's effect differs across the strength of respondents' American identity. To test for this possible heterogeneity, I interact the American identity value from the manipulation check with a dichotomous treatment variable that takes on the value of 1 for respondents who are in the treatment group and a value of 0 for respondents in the control group. I use this interaction and its individual components to predict levels of positive (PPID) and negative partisanship (NPID).

While the interaction of the treatment and American identity is insignificant in both models, preexisting strong American identity on its own (i.e. independently of the prime) is associated with weaker positive party attachments as indicated by its negative coefficient (see column 1 in Table 10.3). At the same time, it is also related to a slight increase in negative partisanship as suggested by its positive coefficient when predicting NPID (see column 2 in Table 10.3).

When examining PPID separately for Democrats and Republicans, I find that the negative effect of American identity is particularly pronounced among Republicans while there is no significant effect for Democrats. When examining NPID separately for Democrats and Republicans, I find diverging results for the effect of strong American identity; it is associated with a reduction in Republicans' negative partisanship toward the Democratic Party, but it strengthens Democrats' negative partisanship toward the Republican Party. Thus, among Republicans, a strong American identity might be more likely to foster the recategorization of Democrats, suggesting that, among Republicans, the treatment worked as expected: American identity is associated with the recategorization of Democrats from an out-group to an in-group – as predicted by the Common Ingroup Identity Model.

At the same time, American identity might exacerbate Democrats' negative partisanship toward the Republican Party – most likely because many Democrats associate the American identity with conservatism and the Republican Party. Indeed, some of the written responses of participants in the treatment group describe a dark side of being American:

I think Americans are so proud of their country because they are legitimately ignorant of the rest of the world . . .. If you have been stuck in a country all of your life, lived middle-upper class, and are not a minority, it is extremely easy to feel like the country has the innovation, beauty, and technology mentioned before. It is something to be proud of when it works for you. The question "what do you think is the most important reason people like America and are proud to be an American" sounds like it was written by a white man for white men. Ask this question to minorities and then ask it to white people and the answers will a whooooole [*sic*] lot different.

While all of those categories did list improvements made throughout the years and how successful our country is, the hardships and tragedy that had to happen to get where we are was not mentioned. If the poor working conditions, the continuing racial disparities, and selfishness in the business world were mentioned then those successes would not be as important.

Greed and ownership. Americans like having control and saying WE ARE THE BEST. We have the best parks, the best music, the. best population, the best innovation . . .. Also that article was hypocritical as heck. How can Americans say they HAVE the best when it wasn't theirs to start with. Beautiful parks = stolen from indigenous people. Best entertainment = stolen from minority populations after white people oppressed them so much that THEY HAD to form their own culture (and then we stole that too). "Best Innovation/technology: Facebook" = did mark Zuckerberg not steal the idea of Facebook from peers? Did he not then use Facebook to invade millions of people's privacy and spread false information, harboring a toxic community? We Americans do not have The Best, we have The Most and all the Best parts were stolen, not created nor earned.

Patriotism is a key reason. People want to be the best, but that is not always true, much like patriotism is not always productive. I would say I am not proud to be an American at this point. It's not that I'm embarrassed of it I simply don't believe it's anything particularly impressive to be bragging about.

I see America as having an abundance of flaws that other nations, namely other European nations don't have. We have a terrible healthcare system as well as having some of the largest wealth inequalities we've ever seen. We lack a system that cares for its laborers enough to even compensate them fairly. I think Americans who are proud of this country are too immersed in this idea that America is the greatest to see even the most basic of flaws within our governing system . . .. As of now, we live in a hypercapitalist state that favors the few. America isn't a great country unless you're rich and white.

Americans are proud of their country for two reasons: because it is their birthplace, and most people have a sense of adoration for their birthplace just because it was their first home, and because they haven't recognized the misfortunes and inhumanity that have come along with all the glory and power the US has cultivated since industrialization. I think once Americans learn about how the US and its people have stepped on other less fortunate populations in order to rise to the top, it gets harder to see the US as being this great caring nation with "southern hospitality" and good morals.

Given the strong emphasis on race in these responses, it is possible that the heterogeneity in the treatment's effects is not just related to partisanship but also to respondents' race. I thus examine levels of positive and negative partisanship for White Democrats and Republicans to control for race and to preserve sample size: Among both partisan groups, their positive partisanship remains unaffected by the treatment, suggesting that priming American identity does not impact the strength of positive partisan identity among White respondents. However, negative partisanship toward Republicans is higher in the treatment group than in the control group, indicating that White Democrats' disdain for Republicans is slightly exacerbated if their common American identity is highlighted (0.45 versus 0.40). While this difference does not reach conventional levels of statistical significance ($p < 0.12$), it is trending toward that direction despite the much smaller sample size ($N = 158$). Surprisingly, negative partisanship toward Democrats is affected in the exact opposite way whereby White Republicans' negative partisanship toward the Democrats is significantly lower when primed with their common American identity (0.37 versus 0.42; $p < 0.08$).

10.5.2 Discussion Study #2

Overall, these results provide insights into the differential effects of highlighting common identities. Evidently, it must be an identity that can truly be claimed by both sides for it to improve relations between partisans. In this case, priming American identity reduced negative partisanship toward Democrats among White Republicans, but it slightly exacerbated negative partisanship toward Republicans among White Democrats. Based on the written responses from several respondents, American identity has different connotations across party and racial groups. If being a proud American is considered a prerogative of the Republican Party, it might be challenging to develop an American identity prime that has uniformly positive effects. Klar (2018) provides experimental evidence for partisan differences in the internalization of another common in-group identity, namely gender. Relying on predictions from the Common In-Group Identity Model (CIIM), Klar (2018) shows that a common gender identity is not sufficient to reduce intergroup bias between Democratic and Republican women since "CIIM requires that members of both rival groups conceive of the superordinate group membership in the same terms" (p. 610) – a condition that is not always met among Democratic and Republicans women when they do not share a common understanding of what it means to be a woman. As a consequence – rather than bridging the partisan divide – increasing the salience of their common gender identity intensifies the mistrust between women from competing parties. From this perspective, it might not be too surprising that priming American identity differentially impacted Republicans and Democrats since "being American" simply has different meanings to them. This is an interesting finding that suggests that unifying identities are hard to come by, especially in a polarized political climate that affects social identities outside of politics. If this is the case for gender and nationality, it likely also applies to other identities like race, class, and religion. Indeed, the Pew Research Center finds that "Christian Republicans are about twice as likely as Christian Democrats to say their religion is 'the one true faith leading to eternal life in heaven' (40% vs. 21%), while Democrats are more likely to say that 'many religions can lead to eternal life in heaven' (65% vs. 53%)."[3] These partisan divisions among Americans of the same faith reiterates the difficulty of finding an identity that can truly unite partisans, rather than deepen their discord.

10.6 INTERVENTION #3: THE ROLE OF PARTY LEADERS

The third intervention focuses on the role of party leaders in shaping the relations between partisans. Research on intergroup leadership and collaboration has engendered a strong theoretical framework that can be used to study the impact of party leaders. Particularly relevant in this context is the notion of party leaders as identity entrepreneurs (Reicher and Hopkins 2003) who can shape the party's image and thus affect how partisans relate to their own party. For example, the Republicanization of the South (see Chapter 2) was partially driven by the inclusion of more White Southerners in the Republican leadership, thereby shaping the image of the Republican Party as a home for Southerners who might have felt alienated from the Democratic Party.

Yet a party's identity is not just defined by its own values, and beliefs but also by their relationship with other groups, including the opposing party. Party leaders have the power to sculpt this component of the party's identity – something that Hogg and colleagues (2012) refer to as an "intergroup relational identity" – through their rhetoric and behavior toward out-party leaders. In other words, The way in-party leaders choose to engage with out-party leaders – publicly or privately – influences how their partisans feel and behave toward members of the out-party and vice versa. From this perspective, this approach can be considered top-down since it starts with party leaders and examines their behaviors' downstream effects on their supporters' party attachments.

---

[3] Pew Research Center, Republicans more likely than Democrats to believe in heaven, say only their faith leads there, www.pewresearch.org/fact-tank/2021/11/23/republicans-more-likely-than-democrats-to-believe-in-heaven-say-only-their-faith-leads-there/ (last accessed December 11, 2022).

Huddy and Yair (2021) test this model, arguing that "partisan leaders can improve or worsen partisan animosity. Negative rhetoric, insults, threats, and hostile actions between leaders of rival parties very likely intensify affective polarization whereas polite rhetoric and warm relations can reduce it . . .. In that sense, the creation of positive relations between leaders is a form of extended contact. Party supporters develop warmer feelings toward an out-party because they witness warm relations among, and mutual respect between, party leaders" (p. 8). To test one of their predictions,[4] the authors create three different experimental groups: one that portray warm relations between party leaders Schumer (a Democrat) and McConnell (a Republican), one that portrays hostile relations, and a control group that omits any details about the nature of the relationship. In the "warm relations" condition, respondents read a short paragraph about a pleasant encounter between the two party leaders; in the "hostile relations" condition, the interaction between them is described as argumentative and uncivil. Huddy and Yair find that the tenor of the interaction between the two leaders matters: Warm relations between rival partisan leaders significantly increased positive ratings of the out-party while hostile relations led to lower ratings of the out-party – regardless of whether party leaders were described as agreeing on policy issues or not. Notably, ratings of the in-party remain unaffected by the depiction of warm or cold relations between the two leaders.

If these in-party and out-party ratings are indicative of positive and negative partisanship, then I expect that friendly and civil relations between party leaders should decrease levels of negative partisanship toward the opposing party while hostile relations should exacerbate them. Positive partisanship, on the other hand, should remain unaffected by either portrayal. To test these predictions, I create a simplified version of the experiment by Huddy and Yair that includes only the random manipulation of the social relations between the two senate party leaders, McConnell and Schumer. The description of the leaders' warm or cold encounter is shown in Figures 10.3 and 10.4. To create a harder test, all conditions suggest disagreement between Democrats and Republicans on key policies such as immigration and climate change. This design feature resembles more closely the current gridlock on these issues in the real world and prevents respondents from assuming that warm relations between the party leaders are indicative of policy agreement between the parties.

Once again, I utilize a sample of 546 undergraduate students from a public university in the South. The sample consisted of 47% Democrats and

---

[4] The authors' experiment is designed to test and differentiate the effects of positive and negative social contact between leaders, on one hand, and policy issue compromise (or its absence), on the other. In the context of this study, I focus only on the social aspect of interparty relations.

Democratic and Republican Senators seen at a local DC restaurant

You can't escape politics in Washington D.C., not even over dinner. This was made clear to diners eating at a well-known DC restaurant this past weekend. Senator Chuck Schumer (D-NY), the Democratic majority leader, was seen dining and laughing with Republican Senate minority leader Mitch McConnell (R-KY).

The two men looked very happy together and parted with a hug.

Their fellow diners were surprised by the degree of public warmth shown by the two senators whose parties in Congress have been fighting fierce battles over many important policies, including immigration, infrastructure, and climate change.

FIGURE 10.3 Experimental treatment "warm relations"
Note: Taken from Huddy and Yair (2021) with slight modifications.

Democratic and Republican Senators seen at a local DC restaurant

You can't escape politics in Washington D.C., not even over dinner. This was made clear to diners eating at a well-known DC restaurant this past weekend. Senator Chuck Schumer (D-NY), the Democratic majority leader, was heard arguing loudly with Republican Senate minority leader Mitch McConnell (R-KY).

The two men looked extremely angry and left each other shaking their heads and muttering to themselves.

Their fellow diners were surprised by the degree of public hostility shown by the two senators whose parties in Congress have been fighting fierce battles over many important policies, including immigration, infrastructure, and climate change.

FIGURE 10.4 Experimental treatment "cold relations"
Note: Taken from Huddy and Yair (2021) with slight modifications.

47 % Republicans, 62% women, and 73% White respondents. Participants were randomly assigned to either the warm relations conditions, the cold relations conditions, or the control group with no information about the nature of the hypothetical encounter between Senators Mitch McConnell and Chuck Schumer. As a manipulation check, respondents were subsequently asked to rate the two party leaders on a scale from 0 to 100, followed by the PPID and NPID scales. For better comparability across analyses, I rescale all variables to range from 0 to 1.

10.6.1 Analyses

First, I examine the feeling thermometer values for the two party leaders across conditions (see Table 10.4). If the treatment was successful, we should find significantly higher values for the opposing party's leader in the "warm relations" condition, compared to the "cold relations" conditions and the control group. Indeed, the feeling thermometer values for the respective out-party leader in the "warm relations" condition and the "cold relations" condition are significantly different from each other ($p < 0.001$). In the "warm relations" condition, Republicans assign a feeling thermometer value to Democratic Party leader Chuck Schumer that is significantly higher than in the "cold relations" condition (0.36 versus 0.21). The same is true for the values that Democratic respondents assign to Republican leader Mitch McConnell in the "warm relations" and "cold relations" condition (0.26 versus 0.18).

When using the control group as a baseline for comparison, the feeling thermometer values for both party leaders are significantly lower in the "cold relations" condition, compared to the control group ($p < 0.01$). However, there is no significant difference between the feeling thermometer values assigned to the out-party leaders in the "warm relations" condition and in the control condition, suggesting that the treatment worked only partially; while the portrayal of hostile leader relations led to more negative affect toward the out-party leader, friendly relations seemed to exert no effect, compared to the control.

Next, I test whether these affective assessments of out-party leaders also correspond to changes in respondents' positive and negative partisanship. I find no significant impact on positive party attachments (see column 1 in

TABLE 10.4 Manipulation check, party leaders experiment

	Warm relations	Cold relations	Control
FT Schumer among Republicans	0.36 (N = 87)	0.21 (N = 83)	0.36 (N = 82)
FT McConnell among Democrats	0.26 (N = 87)	0.18 (N = 80)	0.25 (N = 83)

TABLE 10.5 PPID, NPID, and party leaders

	PPID	NPID	PPID Republicans	PPID Democrats	NPID Democrats	NPID Republicans
Warm relations	0.40 (N = 178)	0.36 (N = 178)	0.41 (N = 87)	0.39 (N = 91)	0.33 (N = 87)	0.38 (N = 91)
Cold relations	0.39 (N = 163)	0.48 (N = 163)	0.43 (N = 83)	0.35 (N = 80)	0.46 (N = 84)	0.50 (N = 80)
Control condition	0.42 (N = 167)	0.41 (N = 166)	0.45 (N = 83)	0.38 (N = 84)	0.36 (N = 82)	0.45 (N = 84)

Table 10.5). The PPID values remain almost identical across all three conditions, rendering any comparison between the "warm"/"cold" conditions and the control condition statistically insignificant. This null finding suggests that positive relations between party leaders do not seem to impact partisans' attachments to their own party. On the other hand, negative partisanship is significantly lower in the "warm relations" conditions compared to the control (0.36 versus 0.41, p < 0.05), suggesting that the friendly encounter between the two party leaders has the desired impact of lowering negative partisanship. The exact opposite pattern emerges for the "negative relations" conditions: Here, levels of negative partisanship are significantly higher compared to the control (0.48 versus 0.41, p < 0.001). These effects highlight the power of party leaders in shaping negative partisanship; their hostile rhetoric and behavior toward the other side is being mirrored by their partisans.

I subset the analysis to examine whether these effects are similar for both Democrats and Republicans. Consistent with prior results, there are no significant differences in positive party attachments across conditions, neither for Democrats nor for Republicans. The main effects are concentrated in the levels of negative partisanship: While Republicans' negative partisanship toward Democrats in the "warm relations" condition is not significantly different from its the value in the control condition (0.32 versus 0.36), their negative partisanship in the "cold relation" condition is significantly higher than in the control condition (0.46 versus 0.36, p < 0.001). Thus, the depiction of hostile relations between their in-party leader McConnell and Democratic out-party leader Chuck Schumer impacted Republican respondents and heightened their negative partisanship toward Democrats.

A slightly different pattern can be found among Democrats. Their negative partisanship toward Republicans is significantly lower in the "warm relations" condition compared to the control condition (0.38 versus 0.45, p < 0.001), suggesting that positive interactions between party leaders *can* lower negative partisanship. Similar to their Republican counterparts, Democrats' negative partisanship toward Republicans is significantly higher in the "cold relations" condition, compared to the control condition (0.50 versus 0.45, p < 0.08). Thus, Democrats also show higher levels of negative partisanship after being exposed to a hostile encounter between their in-party leader Chuck Schumer and Republican out-party leader Mitch McConnell.

Taken together, these results strongly support the notion that relations between party leaders can be a two-way street when it comes to shaping relations between their supporters. Leaders can exacerbate or ameliorate negative partisanship toward the opposing party and its members – a finding that highlights party leaders' responsibility to set a good example for their supporters when interacting with their colleagues of the opposite aisle.

10.6.2 Discussion Study #3

As American politics has become polarized, party leaders have also been more willing to publicly demonize and humiliate the opposition's party leaders. There is no shortage of examples in America's contemporary political discourse, such as former President Trump's repeated references to Democratic Senator Elizabeth Warren as "Pocahontas" or his description of House Majority Leader Nancy Pelosi as a "nasty, vindictive, horrible person" but also Democratic Representative Rashida Tlaib's remark about her intention to "impeach the motherf—er!" (referring to President Trump when he was still in office). Equally hostile are recent comments by Republican Representative Matt Gaetz who publicly stated that abortion rights protesters "are just disgusting" and "odious from the inside out." Indeed, there is evidence that that violent rhetoric in American politics is growing on both sides of the aisle and that it poisons the political discourse long term. As Daniel Byman (2021) from the Brookings Institution astutely observed: "Part of the problem is that leaders' remarks do not fade away after they are given. Incendiary rhetoric from political leaders against their political opponents, minority groups, and other targets is often quickly magnified. Leaders with large social media followings will see their remarks retweeted and otherwise shared with millions of followers. Leaders' rhetoric then drives the coverage of more traditional news outlets, which broadcast it to their viewers and listeners."

This magnifying effect also exacerbates the so-called incivility spiral (Andersson and Pearson 1999) whereby those who experience rudeness from the other side are likely to respond in kind, perpetuating the vicious cycle. This repeated, hostile exchange can reach a tipping point where it escalates into violence. From this perspective, a crude remark or even just a Tweet can set this spiral into motion and "incur aggressive retaliation and undermine diplomatic relations – and put citizens everywhere off politics altogether" (Irwin 2018).

At the same time, a single friendly interaction between party leaders might do little to improve the current climate of partisan animosity. As the experiment here showed, the depiction of warm relations between the two party leaders did not reduce negative partisanship in this experiment, raising the question of whether partisans even register courteous behavior between party leaders. Hogg and colleagues (2012) acknowledge this difficulty and note that the creation of a positive intergroup relational identity cannot be instantaneous (p. 242). It takes time and repeated exposure to courteous and civil interactions between party leaders to change norms and expectations among their supporters, especially when resentment and distrust run deep.

10.7 SUMMARY

With the help of prior scholarship, I implemented three distinct experiments to investigate the effect of cross-cutting identities, unifying identities, and party elite rhetoric on levels of negative and positive partisanship. Each intervention produced unique outcomes: Priming cross-cutting identities weakened positive and negative partisanship; highlighting a unifying identity – being American did not seem to impact levels of positive and negative partisanship, though there were a few interesting partisan differences in the relationship between American identity strength and positive/negative partisan identity strength. Last, relations between party leaders can significantly heighten levels of negative partisanship if party elites choose to engage in an openly hostile and aggressive manner with each other. Taken together, these results also suggest that negative partisanship is slightly more malleable than positive partisanship, which might make strategies to reduce negative partisanship more attainable.

11

Future Outlook

11.1 WHAT IS IN THIS CHAPTER?

Scholarship on partisanship has been transformed by the integration of social and cognitive psychology over the past few decades. Since then, the concept of partisan identity has become widely known beyond the narrow subfield of political psychology. Indeed, the sheer volume of research on the origins, measurement, and effect of partisan identity on political behavior is indicative of its centrality in the general discipline of political science. This book pays tribute to the pioneering past and present scholarship on partisanship.

In this final chapter, I sketch out a few thoughts and suggestions on the complexities and caveats of current research on partisanship as well as possible avenues for future research, including a plea for more research on the interaction of partisanship with other identities, the necessity of studying partisanship in more externally valid contexts, the pitfalls of unifying identities, and the power of party leaders in bridging partisan divisions. I title these suggestions "A Closer Look at . . ." because none of the research avenues I sketch out here are entirely new. Yet I believe that revisiting some of them can significantly advance our understanding of partisanship.

SUGGESTION #1: A CLOSER LOOK AT EXPRESSIVE AND INSTRUMENTAL PARTISANSHIP, AND THEIR INTERPLAY

As I have argued throughout this book, partisanship originates in a mix of both expressive and instrumental factors. More research is needed to assess this claim, not just among different groups of voters across age, personality traits (see Arceneaux and Vander Wielen 2013; Lavine, Johnston, and Steenbergen 2012), political sophistication, ideological orientation, and intensity but also across different political systems. The analyses in Chapters 8 and 9 underscored that point: Among European partisans, the predictive power of instrumental factors was significantly stronger than among partisans in the United States. Multi-party systems might be more prone to instrumental considerations like ideology since it is a salient political dimension that helps voters categorize political parties and coalition blocs (see Bankert, Del Ponte, and Huddy 2017; Huddy, Davis, and Bankert 2018), while salient political issues might help voters distinguish between political parties of the same ideological bloc. From this perspective, these instrumental facets of partisanship might be as powerful in predicting political behavior as their expressive counterparts. Rather than asking which model is "correct," political scientists should investigate the conditions under which each model is more applicable. This type of work requires bridging the gap between individual-level political psychology work on the one hand, and scholarship on political institutions on the other – a challenging task both from a theoretical and methodological standpoint but nevertheless a fruitful one that could answer many questions about the contextual factors that drive expressive and instrumental partisanship and their interplay. In this endeavor, scholars could focus on a range of institutional factors, including the number and ideological distinctiveness of political parties, the voting system, the campaign finance laws, the regulation and distribution of public and private media ownership, and the length of the campaign cycle.

SUGGESTION #2: A CLOSER LOOK AT SOCIAL AND POLITICAL POLARIZATION AND THEIR INTERPLAY

The conceptual difference between instrumental and expressive partisanship has been particularly beneficial for the study of polarization in the United States and beyond (e.g., Ivengar and Westwood 2015; Mason 2016). Expressive and instrumental partisanship correspond almost directly to the crucial distinction between social and political polarization. While the latter assumes polarization along politically substantive divisions such as ideology and policy position, the former can be independent of these instrumental concerns and foster in-party favoritism and out-party disdain despite agreement on substantive policies (Mason 2015). Put differently, social and political polarization are distinct phenomena that can – but do not necessarily – occur together. While a large share of research has been dedicated to figuring out whether partisans are socially or politically polarized, I think it is once again important to give credence to both models and to develop strategies that can reduce partisan hostility – caused either by social or political polarization. This is an important step forward since different sources of polarization also demand different solutions. This is a lesson we learned especially during the COVID-19 pandemic: Partisanship played a particularly prominent role in shaping reactions to the pandemic, mask mandates, as well as social distancing and vaccine requirements (e.g., Druckman et al. 2020; Gadarian et al. 2021; Grossman et al. 2020; Pickup et al. 2020). In fact, some studies show that, in the United States, partisanship was the most consistent predictor of people's attitudes toward COVID-19–related health attitudes and behaviors (Gadarian et al. 2021) than any other demographic factor such as age, race, and education.

Yet health care is not the only area affected by partisanship. There is now a large body of literature that documents the impact of partisanship on less political attitudes such as food (Mosier and Rimal 2020), investor decisions (Cookson et al. 2020), consumer decisions (Endres et al. 2020; Panagopoulos et al. 2020), and even roommate selection (Shafranek 2021). Clearly, partisanship has expanded beyond the political realm and infiltrated people's social and economic life. It is thus important to understand the nature of polarization as well as its origins. I think more work is needed to assess the relationship between political and social polarization. When does political polarization lead to social polarization? Can social polarization lead to political polarization and if so, under what conditions? More research on the (dis-) alignment of social and political polarization could be useful to answer these questions and to develop solutions for them.

SUGGESTION #3: A CLOSER LOOK AT INDEPENDENT IDENTITY

In this book, I have shown that even among independent voters without any prior positive party attachments, negative partisan identity has a significant effect on their political participation as well as political attitudes. In those analyses, I treated independents as an expression of a negative identity. However, being an independent could also be a positive identity if it is grounded in voters' self-image as an unbiased and objective participant in politics. Future research can examine this prediction by adapting the partisan identity scale accordingly with items such as "I have a lot in common with other independents" or "When I speak about independents, I say 'we' versus 'them.'" With this positive independent identity scale, it would be possible to distinguish between "independent" as a negative identity (like in this book) and "independent" as a positive identity. It is likely that we find both versions of such an independent identity among unaffiliated voters. It would be interesting to assess their prevalence as well as their possibly differential effects on political behavior. This type of research, ideally, extends beyond the US two-party system and investigates other established democracies that have been struggling with declining levels of partisanship.

SUGGESTION #4: THE (DE-)ALIGNMENT OF POSITIVE AND NEGATIVE PARTISANSHIP

It is important to understand the conditions that foster the alignment and dealignment of negative and positive partisanship. Such an endeavor most likely includes studying partisanship over the course of several election cycles to see how the fervor of election campaigns might activate negative and positive partisanship. For example, following the aftermath of an election, we might observe higher levels of positive partisanship among the victorious partisans and higher levels of negative partisanship among the losing ones. I find some empirical evidence for that prediction in one of my prior studies: In the 2016 US presidential elections, Democrats' vote for Hillary Clinton was mostly driven by their strong positive attachment to the Democratic Party while Republicans' vote for Trump was influenced by Republicans' strong in-party attachments as well as their negative partisanship toward the Democratic Party. However, I find a reversed pattern for the vote choice in the 2018 US House election in which Democrats' decision to vote for a Democratic candidate was first and foremost driven by their opposition to the Republican Party. These results suggest that the power of negative and positive partisanship is not static but rather influenced by fluctuating factors such as party's status and power but also conflicts within the party. The latter can be found in both the Republican and Democratic Party as they struggle to identify the party's future leadership and ideological direction. These contemporary developments can serve as real-world case studies to examine how positive and negative partisanship wax and wane over time.

SUGGESTIONS #5: NEGATIVE PARTISANSHIP IN MULTI-PARTY SYSTEMS

The development of negative partisanship in multi-party systems requires more attention than I have been able to give within the constraints of this book. As I point out in various sections, partisans might develop negative partisanship toward several parties on the opposing end of the ideological spectrum. At the same time, even parties from the same ideological camp could be considered out-parties if they pose a threat to the electoral success of the in-party. Thus, ideological (dis-)similarity is not necessarily the only predictor of positive and negative partisanship.

Another avenue for research on negative partisanship in multi-party systems relates to the distinction between system and anti-system or anti-establishment parties. For example, Mudde and Kaltwasser (2018) report rising levels of negative partisanship toward populist parties in Western European democracies despite declining levels of positive attachment to mainstream parties. In this scenario, negative partisanship might function as a superordinate identity that attracts partisans from across the ideological spectrum, mobilizing them in opposition to an anti-establishment party that challenges the democratic core values of the political system. If that is the case, future research might examine under what conditions this opposition eventually translates into stronger attachment to mainstream parties, if at all.

Positive and negative partisanship could even develop in response to party coalitions – another complexity in the development of political identities. Indeed, in many European countries, coalition blocs even have their own names and logos, thereby further promoting an identity that can be somewhat decoupled from the individual parties the bloc consists of. Aligned with that expectation, González and colleagues (2008) show, with the example of Chile, that coalitional identities are a possible feature of multi-party systems (see also Huddy, Bankert, and Davis 2018) but it remains unclear to what extent negative partisanship could develop in response to an "out-coalition." These coalitional identities might also impact positive partisanship toward the in-party and other coalition members as well as negative partisanship toward the out-party and members of the opposition coalition.

SUGGESTION #6: A CLOSER LOOK AT THE LIMITS OF AFFECTIVE POLARIZATION

While research on partisanship has been flourishing, especially in the context of affective polarization, political scientists have also been revising prior scholarship and identified more of its nuances and limitations. One notable nuance relates to the measurement of affective polarization and the conclusions we draw about its prevalence among the electorate. For example, Druckman et al. (2021) argue that affective polarization is "more of an illusion" since feeling thermometer values – the conventionally used measure of affective polarization – greatly overstates its extent: When asked to rate their feelings toward the out-party, respondents think of ideologically extreme and politically engaged members. Indeed, Druckman and colleagues show that partisan animus declines sharply when respondents are asked to evaluate out-partisans who are less politically engaged or who are ideologically moderate – in other words, those who represent the majority of the electorate.

Similarly, Klar, Krupnikov, and Ryan (2018) provide evidence for measurement error relating to another common measure of affective polarization, namely a survey item that asks respondents about their child marrying a supporter of the other party. The measure is vulnerable to confounding a general dislike for partisanship, on the one hand, and a specific dislike for out-partisans, on the other. The two are conceptually quite different but could generate similar empirical results. As Klar and colleagues explain: "What seems like negative affect toward the other party is, in fact, negative affect toward partisans from either side of the aisle and political discussion in general . . .. In fact, many people do not want their child to marry someone from their own party if that hypothetical in-law were to discuss politics frequently." The authors support their argument by showing that, as affective polarization has supposedly increased in the United States, feeling thermometer values for the in-party have decreased among weak partisans and partisan leaners. These results suggest that what looks like broad affective polarization among the electorate might, in fact, be a more targeted disdain toward highly engaged partisans from either side.

Why should we care about these nuances? We *should* care about them because possibly erroneous narratives about our party attachments come with crucial normative implications: Research on affective polarization is increasingly featured in popular media outlets such as *Vox* and *National Public Radio*, disseminating the message that citizens are polarized and uncritical, hostile partisans. We might create a self-fulfilling prophecy if our results overestimate the actual level of polarization among the electorate. This concern has been a motivating factor for this book and its emphasis on the positive force that strong partisanship can be when it comes to promoting political engagement.

Admittedly, the same caution should also be applied to the estimation of partisanship's effect: While most studies propose a direct downstream effect on political attitudes, propelled by partisan motivated reasoning, Klar (2014) convincingly demonstrates that partisanship's effect is conditioned by the social setting people find themselves in. These social settings can be homogenous (i.e., including only fellow partisans) as well as heterogeneous (i.e., including out-partisans). Klar's results show that heterogeneous settings lead to more bipartisan evaluations and preferences, including more favorable attitudes toward the opposing party's policies, as compared to those in nonsocial settings. Thus, partisanship is not an immutable force that operates in a vacuum. Instead, it is embedded in a real-world environment that can weaken or strengthen its effects. In turn, this may suggest that prior work, including this book, possibly overestimate partisanship's impact. To address this concern, future work should investigate the effect of partisanship in more externally valid contexts. Field experiments provide a particularly useful toolbox in this endeavor.

SUGGESTION #7: A CLOSER LOOK AT PARTISANSHIP IN COMBINATION WITH OTHER SOCIAL AND POLITICAL IDENTITIES

A closer look at partisanship's interaction with other social and political identities would also contribute to a more externally valid assessment of partisanship. In *The American Voter Revisited*, Lewis-Beck and his colleagues (2008) demonstrate that the strength of other group identities such as religion, union membership, and ethnicity is strongly related to vote choice (p. 312). For example, weak Catholic identifiers are significantly more likely to vote Democratic than strong Catholic identifiers (63% versus 48% respectively), presumably because of the cross-pressure between their Catholic identity and Democratic partisanship. Following this logic, Mason (2015) suggests that contemporary partisanship in the United States has become so powerful since it encompasses multiple other identities such as race, religion, and ideology (see also Mason and Wronski 2018). Yet, even in polarized climates, most partisans are members of various groups that do not always neatly align with their partisanship or even conflict with it. More work on this identity (mis-)alignment would be useful to understand the current level of partisan animus in the American context and beyond. While it is certainly a complicated task to account for even just a small share of existing social and political identities, it is another step toward a more valid evaluation of partisanship's effects in the real world.

SUGGESTION #8: A CLOSER LOOK AT COMMON IDENTITIES (AND THEIR PITFALLS)

Research in social psychology emphasizes the importance of overarching goals and common identities in diminishing intergroup conflict (Brewer 2000; Gaertner et al. 1999). There is some evidence for the validity of this argument in the context of inter-party hostility. For example, Levendusky (2017) shows that priming American national identity can unite partisans and reduce affective polarization – a finding that served as the foundation for one of the three experiments in Chapter 10. Yet I found evidence for diminished levels of negative partisanship only among Republicans, while priming American identity even strengthened Democrats' negative partisanship toward Republicans. These diverging results might be indicative of a "growing trend toward the continued polarization of increasingly incompatible visions of U.S. national identity" (Barreto and Napolio 2020). The partisan appropriation of a formerly superordinate identity might be a crucial consequence of polarization that deserves more theoretical and empirical attention.

Klar (2018) provides experimental evidence for partisan differences in the internalization of another common in-group identity, namely gender. Relying on predictions from the Common In-Group Identity Model (CIIM), Klar (2018) shows that a common gender identity is not sufficient to reduce intergroup bias between Democratic and Republican women since "CIIM requires that members of both rival groups conceive of the superordinate group membership in the same terms" (p. 610) – a condition that is not always met among Democratic and Republicans women when they do not share a common understanding of what it means to be a woman. As a consequence – rather than bridging the partisan divide – increasing the salience of their common gender identity intensifies the mistrust between women from competing parties. From this perspective, it might not be too surprising that priming American identity differentially impacted Republicans and Democrats; "being American" simply has different meanings to them. As societies become more diverse, what kind of common in-group identity can effectively serve as a superordinate identity that unites people?

11.9 SUGGESTION #9: THE ROLE OF PARTY LEADERS

More future work could focus on the role of party elites in intensifying or ameliorating partisan animus. It seems to me that, for this endeavor, it is fruitful to take a step back and examine more closely the origins of party elites' appeal among their supporters. While partisanship and leader evaluations are certainly related, support for in-party leaders can also be grounded in other factors. For example, Mason et al. (2021) demonstrate that support for Donald Trump in 2018 was driven by animus toward Democratic-linked minority groups in 2011. Interestingly, this animus was not related to support for other party leaders on either the Republican or the Democratic side. The authors conclude: "Trump's support is thus uniquely tied to animus toward minority groups" (p. 1508). The extent to which party leaders can activate this animus and translate it into support for their party should be of interest to scholars of partisanship since it suggests that party elites are not just passive beneficiaries of partisan loyalties but also active party entrepreneurs who can re-draw the boundaries of their party's identity. Mason and colleagues' findings also raise questions about the difference between support for the in-party and support for in-party leaders. The strong support for Trump might be grounded in Republicans' strong positive partisanship but it is also feasible that Trump support operates independently of the Republican Party. The latter scenario might, in the long run, even change what it means to be Republican. Indeed, Social Identity Theory emphasizes the role of group leaders as identity entrepreneurs who can change the perceived typicality of the group and its members. As Hogg and Reid (2006) explain: "[Leaders] ... can target deviants or marginal members so as to highlight their own proto-typicality or construct a prototype for the group that enhances their own prototypicality. They can secure their own leadership position by vilifying contenders for leadership and characterizing them as non-prototypical" (p. 20). There is evidence of this leadership struggle within both the Democratic and Republican Party. From this perspective, future research might benefit from collecting panel data to examine the emergence and retreat of party leaders as well as their impact on the meaning and shape of their partisans' identity over the course of an election cycle.

SUGGESTION #10: A CLOSER LOOK AT PARTISANSHIP AMONG PEOPLE OF COLOR

Despite the impressive amount of research on partisanship, we know little about its origins and effects among people of color. This gap is at least partially driven by the limited availability of data on these populations, let alone panel data that could trace the development of their partisanship over time. However, since racial and ethnic minorities constitute some of the fastest-growing demographics in the United States, more effort is necessary to increase their representation in our data collection. Indeed, many people of color do not report any party affiliation (Hajnal and Lee 2011), which might hint at a negative independent identity that is driven by a feeling of exclusion and neglect from both political parties. From this perspective, studying people of color is not just normatively an important goal but it can also advance our understanding of independent identities, the alignment of partisanship with race and ethnicity, and the role of substantive and descriptive representation in mobilizing new groups of partisans. These research avenues could generate a host of predictions regarding the impact of negative and positive partisanship on the political behavior of Black Americans, Latino Americans, and Asian Americans.

FINAL WORDS

This book started with anecdotes of partisan hostility and violence across the United States and Europe. Many more recent examples could be added such as the violent attack on Paul Pelosi – the husband of Nancy Pelosi, Speaker of the US House of Representatives – in October 2022, when an intruder assaulted him with a hammer in the family's San Francisco home, leaving him hospitalized with a skull fracture. While many Republican leaders strongly condemned the incident, there were also many other prominent Republican voices that mocked the Pelosis and the Democratic Party over the attack. Donald Trump Jr., for example, posted a photo online of underwear and a hammer, with the title "Got my Paul Pelosi Halloween costume ready."[1] I would interpret this kind of incivility as a symptom of negative partisanship. As pointed out earlier, there are clear benefits attached to demonizing and humiliating the out-party and its members: It can draw attention away from poor performance of one's own party, it can serve as a temporary substitute for an actual policy platform (it is easier to define a party over what it is not rather than what it is), and it can help to draw in and mobilize voters who might not be completely dedicated to one's own party but who really disdain the other party. In its extreme form, as this book has demonstrated, negative partisanship can even lead to a weakening of partisans' commitment to democratic norms and values. Yet it does not have to be this way. It is every citizen's responsibility to condemn and denounce politicians who contribute to the partisan-fueled disintegration of society with their divisive and hostile rhetoric and actions – especially when they belong to one's own party. Being deeply committed to one's own party does not have to

---

[1] Salon, "Too soon?": Don Jr. mocks brutal hammer attack with meme – "Got my Paul Pelosi Halloween costume," www.salon.com/2022/10/31/too-soon-don-jr-mocks-brutal-hammer-with-meme–got-my-paul-pelosi-halloween-costume/ (last accessed, December 12, 2022).

come at the cost of the out-party's humanity – a point that I theoretically and empirically supported in this book with its strong focus on the distinction between positive and negative partisanship.

Above all, I hope that this book changes the reader's evaluation of strong positive party attachments. Despite the negative image that is frequently attached to partisanship in the United States and beyond, it is important to remember that partisanship also firmly anchors people in their political system and can foster democratic citizenship. Indeed, well-established partisan attachments can stabilize a political system even in times of economic and political turbulences. This resilience is especially important as a counterforce to anti-establishment and populist appeals that undermine core democratic values. Indeed, there is a substantial body of research that documents partisanship's positive effects, including a lower support for anti-establishment parties (e.g., Bankert et al. 2022; Ezrow et al. 2014), greater electoral stability (Lupu and Stokes 2010; Norris 2005), and lower levels of political alienation (Dassonneville and Hooghe 2018). All of these factors can fend off and counteract the emergence of anti-system political parties and populist appeals that destabilize the existing political landscape (Bosch and Durán 2017; Bustikova 2009; Rico et al. 2017) and seek to drive a wedge between democracy and liberalism.

From this perspective, partisanship is and remains an essential pillar of representative and liberal democracy – as long as we promote good partisanship that allows citizens to feel deeply attached to their own party without vilifying their opponents.

Appendix

TABLE A1 Comparison of population and sample composition, United States

	US population	Sample
Gender	54% Female, 45% Male	51% Female, 49% Male
Race/Ethnicity	72% White, 27% Non-White	68% White, 32% Non-White
Religious	77%	70%
Ideology	30% Liberal, 22% Moderate, 33% Conservative	32% Liberal, 31% Moderate, 37% Conservative

Note: Data for US population is taken from the 2020 American National Election Study.

TABLE A2 Comparison of population and sample composition, United Kingdom

	UK population	Sample
Gender	53% Female, 46% Male	53% Female, 47% Male
Race/Ethnicity	86% White, 14% Non-White	85% White, 15% Non-White
Religious	50%	55%
Ideology	25% Left, 28% Middle of the Road, 29% Right	33% Left, 44% Middle of the Road, 23% Right

Note: Data for UK population is taken from the 2019 British National Election Study.

TABLE A3 Comparison of population and sample composition, Italy

	Italian population	Sample
Gender	53% Female, 47% Male	54% Female, 46% Male
Race/Ethnicity	95% White, 5% Non-White	98% White, 2% Non-White
Religious	80%	71%
Ideology	39% Left, 23% Middle of the Road, 38% Right	44% Left, 17% Middle of the Road, 40% Right

Note: Data for Italian population is taken from the 2018 Italian National Election Study.

TABLE A4 Comparison of population and sample composition, Sweden

	Swedish population	Sample
Gender	49% Female, 51% Male	46% Female, 54% Male
Race/Ethnicity	98% White, 2% Non-White	97% White, 3% Non-White
Religious	60%	50%
Ideology	35% Left, 15% Middle of the Road, 49% Right	35% Left, 27% Middle of the Road, 37% Right

Note: Data for Swedish population is taken from the 2018 Swedish National Election Study.

TABLE A5 Comparison of population and sample composition, Netherlands

	Dutch population	Sample
Gender	52% Female, 48% Male	47% Female, 53% Male
Race/Ethnicity	81% White, 19% Non-White	91% White, 9% Non-White
Religious	46%	43%
Ideology	28% Left, 12% Middle of the Road, 31% Right	32% Left, 36% Middle of the Road, 33% Right

Note: Data for Dutch population is taken from the 2018 Dutch Parliamentary Election Study.

TABLE A6 Comparison of Independents in population and sample composition, United States

	Bovitz sample	2020 ANES benchmark
Gender	53% Male	48% Male
	47% Female	52% Female
Race and ethnicity	72% White	62% White
	10% Black	8% Black
	3% Asian	5% Asian
	9% Hispanic	13% Hispanic
	2% Native American	6% Native American
	4% Other	5% Other
Education	29% High school or less	29% High school or less
	42% Some college or associate degree	38% Some college or associate degree
	20% Four-year degree	20% Four-year degree
	7% Professional degree	4% Professional degree
	1% Doctorate	8% Graduate degree
Age (Median)	46 years	46 years
Religion	59% Religious	60% Religious
	42% No religious affiliation	40% No religious affiliation

Table A6 (*cont.*)

	Bovitz sample	2020 ANES benchmark
Ideology	61% Moderate/Middle of the Road	71% Moderate/Haven't thought much about this
	19% Liberals	15% Liberals
	20% Conservatives	15% Conservatives
N	724	949

Note: Respondents in both samples are self-declared pure Independents without any partisan leaning.

TABLE A7 Distribution of NPID toward Democrats

Item	Never (%)	Sometimes (%)	Often (%)	Always (%)
When I talk about the Democratic Party, I say "they" instead of "we."	27	18	24	32
When people criticize the Democratic Party, it makes me feel good.	49	29	14	8
I am relieved when the Democratic Party loses an election.	26	39	22	13
When the Democratic Party does well in opinion polls, my day is ruined.	72	16	9	4
I do not have much in common with supporters of the Democratic Party.	22	34	29	15
When I meet somebody, who supports the Democratic Party, I feel disconnected.	45	33	15	7
I get angry when people praise the Democratic Party.	49	31	12	8
When I speak about the Democratic Party and its supporters, I refer to it as 'their party'.	43	26	14	17

Note: Entries are percentages.

TABLE A8 Distribution of NPID toward Republicans

Item	Never (%)	Sometimes (%)	Often (%)	Always (%)
When I talk about the Republican Party, I say "they" instead of "we."	44	33	17	6
When people criticize the Republican Party, it makes me feel good.	37	20	22	21
I am relieved when the Republican Party loses an election.	43	36	12	9

Table A8 (*cont.*)

Item	Never (%)	Sometimes (%)	Often (%)	Always (%)
When the Republican Party does well in opinion polls, my day is ruined.	19	39	24	18
I do not have much in common with supporters of the Republican Party.	25	16	21	38
When I meet somebody, who supports the Republican Party, I feel disconnected.	28	42	17	13
I get angry when people praise the Republican Party.	41	35	15	9
When I speak about the Republican Party and its supporters, I refer to it as 'their party'.	65	22	9	3

Note: Entries are percentages.

TABLE A9 Pairwise correlations of personality traits, US sample

Variables	(1)	(2)	(3)	(4)	(5)	(6)	(7)	(8)
(1) Need for closure	1.000							
(2) SDO	0.132	1.000						
(3) Authoritarianism	0.117	0.285	1.000					
(4) Conscientiousness	−0.113	−0.184	0.087	1.000				
(5) Agreeableness	−0.146	−0.291	0.036	0.440	1.000			
(6) Emotional stability	−0.271	−0.110	0.093	0.534	0.414	1.000		
(7) Openness	−0.280	−0.249	−0.096	0.335	0.323	0.315	1.000	
(8) Extraversion	−0.118	0.100	0.035	0.093	0.035	0.169	0.267	1.000

Note: All variables are scaled to range from 0 to 1 for better comparability.

TABLE A10 Pairwise correlations of personality traits, Sweden sample

Variables	(1)	(2)	(3)	(4)	(5)	(6)	(7)	(8)
(1) Need for closure	1.000							
(2) SDO	0.039	1.000						
(3) Authoritarianism	0.201	0.355	1.000					
(4) Conscientiousness	−0.176	0.073	−0.015	1.000				
(5) Agreeableness	−0.125	−0.188	−0.199	0.102	1.000			
(6) Emotional stability	−0.169	−0.083	−0.079	0.126	0.374	1.000		
(7) Openness	−0.217	−0.160	−0.167	0.053	0.267	0.215	1.000	
(8) Extraversion	−0.215	0.078	−0.041	0.156	0.071	0.082	0.158	1.000

Note: All variables are scaled to range from 0 to 1 for better comparability.

REFERENCES

Abramowitz, A. I., & Webster, S. (2016). The rise of negative partisanship and the nationalization of US elections in the 21st century. *Electoral Studies*, *41*, 12–22.

Abramowitz, A. I., & Webster, S. W. (2018). Negative partisanship: Why Americans dislike parties but behave like rabid partisans: Negative partisanship and rabid partisans. *Political Psychology*, *39*, 119–135.

Achen, C. H., & Bartels, L. M. (2017). *Democracy for realists: Why elections do not produce responsive government*. Princeton Studies in Political Behavior. Princeton University Press.

Adams, J., Ezrow, L., & Somer-Topcu, Z. (2011). Is anybody listening? Evidence that voters do not respond to European parties' policy statements during elections. *American Journal of Political Science*, *55*(2), 370–382. https://doi.org/10.1111/j .1540-5907.2010.00489.x.

Adorno, T., Frenkel-Brunswick, E., Levinson, D., & Sanford, R. (1950). *The authoritarian personality*. Harper.

Ahlander, J., & Johnson, S. (2021, June 24). *After years on the fringe, Sweden Democrats take centre stage*. www.reuters.com/world/after-years-fringe-sweden-democrats-take-centre-stage-2021-06-24.

Ahler, D. J., & Sood, G. (2018). The parties in our heads: Misperceptions about party composition and their consequences. *The Journal of Politics*, *80*(3), 964–981.

Alford, J. R., & Hibbing, J. R. (2007). Personal, interpersonal, and political temperaments. *The ANNALS of the American Academy of Political and Social Science*, *614*(1), 196–212. https://doi.org/10.1177/0002716207305621.

Allport, G. W. (1954). *The nature of prejudice*. Addison-Wesley.

Altemeyer, B. (1988). *Enemies of freedom: Understanding right-wing authoritarianism*. Jossey-Bass.

Altemeyer, B. (2004). Highly dominating, highly authoritarian personalities. *The Journal of Social Psychology*, *144*(4), 421–448. https://doi.org/10.3200/SOCP.144 .4.421-448.

Amaro, S. (2020, April 21). *Coronavirus deepens political fragmentation in Italy as anti-EU sentiment rises*. CNBC. www.cnbc.com/2020/04/21/italys-political-fragmentation-rises-amid-coronavirus-pandemic.html.

Andersson, L. M., & Pearson, C. M. (1999). Tit for tat? The spiraling effect of incivility in the workplace. *Academy of Management Review, 24*(3), 452–471.

Arceneaux, K., & Vander Wielen, R. J. (2017). *Taming intuition: How reflection minimizes partisan reasoning and promotes democratic accountability.* Cambridge University Press. https://doi.org/10.1017/9781108227643.

Arzheimer, K. (2017). Another dog that didn't bark? Less dealignment and more partisanship in the 2013 Bundestag election. *German Politics, 26*(1), 49–64. https://doi.org/10.1080/09644008.2016.1266481.

Avlon, J. (2017). *Washington's farewell: The founding father's warning to future generations.* Simon and Schuster.

Ayala, R. J. de. (2009). *The theory and practice of item response theory.* Guilford Press.

Azevedo, F., Jost, J. T., Rothmund, T., & Sterling J. (2019). Neoliberal ideology and the justification of inequality in capitalist societies: Why social and economic dimensions of ideology are intertwined. *Journal of Social Issues, 75*(1), 49–88. https://doi.org/10.1111/josi.12310.

Bafumi, J., & Shapiro, R. Y. (2009). A new partisan voter. *The Journal of Politics, 71*(1), 1–24.

Baldassarri, D., & Gelman, A. (2008). Partisans without constraint: Political polarization and trends in American public opinion. *American Journal of Sociology, 114*(2), 408–446. https://doi.org/10.1086/590649.

Bankert, A. (2020). The origins and effect of negative partisanship. In G. H. E. Oscarsson & S. Holmberg (Eds.), *Research handbook on political partisanship* (pp. 89–101). Edward Elgar.

Bankert, A. (2021). Negative and positive partisanship in the 2016 US presidential elections. *Political Behavior, 43*(4), 1467–1485.

Bankert, A. (2022). Negative partisanship among Independents in the 2020 US presidential elections. *Electoral Studies, 78*, 102490.

Bankert, A., Del Ponte, A., & Huddy, L. (2023). Partisanship in times of crisis: Evidence from Italy. *Political Science Research and Methods, 11*(1), 1–17.

Bankert, A., Huddy, L., & Rosema, M. (2017). Measuring partisanship as a social identity in multi-party systems. *Political Behavior, 39*(1), 103–132.

Baker, A., Ames, B., Sokhey, A. E., & Renno L. R. (2016). The dynamics of partisan identification when party brands change: The case of the Workers Party in Brazil. *The Journal of Politics, 78*(1), 197–213. https://doi.org/10.1086/683609.

Barbaranelli, C., Caprara, G. V., Vecchione, M., & Fraley, C. R. (2007). Voters' personality traits in presidential elections. *Personality and Individual Differences, 42*(7), 1199–1208. https://doi.org/10.1016/j.paid.2006.09.029.

Barreto, A. A., & Napolio, N. G. (2020). Bifurcating American identity: Partisanship, sexual orientation, and the 2016 presidential election. *Politics, Groups, and Identities, 8*(1), 143–159.

Bartels, L. M. (2000). Partisanship and voting behavior, 1952–1996. *American Journal of Political Science, 44*(1), 35–50. https://doi.org/10.2307/2669291.

Bartels, L. M. (2002). Beyond the running tally: Partisan bias in political perceptions. *Political Behavior, 24*, 117–150.

Bartels, L. M. (2010, February 25). *The study of electoral behavior.* The Oxford Handbook of American Elections and Political Behavior. https://doi.org/10.1093/oxfordhb/9780199235476.003.0014.

Berglund, F., Holmberg, S., Schmitt, H., & Thomassen, J. (2005). Party identification and party choice. In J. Thomassen (Ed.), *The European voter: A comparative study of Modern democracies* (pp. 106–24). Oxford University Press. https://doi .org/10.1093/0199273219.003.0005.

Bisgaard, M. (2015). Bias will find a way: Economic perceptions, attributions of blame, and partisan-motivated reasoning during crisis. *The Journal of Politics, 77*(3), 849–860. https://doi.org/10.1086/681591.

Bolsen, T., Druckman, J. N., & Cook F. L. (2014). The influence of partisan motivated reasoning on public opinion. *Political Behavior, 36*(2), 235–262. https://doi.org/ 10.1007/s11109-013-9238-0.

Bosch, A., & Durán, I. M. (2019). How does economic crisis impel emerging parties on the road to elections? The case of the Spanish Podemos and Ciudadanos. *Party Politics, 25*(2), 257–267.

Bosco, A., & Verney, S. (2020). Polarisation in southern Europe: Elites, party conflicts and negative partisanship. *South European Society and Politics, 25*(3–4), 257–284.

Bosson, J. K., Johnson, A. B., Niederhoffer, K., & Swann, W. B. Jr. (2006). Interpersonal chemistry through negativity: Bonding by sharing negative attitudes about others. *Personal Relationships, 13*, 135–150.

Boudreau, C., & MacKenzie, S. A. (2014). Informing the electorate? How party cues and policy information affect public opinion about initiatives. *American Journal of Political Science, 58*(1), 48–62. https://doi.org/10.1111/ajps.12054.

Bowles, N. (2019, November 3). How to get Trump voters and liberals to talk: Don't make anyone sit in a circle. *New York Times.*

Brader, T., & Tucker, J. A. (2009). *Follow the leader: Party cues, partisans, and public opinion in old and new democracies.* Social Science Research Network. https:// papers.ssrn.com/abstract=1448995.

Brady, H. E., Verba, S., & Schlozman K. L. (1995). Beyond SES: A resource model of political participation. *American Political Science Review, 89*(2), 271–294. https:// doi.org/10.2307/2082425.

Branscombe, N. R., Ellemers, N., Spears, R., & Doosje, B. (1999). The context and content of social identity threat. *Social Identity: Context, Commitment, Content,* 35–58.

Brewer, M. B. (1999). The psychology of prejudice: Ingroup love and outgroup hate? *Journal of Social Issues, 55*(3), 429–444.

Brewer, M. B., & Pierce, K. P. (2005). Social identity complexity and outgroup tolerance. *Personality and Social Psychology Bulletin, 31*(3), 428–437.

Broder, D. S. (1971). *The party's over: The failure of politics in America.* Harper & Row.

Bullock, J. G., Gerber, A. S., Hill, S. J., & Huber, G. A. (2015). Partisan bias in factual beliefs about politics. *Quarterly Journal of Political Science, 10*(4), 519–578. https://doi.org/10.1561/100.00014074.

Bustikova, L. (2009). The extreme Right in Eastern Europe: EU accession and the quality of governance. *Journal of Contemporary European Studies, 17*(2), 223–239.

Byman, D. (2022, April 9). *How hateful rhetoric connects to real-world violence.* www .brookings.edu/blog/order-from-chaos/2021/04/09/how-hateful-rhetoric-con nects-to-real-world-violence/.

Campbell, A., Converse, P. E., Miller, W. E., & Stokes, D. E. (1960). *The American voter.* University of Chicago Press.

Caprara, G. V., Barbaranelli, C., & Zimbardo, P. G. (1999). Personality profiles and political parties. *Political Psychology, 20*(1), 175–197.

Carlson, E. (2016). Finding partisanship where we least expect it: Evidence of partisan bias in a new African democracy. *Political Behavior, 38*(1), 129–154. https://doi.org/10.1007/s11109-015-9309-5.

Caruana, N. J., McGregor, R. M., & Stephenson, L. B. (2015). The power of the dark side: Negative partisanship and political behaviour in Canada. *Canadian Journal of Political Science, 48*(4), 771–789.

Cassese, E.C. (2021). Partisan dehumanization in American politics. *Political Behavior, 43*(1), 29–50. https://doi.org/10.1007/s11109-019-09545-w.

Choma, B. L., & Hanoch Y. (2017). Cognitive ability and authoritarianism: Understanding support for Trump and Clinton. *Personality and Individual Differences, 106* (February), 287–291. https://doi.org/10.1016/j.paid.2016.10.054.

Chua, A. (2019). *Political tribes: Group instinct and the fate of nations.* Penguin.

Cohen, G. L. (2003). Party over policy: The dominating impact of group influence on political beliefs. *Journal of Personality and Social Psychology, 85*(5). https://psycnet.apa.org/doi/10.1037/0022-3514.85.5.808.

Converse, P. E. (2006). The nature of belief systems in mass publics (1964). *Critical Review: A Journal of Politics and Society, 18*(1–3), 1–74. https://doi.org/10.1080/08913810608443650.

Cookson, J. A., Engelberg, J. E., & Mullins, W. (2020). Does partisanship shape investor beliefs? Evidence from the COVID-19 pandemic. *The Review of Asset Pricing Studies, 10*(4), 863–893.

Cooper, C. A., Golden, L., & Socha, A. (2013). The big five personality factors and mass politics. *Journal of Applied Social Psychology, 43*(1), 68–82.

Crawford, J. T., & Pilanski J. M. (2014). Political intolerance, Right and Left. *Political Psychology, 35*(6), 841–851. https://doi.org/10.1111/j.1467-9221.2012.00926.x.

Crewe, I. (1980). *Negative partisanship: Some preliminary ideas using British data.* Planning Session on Problems in Comparative Survey Research in Political Behaviour: Issues in Data Collection and Analysis, Joint Sessions of the European Consortium for Political Research.

Donovan, M. (2008). The center-right: Conflict, unity, and permanent mobilization. In M. Donovan & P. Onofri (Eds.), Italian politics: Frustrated aspirations for change (pp. 68–85). Berghahn.

Dalton, R. J., & Wattenberg, M. P. (Eds.). (2002). Parties without partisans: Political change in advanced industrial democracies. Oxford University Press on Demand.

Dalton, R. J., & Weldon, S. (2007). Partisanship and party system institutionalization. *Party Politics, 13*(2), 179–196. https://doi.org/10.1177/1354068807073856.

Dassonneville, R., & Hooghe, M. (2018). Indifference and alienation: Diverging dimensions of electoral dealignment in Europe. *Acta Politica, 53*(1), 1–23.

Desilver, D. (2020, November 3). *In past elections, U.S. trailed most developed countries in voter turnout.* Pew Research Center. www.pewresearch.org/fact-tank/2020/11/03/in-past-elections-u-s-trailed-most-developed-countries-in-voter-turnout/.

De Vries, W., Tarrance, L., & Tarrance, V. L. (1972). *The ticket-splitter: A new force in American politics*. Eerdmans.

DutchNews. (2019, November 18). *Man jailed for 10 years for plotting "terrorist attack" on Geert Wilders*. Dutch News. www.dutchnews.nl/news/2019/11/man-jailed-for-10-years-for-plotting-terrorist-attack-on-geert-wilders/.

Druckman, J. N., Gubitz, S. R., Levendusky, M. S., & Lloyd, A. M. (2019). How incivility on partisan media (de-)polarizes the electorate. *The Journal of Politics, 81*(1), 291–295.

Druckman, J. N., Klar, S., Krupnikov, Y., Levendusky, M., & Ryan, J. B. (2020). How affective polarization shapes Americans' political beliefs: A study of response to the COVID-19 pandemic. *Journal of Experimental Political Science*, 1–12.

Druckman, J. N., & Levendusky, M. S. (2019). What do we measure when we measure affective polarization? *Public Opinion Quarterly, 83*(1), 114–122.

Druckman, J. N., Peterson, E., & Slothuus, R. (2013). How elite partisan polarization affects public opinion formation. *American Political Science Review, 107*(1), 57–79. https://doi.org/10.1017/S0003055412000500.

Duckitt, J., & Sibley, C. G. (2007). Right wing authoritarianism, social dominance orientation and the dimensions of generalized prejudice. *European Journal of Personality, 21*(2), 113–130. https://doi.org/10.1002/per.614.

Duckitt, J., & Sibley, C. G. (2009). A dual-process motivational model of ideology, politics, and prejudice. *Psychological Inquiry, 20*(2–3), 98–109. https://doi.org/10.1080/10478400903028540.

Dunwoody, P. T., & Plane D. L. (2019). The influence of authoritarianism and outgroup threat on political affiliations and support for antidemocratic policies. *Peace and Conflict: Journal of Peace Psychology, 25*(3), 198–210. https://doi.org/10.1037/pac0000397.

Ellemers, N., Spears, R., & Doosje, B. (2002). Self and social identity. *Annual Review of Psychology, 53*(1), 161–186.

Elsbach, K. D., & Bhattacharya, C. B. (2001). Defining who you are by what you're not: Organizational disidentification and the National Rifle Association. *Organization Science, 12*(4), 393–413.

Endres, K., Panagopoulos, C., & Green, D. P. (2020). Elite messaging and partisan consumerism: An evaluation of President Trump's tweets and polarization of corporate brand images. *Political Research Quarterly, 74*(4), 1–18. https://doi.org/10.1177/1065912920939188.

Ethier, K. A., and Deaux,K. (1994). Negotiating social identity when contexts change: Maintaining identification and responding to threat. *Journal of Personality and Social Psychology, 67*(2), 243–251. https://doi.org/10.1037/0022-3514.67.2.243.

Eysenck, H. J. (1967). *The biological basis of personality*. Thomas.

Ezrow, L., Tavits, M., & Homola, J. (2014). Voter polarization, strength of partisanship, and support for extremist parties. *Comparative Political Studies, 47*(11), 1558–1583.

Federico, C. M., Fisher, E. L., & Deason, G. (2017). The authoritarian Left withdraws from politics: Ideological asymmetry in the relationship between authoritarianism and political engagement. *The Journal of Politics, 79*(3), 1010–1023. https://doi.org/10.1086/692126.

Feldman, S. (2003). Enforcing social conformity: A theory of authoritarianism. *Political Psychology*, 24(1), 41–74. https://doi.org/10.1111/0162-895X.00316.

Feldman, S., & Stenner, K. (1997). Perceived threat and authoritarianism. *Political Psychology*, 18(4), 741–770. https://doi.org/10.1111/0162-895X.00077.

Fernandez-Vazquez, P. (2014). And yet it moves: The effect of election platforms on party policy images. *Comparative Political Studies*, 47(14), 1919–1944. https://doi .org/10.1177/0010414013516067.

Fiorina, M. P. (1981). *Retrospective voting in American national elections*. Yale University Press.

Fowler, J. H., & Kam, C. D. (2007). Beyond the self: Social identity, altruism, and political participation. *Journal of Politics*, 69(3), 813–827. https://doi.org/10.1111/ j.1468-2508.2007.00577.x.

French, D. (2020). *Divided we fall: America's secession threat and how to restore our nation* (1st edition). St. Martin's Press.

Gadarian, S. K., Goodman, S. W., & Pepinsky, T. B. (2021). Partisanship, health behavior, and policy attitudes in the early stages of the COVID-19 pandemic. *Plos One*, 16(4), e0249596.

Gaertner, S. L., Dovidio, J. F., Anastasio, P. A., Bachman, B. A., & Rust, M. C. (1993). The common ingroup identity model: Recategorization and the reduction of intergroup bias. *European Review of Social Psychology*, 4(1), 1–26.

Gaertner, S. L., Dovidio, J. F., Nier, J. A., Banker, B. S., Ward, C. M., Houlette, M., & Loux, S. (2000). The common ingroup identity model for reducing intergroup bias: Progress and challenges. In D. Capozza & R. Brown (Eds.), *Social identity processes: Trends in theory and research* (pp. 133–148). Sage.

Gaertner, L., Iuzzini, J., Witt, M. G., & Orina, M. M. (2006). Us without them: Evidence for an intragroup origin of positive ingroup regard. *Journal of Personality and Social Psychology*, 90, 426–439.

Garzia, D. (2013). The rise of party/leader identification in Western Europe. *Political Research Quarterly*, 66(3), 533–544. https://doi.org/10.1177/1065912912463122.

Garzia, D., & Ferreira da Silva, F. (2022). Negativity and political behavior: A theoretical framework for the analysis of negative voting in contemporary democracies. *Political Studies Review*, 20(2), 282–291.

Gerber, A. S., Huber, G. A., Doherty, D., & Dowling C. M. (2011). Personality traits and the consumption of political information. *American Politics Research*, 39(1), 32–84. https://doi.org/10.1177/1532673X10381466.

Gerber, A. S., Huber, G. A., Doherty, D., & Dowling, C. M. (2012). Personality and the strength and direction of partisan identification. *Political Behavior*, 34(4), 653–688.

Gerber, A. S., Huber, G. A., Doherty, D., Dowling, C. M., & Ha S. E. (2010). Personality and political attitudes: Relationships across issue domains and political contexts. *The American Political Science Review*, 104(1), 111–133.

González, R., Manzi, J., Saiz, J., Brewer, M., De Tezanos-Pinto, P., Torres, D., Aravena, M. T., & Aldunate N. (2008). Interparty attitudes in Chile: Coalitions as superordinate social identities. *Political Psychology*, 29 (January), 93–118. https://doi .org/10.1111/j.1467-9221.2007.00614.x.

Goren, P. (2005). Party identification and core political values. *American Journal of Political Science*, 49(4), 881–896. https://doi.org/10.1111/j.1540-5907.2005 .00161.x.

Goren, P., Federico, C. M., & Kittilson, M. C. (2009). Source cues, partisan identities, and political value expression. *American Journal of Political Science*, *53*(4), 805–820. https://doi.org/10.1111/j.1540-5907.2009.00402.x.

Gosling, S. D, Rentfrow, P. J., & Swann W. B. (2003). A very brief measure of the Big-Five Personality Domains. *Journal of Research in Personality*, *37*(6), 504–528. https://doi.org/10.1016/S0092-6566(03)00046-1.

Green, D. P., Palmquist, B., & Schickler, E. (2002). *Partisan hearts and minds: Political parties and the social identities of voters*. Yale ISPS Series. Yale University Press.

Greene, S. (1999). Understanding party identification: A social identity approach. *Political Psychology*, *20*(2), 393–403.

Greene, S. (2002). The social-psychological measurement of partisanship. *Political Behavior*, *24*(3), 171–197.

Greene, S. (2004). Social identity theory and party identification. *Social Science Quarterly*, *85*(1), 136–153.

Groenendyk, E. W., & Banks, A. J. (2014). Emotional rescue: How affect helps partisans overcome collective action problems. *Political Psychology*, *35*(3), 359–378. https://doi.org/10.1111/pops.12045.

Grossman, G., Kim, S., Rexer, J. M., & Thirumurthy, H. (2020). Political partisanship influences behavioral responses to governors' recommendations for COVID-19 prevention in the United States. *Proceedings of the National Academy of Sciences*, *117*(39), 24144–24153

The Guardian. (2021, September 26). Angela Rayner stands by labelling of Tories as "scum." www.theguardian.com/politics/2021/sep/26/angela-rayner-stands-byre marks-calling-tories-scum.

Guay, B., & Johnston, C. D. (2021). Ideological asymmetries and the determinants of politically motivated reasoning. *American Journal of Political Science*, 12624. https://doi.org/10.1111/ajps.12624.

Hagevi, M. (2015). Bloc identification in multi-party systems: The case of the Swedish two-bloc system. *West European Politics*, *38*(1), 73–92. https://doi.org/10.1080/01402382.2014.911480.

Hajnal, Z., & Lee, T. (2011). Race, immigration, and (non)partisanship in America. Princeton University Press.

Harteveld, E. (2021). Fragmented foes: Affective polarization in the multiparty context of the Netherlands. *Electoral Studies*, *71*, 102332.

Haslam, N. (2006). Dehumanization: An integrative review. *Personality and Social Psychology Review*, *10*, 252–264.

Haslam, N., & Loughnan, S. (2014). Dehumanization and infrahumanization. *Annual Review of Psychology*, *65*, 399–423.

Heeremans, L. (2018). *Affective polarization in the Netherlands – political parties and political orientation*. Universiteit van Amsterdam Department of Political Sciences: Public Policy and Governance. Unpublished Master's Thesis: file:///Users/ab26663/Downloads/Heeremans_11783710.pdf.

Heider, F. (1958). The psychology of interpersonal relations. John Willey & Sons.

Henry, P. J., Jim Sidanius, Shana Levin, and Felicia Pratto. (2005). "Social Dominance Orientation, Authoritarianism, and Support for Intergroup Violence Between the Middle East and America." *Political Psychology*, *26*(4), 569–584. https://doi.org/10.1111/j.1467-9221.2005.00432.x.

Hetherington, M. J., & Weiler, J. D. (2009). *Authoritarianism and polarization in American politics.* Cambridge University Press.

Hetherington, M., & Suhay, E. (2011). Authoritarianism, threat, and Americans' support for the War on Terror. *American Journal of Political Science, 55*(3), 546–560. https://doi.org/10.1111/j.1540-5907.2011.00514.x.

Hiel, A. v., Pandelaere, M., & Duriez B. (2004). The impact of need for closure on conservative beliefs and racism: Differential mediation by authoritarian submission and authoritarian dominance. *Personality and Social Psychology Bulletin, 30*(7), 824–837. https://doi.org/10.1177/0146167204264333.

Hogg, M. A. (2012). Self-uncertainty, social identity, and the solace of extremism. In D. L. Blaylock & M. A. Hogg (Eds.), *Extremism and the psychology of uncertainty* (pp. 19–35). John Wiley & Sons.

Hogg, M. A., and van Knippenberg, D. (2003). Social identity and leadership processes in groups. In M. P. Zanna (Ed.), *Advances in experimental social psychology* (Vol. 35, pp. 1–52). Elsevier Academic Press.

Hogg, M. A., van Knippenberg, D., & Rast, D. E. I. (2012). Intergroup leadership in organizations: Leading across group and intergroup boundaries. *The Academy of Management Review, 37*(2), 232–255.

Hogg, M. A., & Reid, S. A. (2006). Social identity, self-categorization, and the communication of group norms. *Communication theory, 16*(1), 7–30.

Huddy, L. (2001). From social to political identity: A critical examination of social identity theory. *Political psychology, 22*(1), 127–156.

Huddy, L. (2013). From group identity to political cohesion and commitment. In L. Huddy, D. O. Sears, & J. S. Levy (Eds.), *The Oxford Handbook of Political Psychology* (2nd edition) (pp. 737–773). Oxford University Press.

Huddy, L., Bankert, A., & Davies, C. (2018). Expressive versus instrumental partisanship in multiparty European systems. *Political Psychology, 39*, 173–199.

Huddy, L., Feldman, S., & Weber, C. (2007). The political consequences of perceived threat and felt insecurity. *The Annals of the American Academy of Political and Social Science, 614*, 131–153.

Huddy, L., & Khatib, N. (2007). American patriotism, national identity, and political involvement. *American Journal of Political Science, 51*(1), 63–77.

Huddy, L., Mason, L., & Aarøe, L. (2015). Expressive partisanship: Campaign involvement, political emotion, and partisan identity. *American Political Science Review, 109* (1), 1–17. https://doi.org/10.1017/S0003055414000604.

Huddy, L., & Yair O. (2021). Reducing affective polarization: Warm group relations or policy compromise? *Political Psychology, 42*(2), 291–309.

Ignazi, P. (1992). The silent counter-revolution: Hypotheses on the emergence of extreme right-wing parties in Europe. *European Journal of Political Research, 22*(1), 3–34.

Irwin, A. (2018, August 8). *Does rudeness have a legitimate place in politics? The case for and against.* The Conversation. https://theconversation.com/does-rudeness-have-a-legitimate-place-in-politics-the-case-for-and-against-99420.

Iyengar, S., Sood, G., & Lelkes, Y. (2012). Affect, not ideology a social identity perspective on polarization. *Public Opinion Quarterly, 76*(3), 405–431.

Iyengar, S., & Westwood, S. J. (2015). Fear and loathing across party lines: New evidence on group polarization. *American Journal of Political Science, 59*(3), 690–707.

Iyengar, S., Lelkes, Y., Levendusky, M., Malhotra, N., & Westwood, S. J. (2019). The origins and consequences of affective polarization in the United States. *Annual Review of Political Science*, 22(1), 129–146.

Ito, T. A., Larsen, J. T., Smith, N. K., & Cacioppo, J. T. (1998). Negative information weighs more heavily on the brain: The negativity bias in evaluative categorizations. *Journal of Personality and Social Psychology*, 75(4), 887.

John, O., Naumann, L., & Soto C. (2008). Paradigm shift to the integrative Big Five Trait Taxonomy: History, measurement, and conceptual issues. In O. P. John, R. W. Robins, & L. A. Pervin (Eds.), *Handbook of personality: Theory and research* (pp. 114–158). Guilford Press.

Johnston, R. (2006). PARTY IDENTIFICATION: Unmoved mover or sum of preferences? *Annual Review of Political Science*, 9(1), 329–351. https://doi.org/10.1146/annurev.polisci.9.062404.170523.

Johnston, R., Hagen, M. G., & Jamieson, K. H. (2004). *The 2000 presidential election and the foundations of party politics*. Cambridge University Press. https://doi.org/10.1017/CBO9780511756207.

Jost, J. T., Glaser, J., Kruglanski, A. W., & Sulloway, F. J. (2003). Political conservatism as motivated social cognition. *Psychological Bulletin*, 129(3), 339–375. https://doi.org/10.1037/0033-2909.129.3.339.

Kiley, J., & Maniam, S. (2016, October 25). *Lesbian, gay and bisexual voters remain a solidly Democratic bloc*. Pew Research Center. www.pewresearch.org/fact-tank/2016/10/25/lesbian-gay-and-bisexual-voters-remain-a-solidly-democratic-bloc/.

Klar, S. (2014). Partisanship in a social setting. *American Journal of Political Science*, 58(3), 687–704.

Klar, S. (2018). When common identities decrease trust: An experimental study of Partisan women. *American Journal of Political Science*, 62(3), 610–622.

Klar, S., & Krupnikov, Y. (2016). *Independent politics*. Cambridge University Press.

Klar, S., Krupnikov, Y., & Ryan, J. B. (2018). Affective polarization or partisan disdain? Untangling a dislike for the opposing party from a dislike of partisanship. *Public Opinion Quarterly*, 82(2), 379–390

Kalmoe, N. P., & Mason, L. (2019, January). *Lethal mass partisanship: Prevalence, correlates, and electoral contingencies*. National Capital Area Political Science Association American Politics Meeting.

Klein, E. (2021). *Why we're polarized*. Avid Reader Press.

Kludt, T. (2016, September 29). *Harry Reid: "Trump is the GOP's Frankenstein monster."* CNN. www.cnn.com/2016/09/29/politics/harry-reid-donald-trump-frankenstein-monster/index.html.

Kossowska, M., & Hiel, A. V. (2003). The relationship between need for closure and conservative beliefs in Western and Eastern Europe. *Political Psychology*, 24(3), 501–518.

Krastev, I., & Leonard, M. (2021, September 1). *Europe's invisible divides: How Covid-19 is polarising European politics*. ECFR. https://ecfr.eu/publication/europes-invisible-divides-how-covid-19-is-polarising-european-politics/.

Kruglanski, A. W. (2004). *The psychology of closed mindedness*. Psychology Press.

Kruglanski, A. W., Chen, X., Pierro, A., Mannetti, L., Erb, H.-P., & Spiegel, S. (2006). Persuasion according to the Unimodel: Implications for cancer communication.

Journal of Communication, *56*(S1), S105–122. https://doi.org/10.1111/j.1460-2466.2006.00285.x.

Kruglanski, A. W., & Orehek E. (2012). The need for certainty as a psychological nexus for individuals and society. In M. A. Hogg and D. L. Blaylock (Eds.), *Extremism and the psychology of uncertainty* (pp. 3–18). Wiley-Blackwell.

Kruglanski, A. W., & Webster, D. M. (1996). Motivated closing of the mind: "Seizing" and "freezing." *Psychological Review*, *103*(2), 263–283. https://doi.org/10.1037/0033-295X.103.2.263.

Krupnikov, Y., & Ryan, J. B. (2022). *The other divide: Polarization and disengagement in American politics*. Cambridge University Press.

Krupnikov, Y., & Piston, S. (2015). Racial prejudice, partisanship, and White turnout in elections with Black candidates. *Political Behavior*, *37*(2), 397–418.

Kteily, N., Bruneau, E., Waytz, A., & Cotterill, S. (2015). The ascent of man: Theoretical and empirical evidence for blatant dehumanization. *Journal of Personality and Social Psychology*, *109*(5), 901.

Liu, J. H., Huang, L.-L., & McFedries, C. (2008). Cross-sectional and longitudinal differences in social dominance orientation and Right Wing authoritarianism as a function of political power and societal change. *Asian Journal of Social Psychology*, *11*(2), 116–126. https://doi.org/10.1111/j.1467-839X.2008.00249.x.

Lau, R. R., & Redlawsk, D. P. (2001). Advantages and disadvantages of cognitive heuristics in political decision making. *American Journal of Political Science*, *45*(4), 951. https://doi.org/10.2307/2669334.

Lavine, H. G., Johnston, C. D., & Steenbergen, M. R. (2012). *The ambivalent partisan: How critical loyalty promotes democracy*. Oxford University Press.

Layman, G. C. (1997). Religion and political behavior in the United States: The impact of beliefs, affiliations, and commitment from 1980 to 1994. *Public Opinion Quarterly*, 288–316.

Layman, G. C. (2001). *The great divide: Religious and cultural conflict in American party politics*. Columbia University Press.

Layman, G. C., & Carsey, T. M. (2002). Party polarization and "conflict extension" in the American electorate. *American Journal of Political Science*, *46*(4), 786–802. https://doi.org/10.2307/3088434.

Lebo, M. J., & Cassino, D. (2007) The aggregated consequences of motivated reasoning and the dynamics of partisan presidential approval. *Political Psychology*, *28*(6), 719–746. https://doi.org/10.1111/j.1467-9221.2007.00601.x.

Lelkes, Y., & Westwood, S. J. (2017). The limits of partisan prejudice. *The Journal of Politics*, *79*(2), 485–501. https://doi.org/10.1086/688223.

Lerner, J. S., & Tiedens, L. Z. (2006). Portrait of the angry decision maker: How appraisal tendencies shape anger's influence on cognition. *Journal of Behavioral Decision Making*, *19*(2), 115–137. https://doi.org/10.1002/bdm.515.

Levitin, T. E., & Miller, W. E. (1979). Ideological interpretations of presidential elections. *American Political Science Review*, *73*(3), 751–771. https://doi.org/10.2307/1955402.

Levendusky, M. S. (2018). Americans, not partisans: Can priming American national identity reduce affective polarization? *The Journal of Politics*, *80*(1), 59–70.

Lewis-Beck, M., Norpoth, H., Jacoby, W., & Weisberg, H. (2008). *The American voter revisited*. University of Michigan Press. https://doi.org/10.3998/mpub.92266.

Lupia, A. (2016). *Uninformed: Why people know so little about politics and what we can do about it*. Oxford University Press.

Lupu, N. (2015). Party polarization and mass partisanship: A comparative perspective. *Political Behavior, 37*(2), 331–356.

Lupu, N., & Stokes, S. (2010). Democracy, interrupted: Regime change and partisanship in twentieth-century Argentina. Electoral Studies, *29*(1), 91–104.

Luhtanen, R., & Crocker, J. (1992). A collective self-esteem scale: Self-evaluation of one's social identity. *Personality and Social Psychology Bulletin, 18*(3), 302–318.

Luttig, M. D. (2017). Authoritarianism and affective polarization: A new view on the origins of partisan extremism. *Public Opinion Quarterly, 81*(4), 866–895. https://doi.org/10.1093/poq/nfx023.

Luttig, M. D. (2018). The "prejudiced personality" and the origins of partisan strength, affective polarization, and partisan sorting. *Political Psychology, 39*(S1), 239–256. https://doi.org/10.1111/pops.12484.

Luttig, M. D. (2021). Reconsidering the relationship between authoritarianism and republican support in 2016 and beyond. *The Journal of Politics, 83*(2), 783–787.

MacKuen, M. B., Erikson, R. S., & Stimson, J. A. (1989). Macropartisanship. *The American Political Science Review, 83*(4), 1125–1142. https://doi.org/10.2307/1961661.

McClosky, H. (1958). Conservatism and personality. *American Political Science Review, 52*(1), 27–45.

McCourt, K., Bouchard, T. J., Lykken, D. T., Tellegen, A., & Keyes, M. (1999). Authoritarianism revisited: Genetic and environmental influences examined in twins reared apart and together. *Personality and Individual Differences, 27*(5), 985–1014.

Mael, F. A., & Tetrick L. E. (1992). Identifying organizational identification. *Educational and Psychological Measurement, 52*(4), 813–824. https://doi.org/10.1177/0013164492052004002.

Maggiotto, M. A., & Piereson, J. E. (1977). Partisan identification and electoral choice: The hostility hypothesis. *American Journal of Political Science*, 745–767.

Mangum, M. (2013). The racial underpinnings of party identification and political ideology. *Social Science Quarterly, 94*(5), 1222–1244.

Malhotra, N., & Kuo, A. G. (2008). Attributing blame: The public's response to Hurricane Katrina. *The Journal of Politics, 70*(1), 120–135. https://doi.org/10.1017/s0022381607080097.

Malka, A., & Lelkes, Y. (2010). More than ideology: Conservative–Liberal identity and receptivity to political cues. *Social Justice Research, 23*(2–3), 156–188. https://doi.org/10.1007/s11211-010-0114-3.

Marcus, G. E., Russell Neuman, W., & MacKuen M. (2000). *Affective intelligence and political judgment*. University of Chicago Press.

Martherus, J. L., Martinez, A. G., Piff, P. K., & Theodoridis A. G. (2021). Party animals? Extreme partisan polarization and dehumanization. *Political Behavior, 43*(2), 517–540. https://doi.org/10.1007/s11109-019-09559-4.

Mason, L. H. (2013). *The polarizing effects of partisan sorting.* SSRN Scholarly Paper ID 2303254. Social Science Research Network. https://papers.ssrn.com/abstract= 2303254.

Mason, L. H. (2015). "I disrespectfully Agree": The differential effects of partisan sorting on social and issue polarization. *American Journal of Political Science,* 59(1), 128–145. https://doi.org/10.1111/ajps.12089.

Mason, L. H. (2016). A cross-cutting calm: How social sorting drives affective polarization. *Public Opinion Quarterly,* 80(S1), 351–377. https://doi.org/10 .1093/poq/nfw001.

Mason, L. H. (2018). *Uncivil agreement: How politics became our identity.* University of Chicago Press.

Mason, L. H., & Wronski, J. (2018). One tribe to bind them all: How our social group attachments strengthen partisanship. *Political Psychology, 39,* 257–277.

Mason, L., Wronski, J., & Kane, J. V. (2021). Activating animus: The uniquely social roots of Trump support. *American Political Science Review,* 1–9.

Mattes, R., & Kroenke, M. (2020). The consequences of partisanship in Africa. In H. Oscarsson & S. Holmberg (Eds.), *Research handbook on political partisanship* (pp. 368–380). Edward Elger. https://www.e-elgar.com/shop/gbp/research-hand book-on-political-partisanship-9781788111980.html.

McCann, J. A. (1997). Electoral choices and core value change: The 1992 presidential campaign. *American Journal of Political Science,* 41(2), 564–583. https://doi.org/ 10.2307/2111777.

McCrae, R. R., & Costa, P. T. Jr. (2008). The five-factor theory of personality. In *Handbook of Personality: Theory and Research* (3rd edition) (pp. 159–181). The Guilford Press.

McGregor, M. R., Caruana, N. J., & Stephenson, L. B. (2015). Negative partisanship in a multi-party system: The case of Canada. *Journal of Elections, Public Opinion and Parties,* 25(3), 300–316.

Medeiros, M., & Noël, A. (2014). The forgotten side of partisanship: Negative party identification in four Anglo-American democracies. *Comparative Political Studies,* 47(7), 1022–1046.

Meffert, M. F., Gschwend, T., & Schütze, N. (2009). *Coalition preferences in multiparty systems.* Mannheim.

Meléndez, C., & Kaltwasser, C. R. (2021). Negative partisanship towards the populist radical right and democratic resilience in Western Europe. *Democratization,* 28(5), 949–969.

Miller, P. R., & Conover, P. J. (2015). Red and blue states of mind: Partisan hostility and voting in the United States. *Political Research Quarterly,* 68(2), 225–239.

Mondak, J. J. (2010). *Personality and the foundations of political behavior.* Cambridge University Press. https://doi.org/10.1017/CBO9780511761515.

Mondak, J. J., & Halperin, K. D. (2008). A framework for the study of personality and political behaviour. *British Journal of Political Science,* 38(2), 335–362. https://doi .org/10.1017/S0007123408000173.

Mosier, S. L., & Rimal, A. P. (2020). Where's the meat? An evaluation of diet and partisanship identification. *British Food Journal,* 122(3), 896–909. https://doi.org/ 10.1108/BFJ-03-2019-0193.

Mudde, C., & Rovira Kaltwasser, C. (2018). Studying populism in comparative perspective: Reflections on the contemporary and future research agenda. *Comparative Political Studies*, *51*(13), 1667–1693.

Mummolo, J., Peterson, E., & Westwood, S. (2021). The limits of partisan loyalty. *Political Behavior*, *43*(3), 949–972. https://doi.org/10.1007/s11109–019-09576-3.

Nan, J. (2022, January 17). *How do we avoid threats and harassment towards politicians?* Erasmus University Rotterdam. www.eur.nl/en/news/how-do-we-avoid-threats-and-harassment-towards-politicians.

Nicholson, S. P. (2011). Dominating cues and the limits of elite influence. *The Journal of Politics*, *73*(4), 1165–1177.

Nicholson, S. P. (2012). Polarizing cues. *American Journal of Political Science*, *56*(1), 52–66. https://doi.org/10.1111/j.1540-5907.2011.00541.x.

Norris, P., & Inglehart, R. (2019). *Cultural backlash: Trump, Brexit, and authoritarian populism*. Cambridge University Press.

Mudde, C., & Rovira Kaltwasser, C. (2018). Studying populism in comparative perspective: Reflections on the contemporary and future research agenda. *Comparative Political Studies*, *51*(13), 1667–1693.

Oscarsson, H., Bergman, T., Bergström, Annika, & Hellström, J. (2021). *SNS DEMOCRACY COUNCIL REPORT 2021: Polarization in Sweden*. SNS Democracy Council. https://snsse.cdn.triggerfish.cloud/uploads/2021/03/sns-democracy-council-report-2021-polarization-in-sweden-english-summary.pdf.

Oshri, O., Yair, O., & Huddy L. (2021). The importance of attachment to an ideological group in multi-party systems: Evidence from Israel. *Party Politics* (September), https://doi.org/10.1177/13540688211044475.

Panagopoulos, C., Green, D. P., Krasno, J., Schwam-Baird, M., & Endres, K. (2020). Partisan consumerism: Experimental tests of consumer reactions to corporate political activity. *The Journal of Politics*, *82*(3), 996–1007.

Parker, P., & Wright R. (2021, October 15). Fatal attack intensifies concerns about the safety of MPs. *Financial Times*. www.ft.com/content/b9dae520-1713-4cc0-b205-3a5f46847f2a.

Pelling, L. (2022, July 19). Paving the way for radicalised violence. *IPS*. www.ips-journal.eu/topics/democracy-and-society/paving-the-way-for-radicalised-violence-6075/.

Perry, R., & Sibley, C. G. (2013). A dual-process motivational model of social and economic policy attitudes: Dual process model of political attitudes. *Analyses of Social Issues and Public Policy*, *13*(1), 262–285. https://doi.org/10.1111/asap.12019.

Peterson, E. (2019). The scope of partisan influence on policy opinion. *Political Psychology*, *40*(2), 335–353. https://doi.org/10.1111/pops.12495.

Pettigrew, T. F., Tropp, L. R., Wagner, U., & Christ, O. (2011). Recent advances in intergroup contact theory. *International Journal of Intercultural Relations*, *35*(3), 271–280.

Pew Research Center. (2019, March 4). *Political independents: Who they are, what they think*. www.pewresearch.org/politics/2019/03/14/political-independents-who-they-are-what-they-think/.

Pickup, M., Stecula, D., & Van Der Linden, C. (2020). Novel coronavirus, old partisanship: COVID-19 attitudes and behaviours in the United States and

Canada. *Canadian Journal of Political Science/Revue canadienne de science politique, 53*(2), 357–364

Public Agenda. (2021, December 8). *America's hidden common ground: Putting partisan animosity in perspective.* www.publicagenda.org/reports/partisan-animosity/.

Pratto, F., Sidanius, J., Stallworth, L. M., & Malle B. F. (1994). Social dominance orientation: A personality variable predicting social and political attitudes. *Journal of Personality and Social Psychology, 67*(4), 741–763. https://doi.org/10.1037/0022-3514.67.4.741.

Reicher, S. and Hopkins, N. (2003). On the Science of the Art of Leadership. In D. van Knippenberg & M. A. Hogg, (Eds.), *Leadership and power: Identity processes in groups and organizations* (p. 197). Sage.

Reiljan, A. and Ryan, A. (2021). Ideological tripolarization, partisan tribalism and institutional trust: The foundations of affective polarization in the Swedish multiparty system. *Scandinavian Political Studies, 44*(2), 195–219.

Reilly, K. (2016, September 10). Read Hillary Clinton's "basket of deplorables" remarks about Donald Trump supporters. *Time.* https://time.com/4486502/hillary-clinton-basket-of-deplorables-transcript/.

Rico, G., Guinjoan, M., & Anduiza, E. (2017). The emotional underpinnings of populism: How anger and fear affect populist attitudes. *Swiss Political Science Review, 23*(4), 444–461.

Roberts, B. W., & Mroczek, D. (2008). Personality trait change in adulthood. *Current Directions in Psychological Science, 17*(1), 31–35.

Roccas, S., & Brewer, M. B. (2002). Social identity complexity. *Personality and Social Psychology Review, 6*(2), 88–106.

Rogowski, J. C., & Sutherland, J. L. (2016). How ideology fuels affective polarization. *Political Behavior, 38*(2), 485–508.

Rose, R., & Mishler, W. (1998). Negative and positive party identification in post-communist countries. *Electoral Studies, 17*(2), 217–234.

Rydell, R. J., Mackie, D. M. , Maitner, A. T., Claypool, H. M., Ryan, M. J., & Smith, E. R. (2008). Arousal, processing, and risk taking: Consequences of intergroup anger. *Personality and Social Psychology Bulletin, 34*(8), 1141–1152. https://doi.org/10.1177/0146167208319694.

Samuels, D. J., & Zucco, C. (2018). *Partisans, antipartisans, and nonpartisans: Voting behavior in Brazil.* Cambridge University Press.

Sanders, L., Smith, M., & Ballard, J. (2021, November 9). *Most voters say the events at the US Capitol are a threat to democracy.* YouGovAmerica. https://today.yougov.com/topics/politics/articles-reports/2021/01/06/US-capitol-trump-poll.

Santoro, E. and Broockman, D. E. (2022). The promise and pitfalls of cross-partisan conversations for reducing affective polarization: Evidence from randomized experiments. *Science Advances, 8*(25), eabn5515.

Satherley, N., Sibley, C. G., & Osborne, D. (2021). Ideology before party: Social dominance orientation and right-wing authoritarianism temporally precede political party support. *British Journal of Social Psychology, 60*(2), 509–523. https://doi.org/10.1111/bjso.12414.

Schattschneider, E. E. (1960). *The semisovereign people: A realist's view of democracy in America.* Holt, Rinehart and Winston.

Schumacher, S. (2019, October 28). *Brexit divides the UK, but partisanship and ideology are still key factors.* Pew Research Center (blog). www.pewresearch.org/fact-tank/2019/10/28/brexit-divides-the-uk-but-partisanship-and-ideology-are-still-key-factors/.

Shafranek, R. M. (2021). Political considerations in nonpolitical decisions: A conjoint analysis of roommate choice. *Political Behavior, 43*(1), 271–300.

Sibley, C. G., Robertson, A., & Wilson, M. S. (2006). Social dominance orientation and right-wing authoritarianism: Additive and interactive effects. *Political Psychology, 27*(5), 755–768. https://doi.org/10.1111/j.1467-9221.2006.00531.x

Silva, B. C. (2018). Populist radical right parties and mass polarization in the Netherlands. *European Political Science Review, 10*(2), 219–244.

Slothuus, R., & Bisgaard, M. (2021). How political parties shape public opinion in the real world. *American Journal of Political Science, 65*(4), 896–911. https://doi.org/10.1111/ajps.12550.

Slothuus, R., & de Vreese C. H. (2010). Political parties, motivated reasoning, and issue framing effects. *The Journal of Politics, 72*(3), 630–645. https://doi.org/10.1017/s002238161000006x.

Southern Poverty Law Center. (2022, June 1). *SPLC poll finds substantial support for "great replacement" theory and other hard-Right ideas.* www.splcenter.org/news/2022/06/01/poll-finds-support-great-replacement-hard-right-ideas.

Stenner, K. (2005). *The authoritarian dynamic.* Cambridge Studies in Public Opinion and Political Psychology. Cambridge University Press.

Tajfel, H. (1970). Experiments in Intergroup Discrimination. *Scientific American, 223*(5), 96–102. https://doi.org/10.1038/scientificamerican1170-96.

Tajfel, H. (1978). *Differentiation between social groups: Studies in the social psychology of intergroup relations.* Academic Press.

Tajfel, H. (1981). *Human groups and social categories.* Cambridge University Press.

Tajfel, H., Billig, M. G., Bundy, R. P., & Flament, C. (1971). Social categorization and intergroup behaviour. *European Journal of Social Psychology, 1*(2), 149–178.

Tajfel, H., & Turner J. C. (1979). An integrative theory of inter-group conflict. In W. G. Austin & S. Worchel (Eds.), *The social psychology of inter-group relations* (pp. 33–47). Brooks/Cole.

Tajfel, H. and Turner, J. C. (2004). The social identity theory of intergroup behavior. In J. T. Jost & J. Sidanius (Eds.), *Political psychology: Key readings* (pp. 276–293). Psychology Press.

Tajfel, H., and Wilkes, A. L. (1963). Classification and quantitative judgement. *British Journal of Psychology, 54*(2), 101–114.

Turner, J. C., Hogg, M. A., Oakes, P. J., Reicher, S. D., & Wetherell, M. S. (1987). *Rediscovering the social Group: A self-categorization theory.* Basil Blackwell.

The Conversation. (2016, January 25). Direct democracy may be key to a happier American democracy. *US News & World Report.* www.usnews.com/news/articles/2016-01-25/direct-democracy-may-be-key-to-a-happier-american-democracy.

Tomz, M., & Van Houweling, R. P. (2009). The electoral implications of candidate ambiguity. *American Political Science Review, 103*(1), 83–98. https://doi.org/10.1017/S0003055409090066.

Tondo, L., & Giuffrida A. (2018, August 3). Warning of "dangerous Acceleration" in attacks on immigrants in Italy. *The Guardian*. www.theguardian.com/global/2018/aug/03/warning-of-dangerous-acceleration-in-attacks-on-immigrants-in-italy.

Tsatsanis, E., Teperoglou, E., & Seriatos, A. (2020). Two-partyism reloaded: Polarisation, negative partisanship, and the return of the left-right divide in the Greek elections of 2019. *South European Society and Politics, 25*(3/4), 503–532.

Valentino, N. A., Brader, T., Groenendyk, E. W., Gregorowicz, K., & Hutchings, V. L. (2011). Election night's alright for fighting: The role of emotions in political participation. *The Journal of Politics, 73*(1), 156–170. https://doi.org/10.1017/s0022381610000939.

Van Assche, J., Dhont, K., & Pettigrew, T. F. (2019). The social-psychological bases of far-right support in Europe and the United States. *Journal of Community & Applied Social Psychology, 29*(5), 385–401. https://doi.org/10.1002/casp.2407.

Verba, S., Schlozman, K., & Brady, H. (1995). *Voice and equality: Civic voluntarism in American democracy.* Harvard University Press.

Wattenberg, M. P., & Brians C. L. (2002). Partisan turnout bias in midterm legislative elections. *Legislative Studies Quarterly, 27*(3), 407–421. https://doi.org/10.2307/3598570.

Webster, S. W. (2018). It's personal: The big five personality traits and negative partisan affect in polarized US politics. *American Behavioral Scientist, 62*(1), 127–145.

Weisberg, H. F. (1980). A multidimensional conceptualization of party identification. *Political Behavior, 2*(1), 33–60.

Westwood, S. J., Iyengar, S., Walgrave, S., Leonisio, R., Miller, L., & Strijbis, O. (2018). The tie that divides: Cross-national evidence of the primacy of partyism. *European Journal of Political Research, 57*(2), 333–354.

Wilson, M. S., & Sibley, C. G. (2013). Social dominance orientation and right-wing authoritarianism: Additive and interactive effects on political conservatism. *Political Psychology, 34*(2), 277–284. https://doi.org/10.1111/j.1467-9221.2012.00929.x.

Winter, N., & Berinsky, A. J. (1999). *What's your temperature? Thermometer ratings and political analysis.* Annual meeting of the American Political Science Association.

Wronski, J., Bankert, A., Amira, K., Johnson, A. A., & Levitan L. C. (2018). A tale of two Democrats: How authoritarianism divides the Democratic party. *The Journal of Politics, 80*(4), 1384–1388.

Zaller, J. (2004). Floating voters in US presidential elections, 1948–2000. In *Studies in Public Opinion: Attitudes, Non Attitudes, Measurement Error, and Change* (pp. 166–215). Princeton University Press. https://doi.org/10.1515/9780691188386-008.

Zhong, C. B., Galinsky, A. D., & Unzueta, M. M. (2008). Negational racial identity and presidential voting preferences. *Journal of Experimental Social Psychology, 44*(6), 1563–1566.

Zhong, C. B., Phillips, K. W., Leonardelli, G. J., & Galinsky, A. D. (2008). Negational categorization and intergroup behavior. *Personality and Social Psychology Bulletin, 34*(6), 793–806.

Zomeren, M. v., Postmes, T., & Spears, R. (2008). Toward an integrative social identity model of collective action: A quantitative research synthesis of three socio-psychological perspectives. *Psychological Bulletin*, *34*(4), 504–535. https://doi.org/10.1037/0033-2909.134.4.504.

Zomeren, M. v., Spears, R., & Leach, C. W. (2008) Exploring psychological mechanisms of collective action: Does relevance of group identity influence how people cope with collective disadvantage? *The British Journal of Social Psychology*, *47*(Pt 2), 353–372. https://doi.org/10.1348/014466607X231091

INDEX

For EU product safety concerns, contact us at Calle de José Abascal, 56–1°,
28003 Madrid, Spain or eugpsr@cambridge.org.